KANGAROO

PORTRAIT *of an* EXTRAORDINARY
MARSUPIAL

STEPHEN JACKSON
and KARL VERNES

ALLEN&UNWIN

Allen & Unwin
83 Alexander Street
Crows Nest NSW 2065
Australia
Phone: (61 2) 8425 0100
Fax: (61 2) 9906 2218
Email: info@allenandunwin.com
Web: www.allenandunwin.com

Cataloguing-in-Publication details are available
from the National Library of Australia
www.trove.nla.gov.au

ISBN 978 1 74175 903 7

Set in 11/14.5 pt Garamond 3 by Midland Typesetters, Australia

10 9 8 7 6 5 4

Printed and bound in Australia by The SOS Print + Media Group.

Dr Stephen Jackson has worked in the wildlife industry for the past two decades, as a field biologist, wildlife consultant, zoo keeper, wildlife park curator and government regulator, among other roles. He has a PhD in zoology and has worked extensively with macropods in captivity, giving him a unique insight into their biology and behaviour. Dr Jackson is the author of *Koala: Origins of an Icon*, *Biology of Australian Possums and Gliders* and *Australian Mammals: Biology and Captive Management*, for which he received the prestigious Whitley Medal, and has published numerous papers on various areas of Australian mammalogy.

Dr Karl Vernes has been studying the ecology of Australia's native mammals for more than 20 years. He first worked on kangaroos as a Masters student in north Queensland where he examined the Red-legged Pademelon in tropical rainforest before undertaking a PhD on the endangered Northern Bettong. Since 2003 Dr Vernes has lectured in conservation biology and wildlife ecology at the University of New England in New South Wales, where he has studied various macropods and worked on other kangaroos from as far afield as Tasmania and Papua New Guinea. Dr Vernes has published more than 40 scientific papers and book chapters.

To our own little 'joeys': Olivia, James
and Theo; and 'young at foot' Emma and Cole

CONTENTS

ACKNOWLEDGEMENTS

Many thanks to the experts who have added considerably to this book by reviewing sections or chapters, including John Bradley (Monash University), Hilary Carey (University of Newcastle), Andrew Claridge (NSW Department of Environment, Water and Climate Change), Danielle Clode (University of Melbourne), Jacqui Coughlan, Graeme Coulson (University of Melbourne), Chris Dickman (University of Sydney), Gordon Grigg (University of Queensland), Thomas Heinsohn (University of Canberra), Kris Helgen (Smithsonian Institution, Washington, DC), Cathy Herbert (University of Sydney), Chris Johnson (James Cook University), Ben Kear (La Trobe University), Athol Klieve (Queensland Primary Industries and Fisheries), John McDonald, Tony Pople (Biosecurity Queensland), Euan Ritchie (Deakin University), Tanya Vernes (World Wide Fund for Nature) and George Wilson (Australian Wildlife Services).

Isabelle Devos read and commented on the penultimate draft of this book, and made several excellent recommendations for improvement, for which we are also grateful.

Many other researchers and experts have been generous with their time and assistance. Andrew Woolnough, Steve Van Dyck and David Alonso Love, along with the Australian Museum and its staff, including Anina Hainsworth, Fiona Simpson, Fran Smith and Leone Lemmer, were a great help with obtaining various references. Thanks also to Francine Gilbert (la Bergerie Nationale de Rambouillet, France), Bruno Munilla (Centre d'Etude de Rambouillet et de sa Forêt, France), Derek Yalden (University of Manchester, UK), and Philippe Devos (Deputy Foreign Editor, *Globe and Mail*, Canada) who provided information about expatriate wallabies in Europe and North America. Enormous thanks go to Professor Iain Young, Head of the School of Environmental and Rural Science at the University of New England, who generously provided the funds we needed to purchase many of the wonderful images seen throughout the book. Other images were made freely available to us—thank you to all of the people and organisations who so quickly and generously responded to our requests for material, especially Gerhard Körtner and James Turner who provided most of the stunning colour photos of macropods. Isabelle Devos did the beautiful sketches that open each chapter.

Finally, sincere thanks go to our partners, Kerstin and Isabelle, for their enduring support and patience during this project.

INTRODUCTION

Picture a large Red Kangaroo lying under the shade of a tree on a hot day, its head up and its ears swivelling like antennae, tuned for the slightest sound of danger. The alarm given, the animal bounds into action, its muscular body and unique, spring-like hind-legs allowing it to leap effortlessly over the red sands of central Australia. It's an image of power, grace and efficiency.

The Red Kangaroo may be the archetypal image of 'the kangaroo' but there are, in fact, nearly 80 species of 'kangaroo' in Australia, New Guinea and their surrounding islands. Strictly speaking, only the largest of these magnificent hopping animals are, officially, 'kangaroos'. Those that are medium-sized are known as wallabies, while the smaller species go by fascinating names like pademelon, narbalek, quokka, mala, boodie, woylie, potoroo and bettong—to name just a few. All of these animals are known as 'macropods' (literally meaning 'big foot'), and we will use this term interchangeably with the generic 'kangaroo' throughout this book for all the kangaroos, wallabies, rat-kangaroos and their relatives.

Evolutionarily speaking, kangaroos are stamped 'Made in Australia'. They evolved on that fragment of Gondwana we call Australia, and have adapted superbly to its range of habitat types, and its unpredictable and often fickle climate. Throughout Australia and New Guinea you will find kangaroos living in almost every habitat type—lush forest to the driest of deserts, alpine meadows to steep rocky gorges. The kangaroos' unique and adaptable body form means they can be found living in underground burrows, scurrying about the rainforest floor, following well-worn paths through dense heath, scrambling up and down sheer cliff faces, and climbing into the dizzying heights of the rainforest canopy—and, of course, hopping across the vast open grassy plains, woodlands and deserts that dominate the Australian landscape. Their diet is varied too—grass, leaves, fruit, seeds, tubers, insects and even truffles are on the kangaroos' menu, and some of the extinct species might even have had a taste for flesh. In satisfying their dietary needs kangaroos fulfil many of the same roles played by mammals on other continents, such as grazing antelope and deer, seed-dispersing rodents and even leaf-eating monkeys. However, the large grazing kangaroos differ from other grazing animals in that they can digest plant material without producing methane gas—an evolutionary adaptation that, if harnessed, could quite literally help to save the planet.

What else makes this particular group of marsupials (pouched mammals) so interesting? For one thing, macropods have a remarkable reproductive biology—you won't find anything like it even among other marsupials like possums and wombats. Although macropods have a pouch and a short gestation period, the resemblance to other marsupials stops there—macropods can produce young continually, produce young at three different stages of development and, incredibly, can deliberately stop the development of an embryo. Another defining characteristic of the macropods is their gait. Macropods are exquisite hoppers, their method of locomotion energy-efficient and surprisingly rapid—and probably the first thing that springs to mind when we think of a 'kangaroo'. Why? Because it is such a strange thing for a large mammal to do.

Australia's Indigenous people have lived with and hunted kangaroos for tens of thousands of years, and celebrate them in stories, ceremonies and art. When Europeans arrived in Australia, they too were intrigued by these strange mammals. The journals of the early seafarers, explorers and colonists tell of their fascination, and within a few years of the First Fleet leaving England, kangaroos had been brought back by returning ships and exhibited in London, and would later establish wild populations in England, mainland Europe, Hawaii and New Zealand. Modern preoccupation with macropods seems not to diminish with familiarity either—depictions of kangaroos appeared in art, official currency and the literature of Australia's early European colonists, and continue to be used today by sporting teams, sports fans and advertisers as a symbol of all things Australian. Direct use—in the form of food—has also been a big part of the human experience of kangaroos for as long as people have lived alongside them.

Many smaller macropods have not been able to adapt to the arrival of Europeans in Australia and the release of foxes and cats—a string of extinctions tell that sorry tale. In contrast, a handful of species are not only widespread over vast areas of Australia but overabundant. The response by the agricultural community has been to actively hunt kangaroos to protect pastures, and today many hundreds of thousands of animals are harvested each year by official sanction for their skins and meat as part of successful and environmentally sustainable commercial enterprise.

In the coming chapters we explore these issues in detail— from the ancient origins of kangaroos to modern efforts to conserve and manage them. Along the way we chart the significance kangaroos have to Aboriginal peoples, the amazement that accompanied the first kangaroo sightings by Europeans— and later efforts to manage them—and the sustained fascination people have with kangaroos that leads these animals to be instantly recognised the world over. We also discuss the natural history of kangaroos—reproduction, behaviour, diet and, of course, that amazing hopping ability—all of which make kangaroos such extraordinary marsupials.

1

FANGAROO
TO KANGAROO

The Evolution of Macropods

The Quadrupeds we saw but few and were able to catch few of those that we did see. The largest was call{e}d by the natives Kangooroo. It is different from any European and indeed any animal I have heard or read of except the Gerbua of Egypt, which is not larger than a rat when this is as large as a middling Lamb; the largest we shot weighed 84lb. It may however be easily known from all other animals by the singular property of running or rather hopping upon only its hinder legs carrying its fore bent close to the breast; in this manner however it hops so fast that in the rocky bad ground where it is commonly found it easily beat my greyhound, who tho he was fairly started at several killd only one and that quite a young one.[1]

In the vernacular, a 'kangaroo' is any one of the 77 species of hopping macropod marsupials of Australia and New Guinea. We know that several species have been confirmed as extinct since European settlement but the fossil record shows that

Australia once proliferated in macropods—some the size of rabbits, others giants weighing several hundred kilograms. Many of these ancient species, and all of the largest ones, became extinct shortly after the Australasian region was settled by its indigenous peoples, more than 45,000 years ago, while many others survived until the arrival of the first European settlers.

There were 57 species of macropod known to have occurred in Australia and its islands at the time of European settlement, with a further 23 species found on New Guinea and its surrounding islands, three of which are shared with Australia (see Appendix 1). The 77 modern species of macropods encompass a wide variety of shapes and sizes and range from the diminutive Musky Rat-kangaroo of the Australian Wet Tropics that weighs just 500 grams to the massive Red Kangaroo of the arid centre that can weigh as much as 85 kilograms. The group includes species that burrow, others that climb trees, some that live among the steepest rocky gorges and others that inhabit the seemingly endless desert plains. They live in rainforest, woodland, heathland, grassland and desert—there is not a vegetation type in Australia or New Guinea where you will not find at least one species of macropod.

THE MACROPOD FAMILY TREE

Living macropods are so diverse that they are divided up into three families within the Superfamily Macropodoidea. The most primitive of the three is the strangely named Family Hypsiprymnodontidae. The family has only one living member, the Musky Rat-kangaroo, the smallest of all the macropods and generally considered to be a missing link between the possums and kangaroos. The Musky Rat-kangaroo is unique to the rainforests of North Queensland and retains some of its possum heritage by having five toes on its hind foot. Every other macropod species has four digits, because evolution has done away with the first digit, thus allowing the animals to hop more efficiently. The Musky Rat-kangaroo is the only macropod that does not hop—it appears to have separated from the other macropods before hopping evolved. It is also unique in that it has a simple stomach, and females can give birth to twins and even triplets while all other macropods typically produce only one young at a time.[2]

Distant relatives of the Musky Rat-kangaroo are the potoroos, bettongs and rat-kangaroos of the Family Potoroidae. These small macropods, generally referred to 'potoroids', all weigh less than 3 kilograms, and are represented by 11 species, of which three have become extinct since European settlement. Potoroids once occurred across the length and breadth of Australia—indeed, the Burrowing Bettong once had the greatest geographic range of all the macropods—but the family has no relatives within New Guinea. The potoroos live in the dense rainforest undergrowth of Australia's east coast, and parts of the south-west, whereas the bettongs prefer drier conditions such as open forests and woodlands or scrublands covered in Spinifex and other grass tussocks of central Australia. As we shall see in Chapter 6, the potoroids are also unusual in that their diet is typically dominated by the underground fungi known as truffles.

The third and by far the largest family, in both number and body size, is the Family Macropodidae, generally referred to as the macropodids. There are 65 species in this family, including

KANGAROO

Macropods present in Australia and New Guinea at the time of European settlement (see Appendix 1 for the full species list)

Common name	Genus	Species	Distribution
Family Hypsiprymnodontidae			
Musky Rat-kangaroo	Hypsiprym-nodon	1	Aust
Family Potoroidae			
Rufous Bettong	Aepyprymnus	1	Aust
Bettongs	Bettongia	5	Aust
Desert Rat-kangaroo	Caloprymnus	1	Aust
Potoroos	Potorous	4	Aust
Family Macropodidae			
Tree Kangaroos	Dendrolagus	12	Aust + NG
Dorcopsis Wallabies	Dorcopsis	4	NG
Forest Wallabies	Dorcopsulus	2	NG
Hare-wallabies	Lagorchestes	4	Aust + NG
Kangaroos, Wallaroos and Wallabies	Macropus	14	Aust + NG
Nailtail Wallabies	Onychogalea	3	Aust
Rock-wallabies	Petrogale	16	Aust
Quokka	Setonix	1	Aust
Pademelons	Thylogale	7	Aust + NG
Swamp Wallaby	Wallabia	1	Aust
Banded Hare-wallaby	Lagostrophus	1	Aust

the kangaroos, wallaroos, wallabies, rock-wallabies, nailtail wallabies, hare-wallabies, tree kangaroos, the quokka, pademelons and several species of New Guinea forest wallabies. Macropodids can be found throughout Australia and New Guinea—from the highest mountains to the most arid deserts. The most unusual macropodids are probably the tree kangaroos, which are amongst the family's most recently evolved lineages, in evolutionary terms, but which have taken to the trees to return to an arboreal lifestyle like their early marsupial ancestors.

To this end they have developed several unique features, including forelimbs that are of similar size to the hind limbs, short broad feet, and the ability to move the hind feet alternately, which other macropods only do if they are swimming.[3] Intriguingly, one species of tree kangaroo, the Dingiso—a species from the Indonesian province of Papua (previously known as Irian Jaya) described in 1995 by Professor Tim Flannery—has come full circle and readapted to a terrestrial lifestyle. The Dingiso has a more slender skeleton and longer hind feet than other tree kangaroos and therefore appears to be a tree kangaroo in evolutionary reverse—making the transition back down from the trees to the ground.[4]

WHAT'S IN A NAME?

Common names for many of the macropods such as 'kangaroo', 'wallaroo', 'wallaby', 'pademelon', 'potoroo' and 'bettong' seem to be derived from the multitude of indigenous Australian languages. The local inhabitants of a region would have had specific meanings for these words, in that they would have given each name to an individual species of macropod. The first European explorers and settlers later adopted these names to describe a range of species and even several genera.

The word 'kangaroo' is sometimes used as a generic term for all of the Superfamily Macropodoidea, but it is often reserved for the larger members such as the Eastern Grey Kangaroo, the Western Grey Kangaroo and the Red Kangaroo. There is some disagreement about both the origin of the word and its original meaning. When Lieutenant James Cook was delayed at Endeavour River in 1770 while his ship underwent repairs, he wrote in his journal on 14 July:

KANGAROO

Mr Gore, who went out this day with his gun, had the good fortune to kill one of the animals which had been so much the subject of our speculation .... This animal is called by the natives Kanguroo.[5]

Captain Cook's 'Kanguroo' is now assumed, after considerable debate, to have been the Eastern Grey Kangaroo (for more about Cook's encounter with kangaroos, see Chapter 3). Regardless of the (sometimes heated) discussions about which species was being referred to, it seems certain that the local inhabitants used the word to describe a large macropod. Folklore suggests that, on seeing a large creature hopping around, Cook asked a native what it was called and was told *'kanguroo'* meaning 'I don't know', but this is almost certainly untrue. In the early 1970s, John Haviland's investigation into the language of the area, Guuyu Yimidhirr, concluded that there was no evidence that the language had changed radically between 1770 and the present day. Modern Guuyu Yimidhirr retains the word *gangurru* for 'kangaroo'.[6] The myth perhaps stems from the records of Captain Phillip King, who in 1820 believed he had heard the word *men-u-ah* used as the name for the kangaroo.[7] What King probably heard was *minha*, a Guuyu Yimidhirr word that literally means 'meat' or 'edible animal'.

We are familiar with the term 'wallaby', but what is a wallaby? *Wollabi* is an Eora word, from the language spoken by the people of the Sydney region, and was their name for the Brush-tailed Rock-wallaby. The term was quickly adopted by the earliest settlers around Sydney, along with other Eora words such as *walaru* (wallaroo), *budaru* (potoroo) and *betong* (bettong). Eora also gives us the names for the wombat and the dingo. Today, 'wallaby' is often used loosely to describe the smaller macropodids of the Family Macropodidae, but there is no hard-and-fast rule as to when a kangaroo becomes a wallaby. A quick look over the various body weights suggests that, typically, wallabies weigh less than 20 kilograms and kangaroos weigh more than 20 kilograms, but apart from that there is no real difference between them. One could argue that the only true wallaby is the Swamp Wallaby, as it is the sole member of the genus *Wallabia*, though even this species has recently been proposed to be placed back in with the other wallabies and kangaroos in the genus *Macropus*. The Eora word for Swamp Wallaby is *banggaray*, which brings us no closer to a definition of wallaby! The name Pademelon, which today is given to small forest-dwelling wallabies of the genus *Thylogale*, is also an Eora word, being a transliteration of the word *badimaliyan*.[8]

CLIMATE CHANGE AND THE RISE OF THE MACROPODS

How and when did such a wide variety of macropods evolve? In order to understand this question, we need to first understand how Australia's climate has changed over the last 35 million years. Continental plates have collided, merged and separated again several times during the Earth's history. The super-continent Pangaea ('the entire Earth') began to break up about 250 million years ago, forming two smaller super-continents—Laurasia, which included much of present North America, Europe and Asia; and Gondwana, the major southern land mass. About 160 million years ago, Gondwana began to fragment into the present southern continents (and many smaller fragments), which have been drifting apart ever since. Australia and Antarctica were the last joined fragments of this super-continent. Their rift began about 45 million years ago, a separation which was complete by about 35 million years ago. Australia then began drifting northwards, finally colliding (perhaps 5 million years ago) with an arc of islands lying to the south of South-east Asia. These islands became part of what we now call New Guinea, at the leading northern edge of the Australian plate. Australia is continuing its northward drift towards Asia, causing the highlands of New Guinea to rise and slowly closing the distance between it and the Indonesian archipelago.[9]

The climate trigger for the evolution of the macropods appears to have occurred some 33–23 million years ago when a global cooling episode led to Australia's warm and moist climate becoming progressively cooler and drier.[10] This process was initiated by the opening up of the circumpolar current around Antarctica, which led to a dramatic change in the surrounding ocean currents and associated climate, and the development of ice over Antarctica. Before Gondwana fragmented, its northern tips reached up towards the Equator, but those at the south were still connected to Antarctica. That meant that ocean currents could move only between the Equator and higher latitudes, producing a mixing that kept all oceans at a similar, warm temperature.

Uniformly warm ocean surface temperatures create uniformly warm, wet climates, so prior to the separation of Australia and Antarctica the planet's land masses were covered in forest adapted to the prevailing conditions. The opening up of a route for a circumpolar oceanic current effectively separated a pool of sub-Antarctic waters that rapidly cooled, from the warmer oceans that then circulated water from the tropics to temperate latitudes. This was the first stage in the 'polarisation' of the world's climate: the poles became deeply cold, while the tropics became much warmer. The polarisation of the southern hemisphere's climate, into a polar south, temperate mid-latitudes and a tropical equatorial zone intensified through the Miocene and into the Pliocene (24 million years ago to 2 million years ago) as Australia drifted further into the tropics. The overall effect on Australia's climate was a gradual drying of the interior, leaving only the eastern and northern margins as wet as the whole continent had been at the start of the Miocene.[11]

It was this 'drying out' of Australia which led to the expansion and diversification of the sclerophyllous plants, with their leathery leaves which were better adapted to reducing water loss.[12] The genus *Eucalyptus* became particularly common and widespread from about 120,000 years ago (but in many places only in the last 40,000–50,000 years).[13] The increasing frequency of *Eucalyptus*, grass and forb (non-woody herbaceous plants other than grasses) pollens in lake-bed sediments is matched by a corresponding decrease in rainforest fossil remains and an increase in charcoal particle frequency, indicating a greater frequency or intensity of fires. It was this opening up of the forests and expansion of the grasslands and grassy woodlands which led to such a marked change in the terrestrial marsupial fauna, with the macropod component becoming more conspicuous, providing as it did an abundant supply of food for ground-dwelling browsers and grazers.[14]

Much of Australia's land surface has been exposed to the elements for tens or hundreds of millions of years, so it has been weathered to the point where most of its soluble nutrients have long gone, leaving soils that are generally of low fertility.[15] Much of Australia's vegetation has evolved to tolerate these low-fertility soils and is therefore of low nutritional value. Larger animals are more efficient at digesting low-nutrition foods such as grass as the energy requirements relative to body mass decrease as body mass increases, while gut capacity remains a constant proportion of body mass.[16] The increasing availability of low-nutrient grasses has resulted in an increasing diversity of large marsupials, including giant kangaroos. In contrast, smaller macropods such as the potoroids need food with a higher nutritional value and lower fibre content.[17] Over the last several million years, similar changes in vegetation structure were happening in other parts of the world, leading to the concurrent evolution of the various antelopes, horses and other large, open-country grazing mammals on other continents.[18]

What did the macropod's extinct relatives look like? As it turns out the long-lost relatives of today's macropods were typically larger, sometimes had very different diets, and some may not have hopped. The macropods evolved from tree-dwelling possum-like ancestors that came down from the trees to the rainforest floor, and probably resembled the Musky Rat-kangaroo.[19] Genetic studies suggest the ancestors of modern-day macropods separated from these ancient possum-like relatives in the Eocene some 40 million years ago, but this has yet to be confirmed by the fossil record as the oldest fossils found to date are from some 26–23 million years ago.[20]

How were the ancestors of modern macropods related to each other and, in turn, to the modern species? The relationship between the extinct relatives of the Musky Rat-kangaroo and the potoroids, for example, has been much discussed. Until quite recently, the Musky Rat-kangaroo was placed in the same family as the potoroids, but it is now recognised as a distinct family with a sister lineage to all other macropods.[21] The Musky Rat-kangaroo's primitive status is also supported by DNA research that suggests they diverged from the other macropods shortly after the macropods diverged from their possum-like relatives.[22] The Musky Rat-kangaroo's recognition as a separate lineage gives rise to a number of related issues. Did bipedal hopping and the macropods' other unique characteristics evolve independently in the potoroids and macropodids? Did the Musky Rat-kangaroo's extinct relatives lose these characteristics after evolving into the common ancestor of all macropods or, as seems most likely, did bipedal hopping and a complex digestive system capable of fermenting difficult to digest plant material evolve after the Musky Rat-kangaroo's ancestors separated from the other macropods?[23]

As mentioned above, the first (to date) macropod to appear in the fossil record is a potoroo-like animal found in fossil deposits that are at least 23 million years old.[24] The first Musky Rat-kangaroo ancestor was found in fossil deposits from 25 to 20 million years ago at Riversleigh in North Queensland.[25] The discrepancy between the genetic studies and the current fossil record may be explained by the fossil record being far from complete, which highlights the need for ongoing research to bring to light the many intriguing stories of the evolution of the macropod families.

After the Musky Rat-kangaroos separated from the other ancient macropods, the ancestors of the potoroo-like macropods in turn diverged from the ancestors of the macropods that led to modern wallabies and kangaroos of the Family Macropodidae some 25 million years ago.[26] The Musky Rat-kangaroo's closest relatives appear to be an extinct group known as the 'balbarids'

(Family Balbaridae), while the different groups of potoroo-like animals then further diverged into a variety of species between 22 and 15 million years ago.[27] This diversification of macropods continued with a great expansion in the number of species some 10 million years ago and culminated in an explosion of species approximately 5 million years ago, an event directly linked to the increasing aridity of the Australian climate and the spread of grasslands.[28] The first appearance in the fossil record of larger macropodine fossils (i.e., kangaroos and wallabies) dates from some 11 to 5 million years ago.[29] Between 1.75 million years ago and 45,000 years ago, there was a bewildering array of macropods, including the giant, short-faced kangaroos and the ancestors of modern macropods.[30]

PREHISTORIC MACROPODS

How much of a family resemblance was there between the extinct macropods and their extant relatives? The fossil record to date shows us a wide variety of strange, wonderful beasts, including some that were many times larger than any of today's macropods. The largest were the giant short-faced kangaroos that often weighed over 150 kilograms, with one, *Procoptodon goliah*, weighing in at an incredible 240 kilograms.[31] These giants had only one developed toe, the fourth, with all the other toes having been lost or, in the case of the fifth, reduced to a vestigial digit. A similarly extreme evolutionary modification is found in the horses, whose third digit only is functional, which is what allows them to reach fast running speeds, and may have allowed the macropods to reach or sustain fast hopping speeds.[32]

Numerous other species appear in the fossil record, though there is still much to discover about their body size, let alone

Reconstruction of the giant short-faced kangaroo *Procoptodon goliah*.
(Used with permission of Anne Musser)

their biology. Fossil specimens taken from the World Heritage-listed Riversleigh deposits in north-western Queensland show that at least one of these species possessed enlarged large upper canine teeth. This species was given the name *Balbaroo fangaroo*, with the genus name derived from an Aboriginal word *balba*, meaning 'strange', and the species name in recognition of its unique fang-like dentition.[33] The function of these 'fangs' is unknown; perhaps they were used in defence

Prehistoric kangaroos that died out prior to European settlement

Common Name	Genus	Species	Mass (kg)
Family Balbaridae			
Balbaroo	*Balbaroo*	3	?
Galanarla	*Galanarla*	1	?
Ganawamaya	*Ganawamaya*	3	?
Nambaroo	*Nambaroo*	6	?
Wururoo	*Wururoo*	1	?
Family Hypsiprmnodontidae			
Giant Rat-kangaroos	*Ekaltadeta*	2	?
Musky Rat-kangaroos	*Hypsiprymnodon*	1	?
Rat-kangaroos	*Jackmahoneya*	1	?
Giant Rat-kangaroos	*Propleopus*	3	40?
Family Potoroidae			
Bettongs	*Bettongia*	2	?
Large Rat-kangaroos	*Borungaboodie*	1	10
Rat-kangaroos	*Milliyowi*	1	?
Family Macropodidae			
Kangaroos	*Archaeosimos*	2	?
Kangaroos	*Baringa*	1	?
Large Tree Kangaroos	*Bohra*	4	?
Kangaroos	*Bulungamaya*	1	?
Kangaroos	*Congruus*	1	40
Tree Kangaroos	*Dendrolagus*	1	?
Dorcopsis Wallabies	*Dorcopsis*	1	?
Dorcopsoides	*Dorcopsoides*	1	?
Kangaroos	*Ganguroo*	1	?
Kangaroos	*Hadronomas*	1	?
Kangaroos	*Kurrabi*	3	?
Kangaroos	*Macropus*	8	30–150
Short-faced Kangaroos	*Metasthenurus*	1	55
Kangaroos	*Nowidgee*	1	?
Kangaroos	*Prionotemnus*	1	?
Short-faced Kangaroos	*Procoptodon*	7	50–240

Common Name	Genus	Species	Mass (kg)
Kangaroos	*Protemnodon*	6	40–166
Kangaroos	*Rhizosthenurus*	1	?
Short-faced Kangaroos	*Simosthenurus*	6	55–150
Short-faced Kangaroos	*Sthenurus*	5	70–205
Pademelons	*Thylogale*	2	?
Kangaroos	*Troposodon*	5	40?
Kangaroos	*Wabularoo*	1	?
Wallabies	*Wallabia*	2	30?
Kangaroos	*Wanburoo*	1	?
Kangaroos	*Watutia*	1	?
Family Unknown			
Macropod	*Gumardee*	1	?
Macropod	*Ngamaroo*	1	?
Macropod	*Palaeopotorous*	1	?
Macropod	*Purtia*	1	?
Macropod	*Wakiewakie*	1	?

Source: derived from Kear & Cooke 2001; Long *et al.* 2002; Prideaux 2004; Johnson 2006; Helgen *et al.* 2006; Kear *et al.* 2007; and Kear & Pledge 2007.

or perhaps only in display, as are those of the Mouse Deer of South-east Asia.[34] Most modern large macropods have no canine teeth. Instead, they have a gap—the diastema—between the incisor teeth and the cheek teeth (premolars and molars). The only modern species that still have canine teeth (though typically small) are the small potoroids and the larger tree kangaroos, nailtail wallabies, hare-wallabies and dorcopsis wallabies. In all cases, these teeth are small. The other interesting feature of the balbarids is that they may not have hopped because the forelimbs and hindlimbs were of similar length and they had the first digit on each hind foot, similar to the Musky Rat-kangaroo.

The Riversleigh deposits have also revealed another fanged species, from the same family as *Balbaroo fangaroo*. Given the scientific name *Nambaroo gillespieae*, this macropod dates from the late Oligocene to early Miocene (about 26–23 million years ago), the oldest fossil macropod remains found so far. The uniqueness of this species was described by Dr Benjamin Kear and his colleagues as 'not quite a kangaroo'—this animal may have galloped or bounded on all fours like a brushtail possum, and may even have climbed trees.[35]

Another extinct group of macropods, possibly related to the Musky Rat-kangaroo, were the giant rat-kangaroos, the largest of which was *Ekaltadeta ima*, or 'Powerful-toothed Giant Rat-kangaroo'. Sometimes nicknamed the 'killer rat-kangaroos' because of their enormous serrated third premolar teeth, it is thought that *Ekaltadeta* were at least partly carnivorous and may have used their huge premolars to butcher carcasses.[36] All the extant potoroid species still have serrated premolar teeth, though they vary in size and the angle at which they sit in the mouth. In most species the premolars are relatively long and sit in line with the toothrow, but in the Musky Rat-kangaroo they are more than twice the size of the rest of the cheek teeth and stick out at an angle of about 30 degrees. Other traits that *Ekaltadeta* shared with the modern-day Musky Rat-kangaroo include an apparent non-hopping gait and similar forearm morphology.[37]

The giant extinct kangaroos that we discussed above are part of an extraordinary group of marsupials, known as the mega-fauna, which occurred in Australia from about 1.75 million years ago to 45,000 years ago. The large macropods also shared the continent with other giant marsupials such as the dipro-todontids—heavily built animals similar in some respects to modern wombats but only distantly related to them and a

Reconstruction of the extinct kangaroo *Balbaroo fangaroo*.
(Used with permission of Anne Musser)

great deal larger, being members of a separate family known as the Diprotodontidae.[38] The largest known species, *Diprotodon optatum*, weighed up to 2700 kilograms.

Yet another group of remarkable giant extinct marsupials are the marsupial tapirs, thought to have had a large, flexible proboscis and to have weighed between 100 and 500 kilograms. The largest species, *Palorchestes azael*, was once widespread in eastern Australia and is thought to have had a long, mobile tongue like

Reconstruction of the giant marsupial *Diprotodon optatum*.
(Used with permission of Anne Musser)

that of a giraffe, and long, powerful forelimbs, large paws and sharp claws. These animals were thought to have browsed on the foliage of trees and shrubs and possibly tree bark.[39] Their large size and powerful limbs would have enabled them to reach up and grasp the branches of the small trees upon which they fed.[40] When first discovered and described, *Palorchestes*, or 'ancient leaper', was incorrectly thought to be a giant, extinct macropod. It is now thought to have been quite slow and cumbersome, with claws so big that it has been suggested that they were either knuckle-walkers, like the great apes and giant anteaters, that they walked on the sides of their feet, or that their claws were, in fact, retractable.[41]

Not all the extinct marsupials were herbivores. Eight species of marsupial lions have been described to date, the largest of which, *Thylacoleo carnifex*, is now thought to have weighed in excess of 150 kilograms.[42] Although this species was described as a carnivore in 1858 by the brilliant but controversial anatomist Professor Richard Owen, over the years it was often dismissed as a herbivore—perhaps because of its possum ancestry. Recent work suggests, however, that Owen was right after all—studies of the animal's skull, bone-crushing blade-like cheek teeth and incisors, and post-cranial skeleton all point towards it having been a ferocious predator.[43]

Reconstruction of the giant marsupial *Palorchestes azael*.
(Used with permission of Anne Musser)

Reconstruction of the marsupial lion *Thylacoleo carnifex*.
(Used with permission of Anne Musser)

Imagine Australia's plains and open woodlands filled with these giant kangaroos, wombat-like animals and marsupial lions. Yet, despite their size—or perhaps because of it—the marsupial megafauna, more than 40 species, were extinct by about 45,000 years ago. Why?

Different arguments and counterarguments have been put forward as to why the megafauna became extinct, including climate change as Australia became increasingly arid; and landscape burning and overhunting by the first Aborigines.[44] The overhunting hypothesis has drawn the most controversy, with many authors suggesting that an 'over-kill' scenario is unlikely. Professor Chris Johnson from James Cook University examined the various hypotheses in detail, and concluded that overhunting was indeed the most likely cause of the megafaunal extinctions. Professor Johnson suggests two plausible mechanisms that might explain human-induced megafaunal extinction—the 'blitzkrieg' model proposed by Professor Tim Flannery, where rapid extermination of the fauna occurs as a result of massive overhunting soon after human arrival; and a more gradual 'attrition' model, in which deaths out-run births and a steady population decline occurs over a longer timeframe. Of the two, Professor Johnson feels that the attrition model has the greatest support. Although the megafauna appear to have died out 'suddenly' some 45,000 years ago, these large marsupials would have been long-lived, slow to mature and slow to produce young. Their open habitats and inability to climb trees would have made them obvious targets for human hunters. Professor Johnson therefore argues that modest amount of hunting could cause these species to decline to extinction in a relatively short period of time—many hundreds, or a few thousand years at most—following the arrival of the first humans on the Australian continent, over 45,000 years ago.[45]

2

DREAMTIME

Indigenous Peoples and the Kangaroo

The natives of the Gawler Range, in South Australia, use a method of taking the wallaby which is highly ingenious. They make of long smooth pieces of wood an instrument like {a} fishing-rod, to the thin end of which they attach the skin and feathers of a hawk—so carefully arranged as to represent very accurately a living bird. Taking this in his hand, and his spear, the hunter roams the forest until he spies a wallaby, when, holding aloft his mock-bird, giving a motion to the long flexible rod, such as to cause the mock-bird to appear to fly and stoop, he utters the cry of the hawk, and the wallaby at once takes refuge in the nearest bush. Cautiously stealing onwards, the native throws his spear and secures the game.[1]

For over 45,000 years, indigenous Australasians have utilised native fauna for food, clothing and tools, and have venerated them in religious stories, ceremonies and art. Kangaroos are totems to many Aboriginal groups in both Australia and New Guinea, and central to many Dreamtime stories from all parts of the region. Likewise, of all the animals hunted, the kangaroos were among the most important. In the coming pages we touch upon the complex association between kangaroos and the Aboriginal peoples, an unbroken association that dates from the prehistoric to the present day.

KANGAROO DREAMING

According to the traditional beliefs of Indigenous Australians, all life—human and animal—is part of a vast and unchanging network of relationships that can be traced to the Great Spirit ancestors of the Dreamtime.[2] It was in the Dreamtime that Australia's animals and prominent geographical or astronomical features came into existence. Furthermore, it was in the Dreamtime that the ways of life, the laws and the moral code were laid down, to be followed for all eternity.[3] It is through their 'dreaming' that Aboriginal people express their origins and identity, and maintain their spiritual connection with the land and the ancestral beings.[4] Dreamtime stories are spiritual, their meanings are complex and multifaceted, and they often contain secret knowledge intended only for certain members of a particular tribal group.[5] The telling and retelling of Dreamtime stories via the printed word—often by non-Indigenous Australians—means that many stories have been westernised, and some of their subtler meanings obscured and their emphasis changed. Where possible, the stories presented here are taken from early works in which the writer recorded the story as told by an indigenous storyteller, as we feel these probably represent the truest printed versions of the original stories.

KANGAROO

Many of the stories featuring kangaroos focus on the animal's anatomical oddities—its unusually long hind legs, or strong, muscular tail, for example—and how the creature came to be so endowed. Charles William Peck wrote down stories collected in the 1860s in the Burragorang Valley (which was later flooded to create Sydney's water supply reservoir, Warragamba Dam). *Burragorang* roughly translates as 'place for kangaroo hunting'. One story describes how the kangaroo arrived during a violent windstorm and that it was during this storm that the creature developed its long legs—had it not done so, it would have been drowned at sea:

> During all this terrible wandering and blowing the first kangaroo had a weary time. He could not land. He was blown before that aimless wind and was tossed up and down. In his endeavours to gain a foothold his hind legs stretched out, and if they had not grown long as they did, he would never have alighted except in the sea, where he would have been drowned.[6]

Aldo Massola travelled around Victoria in the 1950s and 1960s writing down stories told to him by Aboriginal people. One such story from the Wotjobaluk people of north-western Victoria recounts how the kangaroo's legs were originally the same length and that it walked on all fours. However, in an attempt to escape without alerting a two-legged human hunter, the kangaroo tiptoed on just two legs:

> One day kangaroo was having a rest in the shade of a large tree, when he heard footsteps approaching. Looking up, he saw a [hunter] with his spear ready in the spear-thrower.

Realizing that he was a kangaroo hunter, he set off at full speed, using the four legs he always did. . . . They ran all that day, and the kangaroo was getting very tired, because he had to use four legs, while the hunter was only using two. Luckily, night came, and the hunter, not being able to see his quarry in the dark, stopped, and made his camp.

Now, he had stopped quite close to the kangaroo, although he did not know it. The kangaroo was afraid to move, lest he reveal his nearness. He therefore waited until the hunter was asleep, and then tiptoed away on his hind legs, in order to make less noise. But the effort to balance upon them was so great that it made them grow, and they have remained much longer ever since.[7]

Katie Langloh Parker collected stories from the Euahlayi people living where her father ran a cattle station in north-western New South Wales in the mid-1800s, and these, originally published in 1896, represent some of the best early European re-telling of Dreamtime stories. One story explores the kangaroo's origins, again focusing on its long legs and ability to hop, but also explaining why it is silent and lacks canine teeth. In this story, Bohra, the kangaroo, is a four-legged creeping animal that is attracted to the sounds of a *corroboree*. He becomes so enthralled in the music that he cannot resist joining the dance:

Bohra felt, as he watched them, a strong desire to dance too. He reared himself on his hind-legs, balancing himself with his tail, and jumped round the ring behind the last man. The singing stopped, the women shrieked, and, shrieking, pointed at Bohra. The men turned and saw him standing on his hind-legs looking in wondering terror at the shrieking women.[8]

'Round the ring they jumped as Borah [*sic*] had done, their long tails waggling behind them.' Nora Heysen, from the original drawings to illustrate *Woggheeguy*, Australian Aboriginal legends collected and written by K. Langloh Parker. (National Library of Australia, nla.pic-an23217591. Used with permission of Lou Klepac)

After their initial shock, the men begin to dance like Bohra by wearing tails made out of grass bound onto switches, and jumping with their hands held in front of them to imitate paws. But there was a problem—Bohra had observed their sacred rituals, and for this he should be killed so that the rituals remained secret. But, because Bohra had taught the men a new dance, they decided to spare his life. Nevertheless, there had to be some consequences. After much debate, the men decided:

> ... so forever shall his tribe move, jumping on their hind-legs, and his fore-feet shall be as hands, and his tail shall balance

him. But before we let him go, we will make him one of us. He and his tribe shall be our brothers, and keep silent [for] they have seen our secret rites. Then, taking Bohra into the bush they knocked his canine teeth out. These teeth... his tribe have never had since.[9]

Storyteller Nugget Jabangadi James recounts the following Warlpiri Dreamtime story from the Tanami Desert region in the Northern Territory:

One day while he was sleeping ... a bushfire blazed across the plains. Kangaroo woke up and tried to run to safety, but he was caught by the flames. As he ran through the fire his front paws were badly burnt. They were now much smaller, and burnt black ... He decided that he would have to run using only his strong back legs and his long tail. And so he hopped ... Kangaroo continued hopping until he was safe. When he tried to walk again on all fours he found he couldn't so he began hopping again and has done so ever since.[10]

Other stories focus on how the kangaroo got its long and powerful tail. The Kulin of central Victoria tell the tale of Wareen, the wombat, and Koim, the kangaroo—another story collected by Aldo Massola on his Victorian travels. Once great friends, the two got into a fight when Koim asked to shelter in Wareen's underground home:

One very wet day Koim came to his friend and asked to be allowed to shelter in the hole, and to dry his fur by his fire. But Wareen would not let him come in. A quarrel ensued, in which Koim cut off Wareen's tail with a blow of his axe, but as he was running off Wareen drove a spear at the base of his back where it stuck fast. This is the reason kangaroos have a heavy tail which sticks straight out behind them, and wombats have no tail at all.[11]

Andrew Leku, a storyteller from northern Australia, tells another story of how the kangaroo got its tail, again through fighting with another Dreamtime animal. Kangaroo had many children, while Bandicoot had none. When Kangaroo refused to let Bandicoot have some of Kangaroo's children for his own, Bandicoot became angry, grabbing Kangaroo by his bottom and holding on tenaciously. Kangaroo pulled and pulled, trying to escape, Bandicoot pulled back, and the result was the long-tailed kangaroo we see today.[12]

Stories about wallabies and how they came to hop on two legs are also found among the many tribal groups that inhabit the islands of New Guinea. A story from West New Britain told by Wilson Salua recounts how Wallaby and Lizard were pilfering *galip* nuts from a tree owned by a fierce giant. Lizard showed Wallaby how to crack the nuts softly with a rock, so as to not attract the attention of the giant, but Wallaby cracked the nuts loudly, rousing the giant who captured him, and beat him until his front legs were badly broken. After this, Wallaby, who until then had moved on all four legs like a dog, could only use his back legs.[13]

The Moni people live high in the mountains of central west Papua, on the main island of New Guinea. Moni children are told the story of the trickster tree kangaroo, Dingiso. It's a cautionary tale, designed to warn children not only of the dangers of gullibility, but also that trickery has its own risks. The story begins when Dingiso meets his friend Bogoso (the Long-beaked Echidna) in the forest one day. The two animals sit down to talk and pass the time of day together. At this time, both animals could climb trees, aided by their long and lovely tails, but Dingiso—the trickster—had sat in such a way that his tail was drawn up across his chest and hidden by his crossed arms. Dingiso remarked on the beauty of Bogoso's tail, adding with tears in his eyes that he had tragically lost his own. Dingiso then encouraged Bogoso to remove his tail so that they could be the same. Bogoso, filled with sympathy for his friend, bit off his own tail. When he found out how he had been tricked, Bogoso was filled with anger towards Dingiso. From that day Dingiso can no longer feed safely on the ground and has to live in the trees, while Bogoso snuffles sadly along the forest floor and hides in hollows in the hope that nobody will see him in his sorry, tail-less state.[14]

Kangaroos also feature in stories that tell how the country was formed. Such stories serve to pass on useful geographical information, as in the Wotjobaluk story of how Purra the Kangaroo, who was being hunted by Doan, the Gliding Possum, hopped northwards. As he hopped, his great tail formed the Wimmera River in north-western Victoria. When Purra realised that the danger had passed, he stopped to feed for a long time, eating the ground bare and thus forming Guru (Lake Hindmarsh). Not completely satiated, he moved a bit further on to browse on sour quandongs, thus forming Ngelbakutya (Lake Albacutya). He continued northwards, but his tracks became fainter (forming the less distinct channel that drains the lake) before disappearing into the sandhill country of the Big Desert.[15] In other stories, kangaroos themselves become the land. A story from around Ramingining, on the edge of the Arafura Swamp in north-eastern Arnhem Land, describes how Garrtjambal the Kangaroo was chased across the land by dingoes, eventually losing his tail, which metamorphosed into rocks, and, later, his head, which became a hill.[16]

In a similar vein, a Djauan story from Arnhem Land in the Northern Territory, the 'Legend and Dreamings of Koopoo, the Red Plain-Kangaroo', traces Koopoo's epic journey across Djauan country, and in doing so describes the locations of billabongs, springs, hunting grounds, camp sites, and deposits of white clay and ochre, as well as regions that should be avoided as they were taboo. During the journey Koopoo '... rubbed himself over with the red ochre and found that it would not come off. And this is why he is the Red Kangaroo'. Other kangaroos also appear in this story: during a flight with Bemmung, the Frilled-neck Lizard, one of Koopoo's smaller kangaroo companions, Kulunjurra, was hit by a spear that broke off and remained in his tail, and so Kulunjurra became the Northern Nailtail Wallaby. Further on, another companion, Doirya, said that he could not follow Koopoo any further, and '... that he would become Doirya the rock-wallaby and would go and live among the tops of the rocks'.[17]

The Gidabal people from the Upper Clarence River region on the border of New South Wales and Queensland tell a story of a *balugan* (a 'hero') who was hunting kangaroo with his aunt. The aunt insisted on holding the kangaroo net, and was dragged away by a big kangaroo. Wherever the kangaroo rested, a swamp or lagoon was formed. Finally, the kangaroo, with the aunt still in tow, entered a lagoon where both aunt and kangaroo became spirits.[18] For this reason, the lagoon features in a 'kangaroo increase ceremony' held in order to increase the numbers of kangaroos in the landscape so that the hunting will be successful. The ceremony involves the performer diving into the lagoon and stirring up the water. It is believed he will see the kangaroo and the aunt in the swirling sediment, and will be able to talk to them.[19]

Kangaroo hunting and increase ceremonies are common to many tribal groups across Australia, although they differ widely in the way they are enacted. Central Australia's Pitjandjara people invoke hot winds at one particular site in the belief that kangaroos can be more easily hunted under such conditions, while at a different site an increase ceremony involves sacred rocks that are believed to be the transformed bodies of mythical kangaroos. This ceremony releases the kangaroos' life-essence from the stones to increase the population.[20] In a similar way, an increase ceremony performed by the Aranda people from Central Australia at major totemic sites for the Red Kangaroo involves striking sacred objects in the belief that every speck of dust that falls to earth will become a kangaroo when next it rains.[21]

Kangaroos also feature in other ceremonies. In western Arnhem Land, male dancers reenact the story about the death of Kundaagi, the Antilopine Wallaroo, who was killed and eaten by the Mimi spirits—and his bones left scattered on the ground. The kangaroo mother found these bones, sung over them, and placed them in a hollow-log coffin so that the soul of the kangaroo could be reborn. Kunwinjku people perform this ceremony today for the human dead in much the same way that the original ceremony was performed for Kundaagi.[22]

KANGAROO AS A FOOD RESOURCE

Kangaroos were probably the major meat source for the first
Aboriginal peoples. Different species were hunted in different

Aboriginal man returning from a hunt, Port Macquarie, northern
New South Wales, with a variety of animals including a Swamp
Wallaby, Koala, Echidna, a goanna, and several snakes. (Mitchell
Library, State Library of NSW, BCP 04764)

Aboriginal man carrying a speared Antilopine Wallaroo at Caledon Bay, Arnhem Land, Northern Territory. (From Dixon and Huxley, 1985)

areas and in different ways; some stalked quietly and speared, others hunted by groups of Aborigines with one chasing the prey and the others waiting in ambush to despatch the animals with a spear or *waddy* (heavy wooden club).[23] In some hilly regions where animal tracks were clearly visible, pitfall traps were the preferred hunting method. In some areas, many different species were hunted. For example, in the early 1970s Jon Altman lived with a group of Gunwinggu in eastern Arnhem Land. Of the 18 mammal species he recorded the Gunwinggu hunting, six were macropods, including the Agile Wallaby, the Antilopine, the Black and Common Wallaroos, and the Short-eared and Little Rock-wallabies. The best times of the year for hunting the macropods were the mid-wet season, when the animals were most plentiful, and the late dry season, when macropods could be driven out of patches of scrub by fire.[24]

There is a broad division of strategies between hunting methods for the larger and smaller species. Large kangaroos have large home ranges and are hunted singly. Success rates are typically low. Smaller wallabies and rat-kangaroos are more numerous over smaller areas and a range of methods such as trapping and driving ensure higher rates of success. Fire is an effective tool for catching large and small species alike—burning provides green pick for the larger species and encourages them to use certain areas, while it drives the smaller species from their densely wooded hiding places.[25]

In open country, the boomerang was deadly. In 1826, Captain Phillip Parker King described it as:

> ... a very formidable weapon; it is a short, curved piece of heavy wood, and is propelled through the air by the hand in so skilful a manner that the thrower alone knows where it will fall. It is generally thrown against the wind and takes a rapid rotary motion. It is used by the natives with success in killing the kangaroo, and is, I believe, more a hunting than a warlike weapon ... Boomerang is the Port Jackson term for this weapon, and may be retained for want of a more descriptive name.[26]

In *The Story of the Flinders Ranges Mammals*, Dorothy Tunbridge recounts the various ways the Adnyamathanha people hunted macropods using pitfall traps, funnel traps and nets. Deep pits, known as *vata*, were dug in tracks used by macropods and covered with fresh vegetation that offered the unsuspecting animal food or shelter. *Vata* were particularly effective for catching rock-wallabies, kangaroos and euros. The captured animals were killed with stones or a long stick before being removed.[27] *Yarru* were V-shaped fences constructed of brush and sticks, intertwined and kept in place with stones. The macropods, and other animals such as emus, were herded into the opening of the V-shaped funnel. At the narrow end of the funnel was a pitfall trap, or a net, or other members of the tribe waiting in ambush. The Adnyamathanha also used nets to entangle kangaroos at waterholes.[28]

Similar hunting methods were observed throughout the time of European exploration and settlement. The first European to travel through Adnyamathanha country and to witness firsthand their techniques for capturing kangaroos, including those described 150 years later by Tunbridge, was the explorer Edward John Eyre who explored the Flinders Ranges in the late 1830s.

Kangaroos are speared, netted, or caught in pit falls. Four methods of spearing them are practised. 1st. A native travelling with his family through the woods, when he sees a kangaroo feeding or sleeping, will steal silently and cautiously upon it, keeping, as he advances, a tree or shrub between himself and the animal, or holding up before him, if he be in an open place, a large branch of a tree, until sufficiently near to throw the fatal weapon. 2ndly. Two natives get upon the track of a kangaroo, which they follow up perseveringly even for two or three days, sleeping upon it at night, and renewing their pursuit in the morning, until, at last, the wearied animal, fairly tired out by its relentless pursuers, is no longer able to fly before them, and at last becomes a prize to the perseverance of the hunters. 3rdly. A small hut of reeds is made near the springs, or water holes, in those districts, where water is scarce; and in this, or in the top of a tree, if there be one near, the native carefully conceals himself, and patiently waits until his game comes to drink, when he is almost sure to strike it with his spear, seldom quitting his lurking place without an ample remuneration for his confinement. 4thly. A large party of men go out early in the morning, generally armed with barbed spears, and take their stations upon ground that has been previously fixed upon in a large semicircle. The women and children, with a few men, then beat up, and fire the country for a considerable extent, driving the game before them in the direction of the persons who are lying in wait, and who gradually contract the space they had been spread over, until they meet the other party, and then closing their ranks in a ring upon the devoted animals, with wild cries and shouts they drive them back to the centre as they attempt to escape, until, at last, in the conflict, many of them are slaughtered. At other times, the ground is so selected as to enable them to drive the game over a precipice, or into a river, where it is easily taken. Netting the kangaroo does not require so large a party; it is done by simply setting a strong net (*mugn-ko*) across the path, which the animal is accustomed to frequent, and keeping it in its place by long sticks, with a fork upon the top. A few natives then shew themselves in a direction opposite to that of the net, and the kangaroo being alarmed, takes to his usual path, gets entangled in the meshes, and is soon despatched by persons who have been lying in wait to pounce upon him.[29]

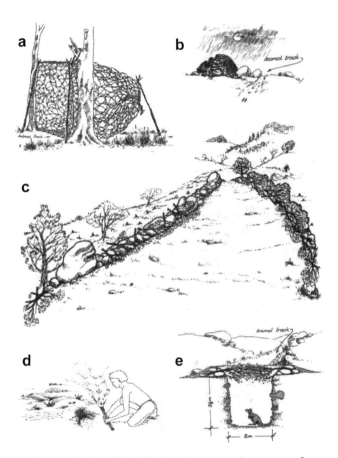

The Adnyamathanha of the Flinders Ranges used a variety of methods to catch macropods. (a) A *mindi* could be used to net animals, (b) hiding places along wallaby tracks were used to ambush prey, (c) a V-shaped funnel or *yarru* was used to herd macropods towards a pit or an ambush, (d) fire could be used to smoke Burrowing Bettongs from their underground burrows and tunnels, and (e) a pit or *vata* covered with vegetation could trap unsuspecting wallabies. (Taken from Tunbridge, 1991)

Other explorers also keenly observed and reported on the methods used in different regions to catch kangaroo. In the late 1830s, George Grey was travelling through Western Australia, and observed:

> Another very ingenious mode of taking wallaby and the smaller kind of kangaroos is to select a thick bushy place where there are plenty of these animals; the bushes are then broken down in a circle round the spot where they intend to hunt, so as to form a space of broken scrub about ten feet wide all round a thick bush, they thus not only destroy the runs of the animals but form with the fallen bushes a place which so embarrasses and entangles them that they find great difficulty in passing it; indeed when these preparations have been made the natives fire the bush and the frightened animals, finding their runs stopped up, rush into the fallen branches, where every jump which they make upon their hind legs only involves them in greater difficulties, so that they fall an easy prey to their pursuers.[30]

KANGAROO TOOLS AND ORNAMENTS

The kangaroo was hunted for more than its flesh. Very little of the kangaroo was wasted; the skin was used to make clothes, rugs and carry bags, the sinews and bones were used as binding to construct weapons and the tools used in basketry, net making, surgery, and as items of personal decoration (the women of the Yarra tribe, for example, inserted a piece of leg bone through their nasal septums). Kangaroo teeth were used as engravers on wooden objects and for personal adornment.[31] Even the animals' fibrous dried dung was used, as tinder to start a fire.

Kangaroo skins were also used to make waterbags. In fact, the kangaroo skin waterbag—a survival tool developed about 5000 years ago, gave people the means to move into areas that previously were inhospitable, such as the Simpson, Great Victoria and Sandy Deserts, thereby completing their occupation of the Australian continent. These waterbags could hold nearly 20 litres of water and were essential tools for living in the drier parts of Australia. Apparently, the explorer Thomas Mitchell borrowed the waterbag idea from Aborigines he encountered in central Australia, making a canvas version of the kangaroo skin original. Like the kangaroo skin waterbags, the canvas bag allowed water to slowly seep through the bag, wetting it, which would evaporatively cool the water within. The canvas bags—sometimes called 'dromedary bags'—seen today strapped to the front of 4WD vehicles continue the 5000-year-old tradition. The making of a kangaroo skin bag involved removing the skin from the kangaroo with the greatest care, cleaning it with a basalt-chip or mussel shell, and then stretching it on pegs until dried by the sun. Once dry, the ends were brought together and tied with strings made of grass. A grass rope was attached to both ends so that the bag could be carried over the shoulder.[32]

To the native people of New Guinea, kangaroos are also an important source of food, clothing and ornaments. In particular, macropods appear to have had a special significance in the construction of ceremonial ornaments. Although there is a lack of records about the cultural significance of macropods to the New Guineans, a fascinating study by anthropologist Alexandra Szalay, which focused on tree kangaroos, found them to be used in necklaces, neck ornaments, hair combs, string bags and head-dresses.[33]

New Guinean ceremonial ornaments containing tree kangaroo body parts. From the top left, clockwise: necklace of tree kangaroo, cuscus, striped possum and pig incisors; hair comb with fur of Vogelkop Tree Kangaroo; necklace with Scott's Tree Kangaroo (or Tenkile) claw; fur head-dress of Doria's Tree Kangaroo fur; ceremonial string bag decorated with hunting trophies including tree kangaroo feet, skulls and jaws. (Paintings by Peter Schouten from the collection of Tim Flannery and reproduced with the kind permission of Peter Schouten and Tim Flannery)

THE KANGAROO IN ABORIGINAL ART

Aboriginal art has a history in Australia that stretches back many tens of thousands of years. The oldest evidence of rock art dates to more than 40,000 years ago, but the tradition is probably older—used pigment fragments excavated from Arnhem Land have been dated at more than 52,000 years old, so art was probably a feature of Aboriginal life right from the time the first people arrived in Australia.[34] So when Europeans reached Australia in the eighteenth century, they encountered a people who for perhaps 50 millennia had been making paintings, carvings and engravings of Australia's most ubiquitous animal inhabitant: the kangaroo.

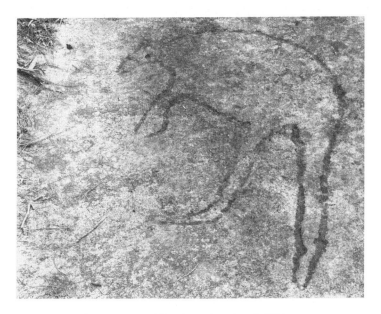

Kangaroo rock engraving, Allambie, New South Wales. (Warringah Shire Library Service)

Art by indigenous Australians was and still is the major means of recording and recreating ancestral events, ensuring continuity with one's ancestry, and for communicating with the spirit world. Art is an expression of ritual knowledge, and a statement of authority—by using ancestrally inherited designs, the artist asserts their identity, rights and responsibilities.[35]

Aboriginal art takes many forms, and we can barely touch upon the subject here. The most enduring forms are of course rock paintings and engravings. Other forms include body decoration, bark paintings, ground paintings, and ceremonial sculpture of wood, stone and bone. Kangaroos are represented in many of these art forms. They adorn rock shelter painting

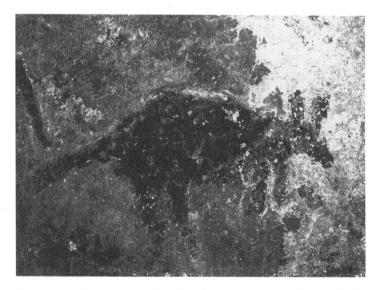

Kangaroo painting at a rock shelter site in northeastern Queensland. (Photo: Karl Vernes)

sites across Australia, and are depicted in bone ornaments, rock engravings, bark paintings and burial poles, as well as in contemporary Aboriginal carvings and paintings.

'Black Rock Kangaroo, Wolerrk Narbelek' by Bobby Barrdjaray Nganjmirra (West Arhem Land, Oenpelli, circa 1970). (Reproduced with permission of Arthur Beau Palmer)

One obvious aspect of Aboriginal images of kangaroos to the artistically trained and layperson alike is the elegance of line and accuracy of the depiction that demonstrate a long history of observation, and intimate knowledge of the animal's physicality. In the coming chapter, by contrast, we will see the difficulty that European artists had in portraying the kangaroo form. This is understandable—kangaroos were new and unusual to the European eye, and culturally, kangaroos may never have the same significance for Europeans as they do for Aboriginal peoples who for millennia had been sustained by these animals. Nevertheless, of all Australia's indigenous fauna it is the macropods that have certainly bewildered, confounded and fascinated Europeans the most since their very first sighting. So, when Europeans began to chart the coastline of Australia in the seventeenth century, new stories about kangaroos would be told in distant lands, and the cultural and economic importance of these animals would enter the consciousness of colonial Australians and their descendants.

3

CIVET-CATS, GIANT RATS AND JUMPING RACCOONS

Early European Observations

Quadrupeds we saw but few and were able to catch few of them that we did see. The largest was calld by the natives Kangooroo. It is different from any European and indeed any animal I have heard or read of except the Gerbua of Egypt, which is not larger than a rat when this is as large as a midling Lamb ... It may however be easily known from all other animals by the singular property of running or rather hopping upon only its hinder legs ... [1]

For at least two hundred years before Lieutenant (later Captain) James Cook charted the east coast of 'New Holland' in 1770, European seafarers—Dutch, Portuguese, English, Spanish and French—had been exploring Australia's west, northern and even southern coastlines. The earliest confirmed observation of an Australian macropod by Europeans was made by the Dutch in 1629; however, the first Europeans to set eyes on macropods might have been sixteenth-century Portuguese mariners. After 1788, the early settlers and explorers recorded numerous observations of these extraordinary-looking animals. It is understandable that the first Europeans compared the macropods with animals they were already familiar with, such as rats and hopping mice, sometimes with unintentionally comic results.

DE JODE'S 'KANGAROO' AND OTHER EARLY ENCOUNTERS

Who were the first Europeans to come across a kangaroo? One of the problems in verifying the earliest depictions of macropods is that, to European eyes, these animals were so unusual that explorers, naturalists and even artists had terrible difficulty in producing a realistic rendition. The cover page of a book of world geography, the *Speculum orbis terrae* published by Flemish cartographer Cornelis de Jode in 1593, appears to illustrate a type of marsupial with young. It's hardly an anatomically accurate depiction of any known species of macropod—the head and neck are camel-like, and the female's pouch appears to hang from below its neck and contains twins, which are exceedingly rare in macropods. Nevertheless, the animal has some tantalisingly macropod qualities, particularly the proportions of its muscular hind quarters compared to the relatively slender forelimbs.[2]

The islands of New Guinea were known to the Portuguese in the sixteenth century, and world maps produced by the French cartographer Nicolas Desliens in 1566 and Gerard and Cornelis de Jode in 1578 (and again in 1593) are clear evidence that there that was some geographical knowledge of the northern shore of Australia.[3] In de Jode's *Speculum orbis terrae* a mysterious land, *Terra Australis Incognita*, is indicated in roughly the actual position of continental Australia, and the northern coastline of this land approximates—in shape, size and relative position to New Guinea and the Indonesian archipelago—the northern coastline of Australia. If northern Australia was indeed charted in the sixteenth century, it would be hard to believe that the seafarers that travelled along those shores would not have encountered macropods, as the 'Top End' is home to some of our larger and more gregarious species, including the Agile Wallaby, which occurs in large mobs across northern Australia's floodplains.

Danielle Clode's recent study of Portuguese activity in the Australasian region in the sixteenth century suggests that de Jode's 'marsupial' might indicate that these Portuguese explorers and cartographers had a greater knowledge of Australia than has been generally assumed. On the cover of de Jode's book, the marsupial in the bottom right-hand corner is accompanied by a horse, camel and lion in the other corners. It is thought that these three animals represent the known continents—the horse for Europe, the camel for Asia and the lion for Africa—but where was de Jode's marsupial-like creature intended to represent? It could be argued that the animal represents the Americas, and that it is an opossum, albeit a larger one than any known from that continent. However, the axes upon which these animals are positioned are thought to represent direction, and de Jode's map of 'the known world' shows South America to the west of Africa, not to the east. Clode argues therefore that the only continent to the east of Africa is Australia, and that the logical origin of this macropod-like marsupial is the Australasian region—New Guinea or the Moluccas, if not continental Australia itself.[4]

Title page of Cornelis de Jode's *Speculum Orbis Terrae*, published in 1593, showing the first possible depiction of a kangaroo (bottom right).

Whether or not de Jode took the inspiration for his marsupial from the stories of Portuguese mariners who might have glimpsed the northern coastline of Australia and its inhabitants is long lost in time. The first indisputable written observation of a macropod was made only a few years later, by Spanish nobleman Captain Don Diego de Prado y Tovar. In 1606, Don Diego de Prado was captain of the *San Pedro y San Pablo* whose crew landed at San Millan Bay, on the southern coast of New Guinea and described what was, most likely, a Dusky Pademelon. After a clumsy and brutal encounter with the 'Indians', where several of the natives were shot dead, Don Diego de Prado made the following observation:

> We also saw a very large field of ginger which God alone cultivates for the natives do not know what it is; here we killed an animal which is in the shape of a dog smaller than a greyhound, with a bare and scaly tail like that of a snake, and his testicles hang from a nerve like a thin cord; they say that it was the castor, we eat it and it was like venison, its stomach full of ginger leaves and for that reason we eat it.[5]

But, it was a far bloodier event that preceded the first confirmed observation of a macropod on Australian soil. Francisco Pelsaert was captain of the *Batavia*, wrecked off the Western Australian coastline in 1629 on her maiden voyage to the Dutch East Indies. *Batavia*'s intended route was to cross the Indian Ocean from the Cape of Good Hope at a latitude of about 40°S of the Equator, as the 'Roaring Forties' could carry a ship in sprightly fashion across the ocean to the western shoreline of Australia, at which point the usual procedure was to turn the prow northwards towards Indonesia. Calculating a ship's true position was not yet an exact science, as the numerous shipwrecks along Western Australia's coast attest. Two hours before dawn, on 4 June 1629, the *Batavia* was wrecked on a reef off West Wallabi Island, one of the Houtman Abrolhos Islands, which lie about 80 kilometres off mainland Western Australia. Her skipper thought she was still about 1000 kilometres from land. Pelsaert took the ship's cutter and set off in search of help, aiming for Batavia—now known as Jakarta on the Indonesian island of Java. This was the signal for a mutiny planned months earlier to explode into systematic and sickening violence. More than 125 men, women and children had been murdered by Jeronimus Cornelisz and his fellow mutineers by the time Pelsaert returned on 17 September. The murderers were dramatically captured and tried, and on 2 October 1629 they became the first criminals to be hanged on Australian soil.[6]

Pelsaert's journal leaves the reader in no doubt that the wreck of the *Batavia* is a great dramatic tragedy in Australian history. For that reason alone, it is remarkable that shortly after justice had been meted out to the worst of the mutineers, Pelsaert, having set sail once more for Batavia, wrote the first detailed observation of an Australian mammal by a European, an insightful and inspired account of the Tammar Wallaby. On 15 November 1629, Pelsaert wrote:

Moreover on these islands there are a large numbers of Cats, which are creatures of a miraculous form, as big as a hare; the head is similar to [that] of a civet-cat, the fore-paws are very short, about a finger long. Whereon there are five small Nails or small fingers, as an ape's fore-paw, and the two hind legs are at least half an ell long [about 35 centimetres], they run on the flat of the joint of the leg, so that they are not quick in running. The tail is very long, the same as a Meerkat; if they are going to eat, they sit on the hind-legs and take the food with the fore-paws, and eat exactly the same as the squirrels or apes do.[7]

The Tammar Wallaby is one of only two mammals that occurred on the Houtman Abrolhos Islands in 1629, the other being the diminutive Bush Rat, and although the Tammar Wallaby now has to share the islands with a raft of introduced species, it is still common there.

The next Australian macropod to be recorded was the Quokka, which was observed in 1656 by another Dutchman, Samuel Volkersen, on what is now known as Rottnest Island, off the coast of Western Australia. Volkertsz wrote:

In slightly under 32-S latitude there is a large island of the South-land ... here certain animals are found, since we saw many excrements, and besides two seals and a wild cat [Quokka], resembling a civet-cat, but with browner hair.[8]

Some 40 years later while travelling along the west coast of Australia on board the *Geelvinck*, Dutch mariner William de Vlamingh also saw the Quokka on Rottnest Island. On 30 December 1696 he recorded in the *Geelvinck* Journal that 'our bookkeeper reported that he and the people with him had gone through and searched everything thoroughly, and that of animals there is nothing there but bush rats of which they shot a few and brought with them on board with various trees with a pleasant fragrance'.[9] De Vlamingh referred to the island as 'Fog Island', 'Isle of Girls', 'Rats' Island' and 'Rat's nest Island', the last of which evidently stuck.[10] The voyage was further reported by the Dutch diplomat Nicolaes Witsen, who had invested in the journey:

> It was at thirty-one degrees and forty-seven minutes south latitude that Vlamingh sighted the land of Hollandia Nova, first landing on an island in sight of the mainland, where he found no people but a large number of rats, nearly as big as cats, which had a pouch below their throat into which one could put one's hand, without being able to understand to what end nature had created the animal like this: as soon as it had been shot dead, this animal smelled terribly, so that the skins were not taken along.[11]

Witsen made further reference to the Quokka in a letter to Dr Martin Lister dated 3 October 1698, in which he describes 'rats as great as cats, in an innumerable quantity; all which had a kind of a bag or purse hanging from the throat upon the breast downwards'.[12]

Another seventeenth-century sighting was that of the beautiful Banded Hare-wallaby by English buccaneer, sea captain and explorer William Dampier on 6 August 1699 on Dirk Hartog Island off the coast of Western Australia:

> The Land-Animals that we saw here were only a sort of Raccoons, different from those of the West Indies, chiefly as to their Legs; for these have very short Fore-Legs; but go jumping upon them as the others do (and like them are very good meat).[13]

By the close of the seventeenth century, European knowledge of macropods was limited to Pelsaert's short but elegant account of the Tammar Wallaby and vague descriptions of giant rats and raccoons. Many of the travel journals of voyages that landed in Australia and New Guinea were written in Spanish and Dutch, and were 'commercial in confidence' so they often did not publish them because keeping these documents secret was the only way they could protect their business from larger maritime powers. The later voyages (such as those of Captain Cook) were voyages of discovery and matters of national pride, so the results were often widely published and distributed. The rather limited data on the biology and appearance of the kangaroos was augmented considerably by the Dutch artist and traveller Cornelis de Bruijn. In 1706, de Bruijn observed a strange animal in captivity in Java. The animal's owners had called it the 'philander' or 'friend of man'—now thought to have been a Dusky Pademelon. It had been brought from its native home in New Guinea to a menagerie owned by a Dutch East India Company official, Cornelis Kastelein. De Bruijn was apparently delighted with this little animal, and his overall description of it and the pouch of the female was, importantly, accompanied by an engraving—the first confirmed illustration of any species of macropod.[14]

CAPTAIN COOK'S KANGAROO

The earliest observations of macropods have been overshadowed by the more widely published observations of Captain James Cook and his botanist Joseph Banks.[15] Cook and his party may or may not have read the earlier European accounts of civet-cats, jumping raccoons, giant rats and de Bruijn's 'friend of man'

The first confirmed image of a macropod. The 'philander' (Dusky Pademelon) drawn by Cornelis de Bruijn in 1706 in Java, and which appeared in his *Reizen over Moskovie door Persie en Indie*. (National Library of Australia, nla.pic-an9927081)

when their ship, the *Endeavour*, struck a coral reef on 11 June 1770—but if they had, those accounts did not prepare them for the strange animals they were going to meet. After unloading the ballast, guns and heavy stores the ship was floated off and three days later beached at the mouth of a large river. It took six weeks to repair and refit the ship, so the crew had numerous opportunities to explore the shoreline near the mouth of what is now known as the Endeavour River, near Cooktown in North Queensland. Here the crew of the *Endeavour* famously encountered what is thought to be, after much controversy, the Eastern Grey Kangaroo, and Cook and Banks made numerous observations.

Banks—22 June 1770—The People who were sent to the other side of the water in order to shoot Pigeons saw an animal as large as a grey hound, of a mouse coulour and very swift ...

Cook—24 June 1770—I saw one of the animals which had been so often described: it was of a light mouse colour, and in size and shape very much resembling a greyhound; and I should have taken it for a wild dog, if instead of running, it had not leapt like a hare or a deer: its legs were very slender, and the print of its foot to be like that of a goat, but where I saw it the grass was so high that the legs were concealed, and the ground was too hard to receive the track.

Banks—25 June 1770—In gathering plants today I myself had the good fortune to see the beast so much talkd of, tho but imperfectly; he was not only like a grey hound in size and running but had a long tail, as long as any grey hounds; what to liken him to I could not tell, nothing certainly that I have seen at all resembles him.

Banks—7 July 1770—We walked many miles over the flats and saw 4 of the animals, 2 of which my greyhound fairly chas'd, but they beat him owing to the length and thickness of the grass which prevented him from running while at every bound [they] leapd over the tops of it. We observd much to our surprize that that instead of Going upon all fours this animal went upon two legs, making vast bounds just as the Jerbua (*Mus jaculus*) does.

But it was more than three weeks of seeing the kangaroo before Cook, Banks and others finally procured a specimen, which must have caused great excitement among the party, especially the naturalist, Joseph Banks:

> *Banks*—14 July 1770—Our second lieutenant who was out shooting today had the good fortune to kill the animal that had so long been the subject of our speculations. To compare it to any European animal would be impossible as it has not the least resemblance of anyone I have seen. Its fore legs are extremely short and of no use to it in walking, its hind again as disproportional long; with these it hops 7 or 8 feet at each hop in the same manner as the Gerbua, to which animal indeed it bears much resemblance except in Size, this being in weight 38lb and the Gerbua no larger than a common rat.

The next day the kangaroo was eaten, followed by many more as the crew made use of this new source of meat which they mostly—but not always—relished:

> *Cook*—15 July 1770—The next day, our Kanguroo was dressed for dinner, and proved most excellent meat.
>
> *Banks*—28 July—Dind today upon the animal, who eat but ill, he was I suppose too old. His fault however was an uncommon one, the total want of flavour, for he was certainly the most insipid meat I eat.

The specimens taken back to London were described and given scientific Latin names that, typically, reflected the idea that these strange new animals were giant rodents, for example *Mus canguru* (Philipp Müller, 1776) suggested they were mice and *Jerboa gigantea* (Eberhard Zimmerman, 1777), suggested that this new animal was a giant hopping mouse, similar to those that occur in Africa.[16] There has been considerable debate as to the true identity of 'Captain Cook's kangaroo', with various species being proposed including the Eastern Grey Kangaroo, Common Wallaroo and Whiptail Wallaby. The debate arose partly because the kangaroo skull brought back to England by Joseph Banks belonged to the museum collection of the Royal College of Surgeons in London that was lost when the museum was bombed in World War II. Thankfully, the skull had been photographed, and those surviving photos suggest that the skull was from an Eastern Grey Kangaroo, though even this has been debated.[17]

In 1770 Cook had observed Eastern Grey Kangaroos almost at their northern geographical limit. In 1777, during his third voyage, he again observed evidence of this species, but this time at the extreme south of their range at Adventure Bay in Tasmania.

> The Kangooroo which is found farther northward in New Holland as describ'd in Captn Cooks Voyage with out doubt also inhabits here, as the natives had some pieces of their skins and we several times saw animals, though indistinctly, run from the thickets when we walk'd in the woods which from the size could be no other. It would also appear that they are in considerable numbers from the dung we saw almost every where and the narrow tracks or paths they have made amongst the shrubbery.[18]

THE FIRST FLEETERS' FIRST IMPRESSIONS

The earliest settlers made numerous observations of kangaroos after the First Fleet arrived in Australia between 18 and 20 January 1788. David Blackburn was Master of the ship *Supply*. In a letter dated 12 July 1788, Blackburn wrote to his friend Richard Knight, back in England that:

> The animals of this country are all curious. The kangaroo is frequently shot by our parties, & is the only fresh meal they can get; some of them are very large weighing upwards of 140 Pounds.
>
> Capt. Cook has describd their form. I shall only remark that a stout greyhound has little chance of overtaking them they hop on their hind legs with great swiftness over the high grass. The tail is certainly their principal Weapon of Defence, which they can use with force sufficient to break a bone. The root of the tail of a large one measured eleven inches round & was near 4 feet long. They have a false belly which is a loose skin which they have the power of expanding or contracting at pleasure—they bring forth the young perfectly formd. Not bigger than a mouse; & in time of cold or danger always take shelter in the false belly—To what age the parent protects them in this manner we do not know but I think not after they are the size of a cat.[19]

British Marine officer Watkin Tench is considered by some to be the father of Australian literature, if not Australian history, and has been often praised for his well-written and lively accounts of the first years at Sydney Cove.[20] In his first book of life in the colony, *A Narrative of the Expedition to Botany Bay* published in 1789, Tench describes in detail the natural history of the kangaroo and demonstrates that he deserves his reputation as a skilled and observant narrator:

Of the natural history of the kangaroo we are still very ignorant. We may, however, venture to pronounce this animal, a new species of opossum, the female being furnished with a bag, in which the young is contained; and in which the teats are found. These last are only two in number, a strong presumptive proof, had we no other evidence, that the kangaroo brings forth rarely more than one at birth. But this is settled beyond a doubt, from more than a dozen females have been killed, which had invariably but one formed in the pouch. Notwithstanding this, the animal may be looked on as prolific, from the early age it begins to breed at, kangaroos with young having been taken of not more than thirty pounds weight; and there is room to believe that when at their utmost growth, they weigh not less than one hundred and fifty pounds. A male of one hundred and thirty pounds weight has been killed...

After this perhaps I shall hardly be credited, when I affirm that the kangaroo on being brought forth is not larger than an English mouse. It is, however, in my power to speak positively on this head, as I have seen more than one instance of it.

In running, this animal confines himself entirely to his hinder legs, which are possessed with an extraordinary muscular power. Their speed is very great, though not in general quite equal to that of a greyhound; but when the greyhounds are so fortunate as to seize them, they are incapable of retaining their hold, from the amazing struggles of the animal. The bound of the kangaroo, when not hard pressed, has been measured, and found to exceed twenty feet. At what time of the year they copulate, and in what manner, we know not: the testicles of the male are placed contrary to the usual order of nature [Tench had noticed that they are placed in front of the opening where the penis is stored instead of behind as in placental or eutherian mammals]...They are not carnivorous, and subsist altogether on particular flowers and grass. Their bleat is mournful, and very different from that of any other animal: it is, however, seldom heard but in the young-ones.[21]

In 1793, Tench updated and expanded his description of the kangaroo in *A Complete Account of the Settlement at Port Jackson*. Here he corrects his earlier statement about the number of teats, and provides more detail about the species' natural history. His description of the ear, and the kangaroo's trademark characteristic of being able to rotate the ear pinnae when sensing danger is particularly well observed:

The elegance of the ear is particularly deserving of admiration. This far exceeds the ear of the hare in quickness of sense and is so flexible as to admit of being turned by the animal nearly quite round the head, doubtless for the purpose of informing the creature of the approach of its enemies, as it is of a timid nature and poorly furnished with means of defence; though when compelled to resist, it tears furiously with its forepaws, and strikes *forward* very hard with its hind legs.[22]

Tench also describes some of the other macropods he had encountered around Sydney Cove, including the Swamp Wallaby and Rufous Bettong. This makes his account the first to describe a community of macropods.

Hitherto I have spoken only of the large, or grey kangaroo, to which the natives give the name of 'patagaran'. But there are (besides the kangaroo-rat) two other sorts. One of them we called the red kangaroo, from the colour of its fur, which is like that of a hare, and sometimes is mingled with a large portion of black: the natives call it 'bagaray' [this is the Swamp Wallaby, *Wallabia bicolor*] ... The third sort is very rare, and in the formation of its head resembles the opossum [Tench was possibly referring to the Red-necked Pademelon, *Thylogale thetis*]. The kangaroo-rat is a small animal ... this is probably the Rufous Bettong, *Aepyprymnus rufescens*]. It joins to the head and bristles of a rat the leading distinctions of a kangaroo, by running when pursued on its hind legs only, and the female having a pouch.[23]

Tench describes beautifully and accurately the nest, and nest-making behaviour, of the Rufous Bettong:

Unlike the kangaroo, who appears to have no fixed place of residence, this little animal constructs for itself a nest of grass, on the ground, of a circular figure, about ten inches in diameter, with a hole on one side for the creature to enter at; the inside being lined with a finer sort of grass, very soft and downy. But its manner of carrying the materials with which it builds the nest is the greatest curiosity: by entwining its tail (which, like that of all the kangaroo tribe, is long, flexible and muscular) around whatever it wants to remove, and thus dragging along the load behind it.

The Long-nosed Potoroo also occurred in the Sydney region and was noted by Governor Arthur Phillip in his journal:

The general shape of the body is not widely different from that of the *Kanguroo,* both in respect to the shortness of the fore legs and the peculiar construction of the hind ones; but the visage being strongly similar to that of the rat, and the colour of the whole not ill resembling that animal, it has obtained the name of the *Kanguroo Rat*. [It is from this incorrect name that the small potoroos and bettongs came, unfortunately, to be known as 'rat-kangaroos'.][24]

The English naturalist George Perry was another observer who thought that Australia's kangaroos were indeed giant jumping rodents. He described the Long-nosed Potoroo as *Dipus muscola* (after one of the genera of hopping rodents called jerboas).

Since the discovery of the extensive Continent of New Holland [Australia], by Capt. COOKE, and other circumnavigators, various species of the Jerboa have been discovered in great variety in that curious region of the Globe. Of these the largest is the brown Kangaroo, the grey and the buff kinds being much smaller and of different character. Next to these is the curious Animal called the Kangaroo Rat [Long-nosed Potoroo], so well described in Governor PHILLIPS Journal of a Voyage to New Holland.[25]

And so, at the start of the nineteenth century, a handful of Australian macropods had been sighted, described, observed in detail or even taken alive back to Europe: Tammar Wallabies, Quokkas and Banded Hare-wallabies, the Eastern Grey Kangaroo, Swamp Wallaby, Rufous Bettong, Long-nosed Potoroo and, possibly, the Red-necked Pademelon and Tasmanian Bettong.

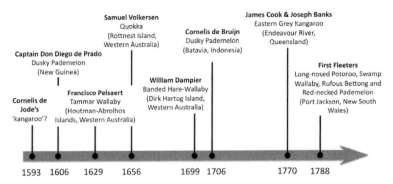

Timeline of European discovery of kangaroos. Spanish, Dutch and English seafarers had all seen macropods before Cook and Banks described 'the kangaroo of New Holland'.

Perry summarises this diversity, stating that 'the different species of the genus, already discovered in New Holland, amount already to five or six, and probably other kinds may be found when the country is more penetrated, for being itself larger than Europe, it is natural to suppose that a great variety of Animals must inhabit so extensive a region'.[26]

The next encounter between macropod and European took place in the interior of New Guinea. Salomon Müller and Heinrich Macklot[27] were naturalists sent to the Dutch East Indies by the Natural History Commission for the Netherlands. In 1828 they visited the Lobo District of New Guinea (now West Papua in Indonesia), where they obtained specimens of a small, blackish kangaroo which local hunters called *wangoerie* and a second species, similar to the first, known as *wakera*. These were the first remarkable macropods known as 'tree kangaroos' ever collected and observed by Europeans.[29] Later, Müller reported:

> In New Guinea ... [we discovered] two kangaroos, which
> differ very characteristically from all others of the class
> hitherto described, in that they live upon trees. For this reason,
> as well as for other physical distinctions, we have formed
> them into a new group, under the name *Dendrolagus* [meaning
> 'tree hare'].[30]

In 1847, HMS *Rattlesnake*, a naval vessel searching for a safe
route between Sydney and India inside the Great Barrier
Reef, was in the vicinity of modern day Innisfail (south
of Cairns) in North Queensland when the ship's naturalist,
John MacGillivray, made the first observation of what we
now know to have been the Red-legged Pademelon, a rainforest wallaby that occurs from northern New South Wales to
New Guinea:

> Near this place, while tacking close in shore, a native dog was
> seen by Lieutenant Simpson, in chase of a small kangaroo,
> which, on being close pressed, plunged into the water and
> swam out to sea, when it was picked up by the boat, leaving
> its pursuer standing on a rock gazing wistfully at its intended
> prey, until a musket ball, which went very near its mark, sent
> it off at a trot. The kangaroo lived on board for a few days, and
> proved to constitute quite a new kind, closely allied to *Halma-
> turus thetidis* [the Red-necked Pademelon].[31]

Discoveries continued through the nineteenth and into the
twentieth century, as naturalists added dozens of species to
the list of known macropods, including oddities such as the
Bridled Nailtail Wallabies with their tails tipped by toenails.

As late as the 1970s, brand-new macropod species were still being discovered. John Seebeck discovered the Long-footed Potoroo in western Victoria; Gerry Maynes discovered the Proserpine Rock-wallaby in north Queensland.[32] In New Guinea, almost 400 years after Don Diego de Prado's first encounter with a strange, 'dog-like' animal, Tim Flannery discovered Scott's Tree Kangaroo (or Tenkile) in 1988 and the Dingiso in 1994.[33] Such recent discoveries make one wonder whether more undiscovered macropod species await scientific attention.

THE FIRST KANGAROOS IN EUROPEAN ART

It was Banks and Cook who first described the Eastern Grey Kangaroo at Endeavour River in 1770, but the credit for the first illustration of an Eastern Grey Kangaroo must go to the ship's draughtsman, Sydney Parkinson. Parkinson made nearly 1300 drawings of the plants and animals collected by Banks and the other naturalists on board, among which was a sketch of a kangaroo that would later be used as the model for the British painter George Stubbs. Parkinson also made a few unfinished pencil drawings of kangaroos, which probably precede the refined version used by Stubbs. Unfortunately, Parkinson did not live to see his drawings transformed into a masterpiece—after leaving New Holland he contracted dysentery in Batavia, and died at sea on 26 January 1771. On his return to England, Banks paid Parkinson's outstanding salary to his brother, Stanfield, believing this gave him ownership of Parkinson's works. A dispute between the two over who owned the rights to the artwork followed, however, with Banks eventually obtaining an injunction against Stanfield from publishing any of Parkinson's work until after the publication of the official account of the voyage.

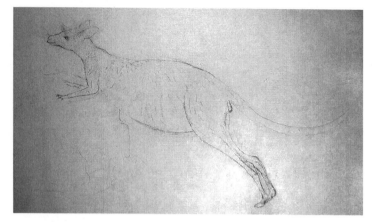

One of Sydney Parkinson's unfinished pencil drawings of the kangaroo seen at Endeavour River. Drawn in 1770, this is possibly the first image made of an Australian macropod by a European. (Original drawing at the Natural History Museum, London)

Cook's editor, Dr John Hawkesworth omitted any mention of Parkinson, nor did he credit him with any of the drawings that were used—including that of the kangaroo. Sadly, the dispute meant that Parkinson became an almost forgotten name in the history of Australia.[34]

It was Joseph Banks who commissioned George Stubbs to paint the subject, which Stubbs entitled *The Kongouro from New Holland, 1770*. This work was exhibited by Stubbs at the *Society of Artists* of Great Britain in 1773, and was used as the frontispiece to the second volume of *The* Endeavour *Journal of Joseph Banks*. It can still be seen on display today at Parham House and Gardens, south of London.[35]

Parkinson's own description of the bizarre animal that had caused so much excitement among the naturalists on the

The Kongouro. Engraved for Bankes's *New System of Geography* after a drawing by Sydney Parkinson—above, and the painting by George Stubbs for which Parkinson's work served as a model—below. (Allport Library and Museum of the Arts, Tasmanian Archive and Heritage)

Endeavour, published posthumously, illustrates the difficulties encountered by naturalists and artists for much of the following century when attempting to describe and depict this unlikely mammal:

> Of quadrupeds, there [is] an animal of a kind nearly approaching the *mus* genus, about the size of a grey-hound, that had a head like a fawn's; lips and ears, which it throws back, like a hare's ... with a short and small neck, near to which are the fore-feet ... the hinder legs are long, especially from the last joint, which, from the callosity below it, seems as if it lies flat on the ground when the animal descends any declivity ... The tail, which is carried like a grey-hound's, was almost as long as the body, and tapered gradually to the end.[36]

The journal of John White, Surgeon-General to the First Fleet and the settlement at Port Jackson, published in 1790, contained many drawings of the flora and fauna that took his fancy, including macropods.[37] Although not trained in natural history, White apparently devoted almost every waking hour of daylight that could be spared from his professional work to collecting plants and animals.[38] The drawings in his journal, which include some of the earliest depictions of the kangaroo and potoroo (although the latter is now thought to be the Rufous Bettong), were not, however, made by White himself but were 'copied from nature' by competent English natural history artists 'with care and accuracy'. Chief among these artists was Sarah Stone, who did the macropod drawings. Her paintings, alongside those done by Parkinson and Stubbs, were the earliest images of macropods seen by the English public.

White's journal described the very earliest days of the colony at Sydney Cove and together with those of Arthur Phillip, Watkin Tench, John Hunter and David Collins,[39] constitutes what is known as the 'basic books' of the colony's history. Although no official artists were sent with the First Fleet, naval officers were trained in drawing to enable them to chart unexplored coastlines. Thankfully, in addition to their training, quite a number of the naval personnel travelling with the First Fleet had natural artistic abilities. In particular, the *Sirius'* crew was seemingly stacked with artists. Among these was John Hunter, Captain of the *Sirius*, whose many drawings include one of a kangaroo. Despite Hunter's drawing being considered 'clumsy and inaccurate',[40] with regard to the animal's proportions it is actually superior to other renditions of the time, including those

'A Kangaroo' and 'A Poto Roo' by Sarah Stone that appear in John White's *Journal of a Voyage to New South Wales*. (Mitchell Library, State Library of NSW, PXA 909/22 and PXA 909/27)

in both White's and Phillip's journals. The kangaroo in Phillip's account is unsigned, but based on limited evidence was possibly done by the First Lieutenant of the *Sirius*, William Bradley.[41] Phillip's journal also contained a depiction of the Long-nosed Potoroo, presumably by the same anonymous artist, and while some elements of the animal are well executed (such as the pouch young), it, too, is poorly proportioned. *Sirius* Midshipman George Raper's depiction of a kangaroo now forms part of the Godman Collection at the British Museum of Natural History.[42] Arthur Bowes, surgeon aboard the First Fleet convict transport ship *Lady Penrhyn* also made a sketch of a kangaroo, but his drawing is an inferior copy of Sydney Parkinson's original.

The colony's naturalists were quick to recruit convict artists who could draw the new flora and fauna in its more natural state. In 1792, soon after White's journal was published in England, a young Scottish artist, Thomas Watling, arrived in the colony on a 14-year transportation sentence. Watling's artistic skills had already been recognised by the English judicial system— he had been transported for forgery, with one of the sentencing judges noting that 'He is a young Man, unmarried, & an ingenious Artist; he will be an acquisition to the new Colony at Botany Bay'.[43] Within weeks of his arrival, Watling was making drawings for White. Feeling that he was required to 'toil as a slave by day', Watling confessed in a letter to his aunt that he tried no harder than he had to, and as a consequence his drawings were 'such as may be expected from genius in bondage to a very mercenary, sordid person'.[44] Watling painted many natural history subjects, and almost all of those that survive are in the Watling Collection of the Zoological Library of the British Museum of Natural History. However, the collection includes many unsigned works

Kang-oo-roo or pa-ta-garang painted by John Hunter, Captain of the First Fleet supply vessel *Sirius*, between 1788 and 1790. (National Library of Australia, nla.pic-an3172052).

that may or may not have been done by Watling, and these are ascribed to the unknown artist or artists termed 'The Port Jackson Painter'. They include a painting of the Eastern Grey Kangaroo, and also the first ever depiction of the Swamp Wallaby, which was accompanied by a description of the animal:

> This Animal was run down by Grey Hounds and the only one of the colour seen; it differs from the Pattegorang or Kangaroo a little in the shape of the Head and in the form of the Ears, but in nothing so much as in the Tail, which has the

THE KANGOOROO.

The kangooroo, possibly drawn by William Bradley. This image, published in *The voyage of Governor Phillip to Botany Bay* in 1789 was among the first images of a kangaroo the British public would have seen. (National Library of Australia, nla.pic-an9939754)

The potoroo, another macropod that appeared in *The voyage of Governor Phillip to Botany Bay*. (State Library of Victoria)

Hair longer near the tip than in any other part—The hinder parts are not so much out of all proportion to the fore parts as in the Kangaroo—I take it to be a kind of mixed Genus between that Animal and some other, perhaps the Kangaroo Rat, I was led to this conclusion because it was found near a Brush or low woody swampy place where the Kangaroo Rats mostly frequent—Governor Phillips has taken home the Skin and Bones of the Head.[45]

Another notable convict artist, Richard Browne, painted animals for Thomas Skottowe, Commandant of the Newcastle Penal

Settlement. Browne has a unique style, but his drawings suffer from inaccuracies that '... have, at most, the charm which comes of awkward execution'.[46] The kangaroo, in particular, is poorly drawn, with hind feet, 'wrists' and ears that are too long and slender.[47] Nevertheless, after receiving his ticket-of-leave Browne went on to become a successful artist in Sydney, producing water-colours of Aborigines and native plants and animals that were popular among the colonists.[48] The 'Kangaroo' in Skottowe's manuscript is the Eastern Grey Kangaroo, although Skottowe describes several kinds in the Newcastle district.

The first painting of the Swamp Wallaby, published with the title *The Native Name Bag-ga-ree, or a species of Kangaroo*. This unsigned work painted between 1788 and 1794 has been credited to convict forger Thomas Watling. (Natural History Museum, London)

Richard Browne's drawing of the Eastern Grey Kangaroo that appeared in *The Skottowe Manuscript*. (Mitchell Library, State Library of NSW, PXA 555)

There are several species, or more properly speaking several sizes of this animal; which it is probable will be of some use to enumerate. First there are two kind[s] of forest kangaroo, viz. large and small; the larger ones when seated on their hind legs, stand near six feet high, and weigh generally from one hundred to one hundred and fifty weight, the smaller kind are scarcely above half that size, but are much swifter and more difficult to catch. The brush kind are of three sizes the smallest which has obtain'd the name of the kangaroo rat.[49]

John Lewin was the first professional artist to settle in the colony
of New South Wales, and his *Two Kangaroos in a Landscape* (1819)
show how skilfully a trained artist could render the macropod form.
(Mitchell Library, State Library of NSW, ML 852)

The first free artist to settle in New South Wales was John
William Lewin. His *Two Kangaroos in a Landscape* (1819) shows
a female and male Red Kangaroo, and the animals' proportions
begin to approach something akin to real life. One of Lewin's
contemporaries was Ferdinand Bauer, an Austrian natural history
artist who accompanied Matthew Flinders on his circumnavigation of the continent in the *Investigator* between 1801 and 1803.
Bauer made exquisite and accurate drawings of the flora and
fauna he encountered, including a Black-footed Rock-wallaby
collected on Mondrain Island in Western Australia.[50] A fellow
naturalist on the expedition, Robert Brown, wrote to Joseph

Black-footed Rock Wallaby (1803) by Ferdinand Bauer. Bauer accompanied Matthew Flinders during his circumnavigation of the Australian continent in the *Investigator*. (Natural History Museum, London)

Banks, referring to Bauer as '... indefatigable and that considering his minute accuracy the number of drawings he has made is astonishing'.[51]

Bauer and Lewin were, however, the exceptions to the rule. Most illustrators would continue to struggle with drawing macropods over the coming decades, not helped by awkward written descriptions of the beasts they were attempting to depict. In his *Arcana,* published in 1810, George Perry's eccentric description of the Eastern Grey Kangaroo was apparently based on his observations of live animals being kept at the Queen's Palace in Kew. Perry's clumsy text is accompanied by a similarly inaccurate illustration:

KANGAROO

[The kangaroo] exhibits to the human mind, as strange an assemblage of forms as the most eccentric fancy can conceive. Its head and neck are small and taper, resembling those of a squirrel; the nose of a dark brown, adorned with whiskers; the neck and fore legs very short, but the body extended like a bag of shot, for four or five feet, with enormous strong hind legs, which are calculated like those of a flea, by a particular springing their motion, to leap up a considerable distance. The tail is also so thick and strong that it frequently rests

The oddly proportioned 'Kangaroo' that appeared in Perry's *Arcana*. (Taken from Perry, 1810)

upon it as if upon a chair, and steadying its upright direction, by its various expansion of the tail.... they carry [the young] in a pouch or apron, where the little creatures may be seen peeping out of the bag, whenever the mother directs herself to sitting up.[52]

Perry continues his inept account with some imaginative descriptions of kangaroo behaviour:

Nature has kindly provided the path for its safety on the swiftness and extent of its leaps, which are reported to be from rock to rock, twenty feet at a time, over bush and brie. When the Kangaroo threatens to fight with its mates, it is said to lean forward upon its forefeet, and to use its long hind toes in a kicking posture, like an Ass.

By 1871, the Director of the Australian Museum, Gerard Krefft, had clearly seen enough poor renditions of kangaroos. In his *Mammals of Australia* he pleaded with artists to take more care:

Few animals are more graceful when running than those of the kangaroo tribe; but ... artists will not take the trouble to observe them, and the consequence is that, when a sketch is attempted, a caricature is the result. We appeal to the rising generation to study nature, and trust they will learn to draw a Kangaroo as carefully as they learn to draw a Horse or a Dog, and that they will discontinue to accept as correct the ludicrous representation of the animals which have hitherto supported the Australian Shield under the names of Kangaroo and Emu.[53]

These early observations and illustrations of the different species of macropods frequently show a degree of amazement in these animals that were so unfamiliar to the observers. Over time, close observation and artistry would reveal these animals as being as extraordinary and beautiful in still life as they are in real life. Nevertheless, the amateur naturalists and artists among the early colonists made an important contribution at the time regarding what was known of the natural history of kangaroos. In the next few chapters, we explore the natural history of macropods in greater detail.

4
SUSPENDED ANIMATION
Kangaroo Reproduction

At its birth, the kangaroo... is not so large as a half-grown mouse... This phenomenon is so striking and so contrary to the general laws of nature, that an opinion has been started that the animal is brought forth not by the pudenda, but descends from the belly into the pouch by one of the teats which are there deposited. On this difficulty, as I can throw no light, I shall hazard no conjecture.[1]

If you were to stop a passer-by on pretty much any street in the world and ask them what they knew about the kangaroo, you would find out that it comes from Australia, it hops, and it carries its young in a pouch. Kangaroo reproduction has fascinated researchers for as long as they have known about kangaroos. Why? Like the other marsupials kangaroos have a relatively short gestation period, at the end of which the female gives birth to an under-developed 'neonate', which completes its development in the pouch, or 'marsupium', from which the entire group gets its name. The similarities stop there. Macropod reproduction is, quite simply, amazing. Female macropods not only have a variety of different reproductive strategies but can produce up to three young simultaneously— at different stages of development. Some species can terminate a pregnancy and sacrifice the unborn embryo if drought conditions make reproductive success unlikely. A kangaroo mother can produce different milk for young of different ages and can even control the sex of the young before it is born. Perhaps the most remarkable thing about these modifications to the basic marsupial breeding plan is that they are natural, evolutionary adaptations, which combine to give the macropods the best possible chance of survival in the harsh and unpredictable Australian environment.

The ability of any species to maximise its reproductive output is critical for its survival. Therefore mothers endeavour to correlate the period of lactation and weaning when the young gain all or most of their nutrients from the mother, to a season in which key resources, such as food and water, are readily available.[2] Eutherian or placental mammals invest much more energy in their pregnancies than marsupials, as the gestation periods are considerably longer. Some species continue this in-utero investment of energy after the young are born. Others wean their young quickly and there is little subsequent contact between the mother and her offspring. The same applies to marsupials. Bandicoots, for example, wean their young as quickly as 60 days after birth. A young Eastern Grey or Red Kangaroo, in contrast, can remain with its mother for 18 months, and the female kangaroos are devoted and attentive carers.[3]

THE MIRACLE OF MACROPOD REPRODUCTION

Any discussion of reproduction has to start with the reproductive system. Like all marsupials, that of the macropods is radically different from those of the monotremes—the platypus and the echidnas—and the placental or eutherian mammals. The first and most striking difference is that marsupials have three vaginas: two lateral vaginas through which the sperm travels after mating, and a larger medial vagina through which the young one passes in the birth process. It appears that in most macropod species, and the Honey Possum, the birth canal remains open after the first birth, while in other marsupials the birth canal is not permanent and a pseudo-vaginal canal forms prior to each birth.[4] In contrast eutherian mammals have only one vagina.

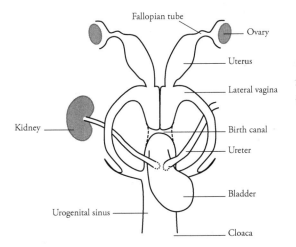

The marsupial reproductive system showing the positions of the lateral and medial vaginas. (Adapted from Jackson, 2007)

After mating the female's fertilised egg forms a zygote that multiplies in cell number until it becomes a ball of about 6–80 cells, after about eight days. At this point, it is referred to as a 'blastocyst'.[5] This is when something intriguing happens in the macropods: if the female already has a young suckling in the pouch, the ovaries enter a period of inactivity and the blastocyst stops developing, which is referred to by marsupial reproductive biologists as 'embryonic diapause'. The blastocyst remains in this suspended state of animation until it is ready to be restarted and continue growing. Embryonic diapause and delayed implantation were first observed in the Quokka and subsequently confirmed in the Tammar Wallaby in the mid-1950s by one of the fathers of marsupial research, Geoff Sharman.[6] Since then, the reproductive strategies of many species of macropods have been studied and most species have been found to undergo embryonic diapause and delayed implantation except for the Western Grey Kangaroo and possibly the Lumholtz's Tree Kangaroo and Musky Rat-kangaroo.[7] While the basic process of embryonic diapause is the same for most macropod species, the triggers for it vary greatly.

In the Tammar Wallaby and Tasmanian Red-necked Wallaby the cessation of breeding through embryonic diapause is regulated each year by the summer and winter solstices and is known, therefore, as 'seasonal embryonic diapause'.[8] In all other macropods embryonic diapause is associated with lactation and is known as 'lactational embryonic diapause'. Kangaroos can also enter a period of non-oestrous or 'anoestrous', where ovulation ceases temporarily. When the cessation of oestrus occurs regularly, such as occurs in winter for some Western Grey Kangaroo and Eastern Grey Kangaroos it is known as seasonal anoestrous.[9]

Seasonal anoestrous can also occur in conditions of prolonged drought, such as occurs in Red Kangaroos of the arid inland regions of Australia, where drought is a common occurence.[10] Therefore female macropods that are not undergoing an oestrous cycle or pregnancy can be in one of four reproductive conditions: seasonal embryonic diapause, lactational embryonic diapause, seasonal anoestrous, or lactational anoestrous.[11]

After a gestation period of 20–38 days for the potoroids and 21–48 days for the macropodids the female gets ready to give birth, typically to a single young (despite having four teats) although there are several records of twins and even triplets.[12] The only real exception to this is the Musky Rat-kangaroo, which routinely has twins and triplets.[13] An empty pouch is lined with brownish-black scale and looks very dirty in appearance. Before giving birth, the female begins to remove this scale by inserting her head into the pouch and cleaning it with her tongue. To give birth, the female typically adopts a 'birth position' in which the tail is passed between the hind legs that are extended straight ahead, though it can sometimes lie behind the animal in the normal position.[14] When in the birthing position the female hunches forward, carrying her weight on the base of her tail. Her back is usually supported by a tree or rock. She may adopt this position 20 or more times before actually giving birth. About half-an-hour before giving birth she begins to lick her urogenital opening vigorously. The actual birth is signalled by the release of fluid from the ruptured yolk sac that is licked up by the mother. She does not appear to lick a path in her fur to allow the young access to the pouch.[15] The joey, known at this stage as a neonate, appears head first and enclosed in a fluid-filled amnion. The neonate is tiny, that of the biggest macropod, the Red Kangaroo, is only 10 millimetres long and weighs about 830 milligrams.[16] Despite its tiny size it breaks free of the amnion by itself and crawls straight up through the mother's fur from the urogenital opening to the pouch, all of which it achieves within five minutes and without the mother's direct help!

A VERY ELUSIVE BIRTH

Though the macropod birth process is now well understood, this was not always the case. The first European observers thought that the young originated from the teat in the female's pouch. Some of the confusion may have arisen from problems in translation of 'Diets' (or Middle Dutch, which is no longer spoken) into English. This 1899 translation of Franciso Pelsaert's observations of the Tammar Wallaby (see Chapter 3) suggests that Pelsaert believed that the young emerge *from* the teat:

> Their manner of generation or procreation is exceedingly strange and highly worth observing. Below the belly the female carries a pouch, into which you may put your hand; inside this pouch are her nipples, and we have found that the young ones grow up in this pouch with the nipples in their mouths. We have seen some young ones lying there [in the pouch], which were only the size of a bean, though at the same time perfectly proportioned, so that it seems certain that they grow there out of the nipples of the mammae, from which they draw their food, until they are grown up and are able to walk.[17]

However, a 1963 translation of the later part of this same passage seems to suggest otherwise:

...[we] found the limbs of the small beast to be entirely in proportion, so that it is certain that they grow there at the nipple of the mammal and draw the food out of it until they are big and can run.[18]

Whatever Pelsaert meant by his statement, the myth that the young grow out of the nipples has been attributed to him, and lingered on for over 200 years.[19] The marsupials' extraordinary reproductive system was first observed in 1698, when a Virginian Opossum from North America was dissected by Edward Tyson, a physician and comparative anatomist.[20] Tyson clearly showed that the genital tract was double from the ovaries to the opening of the urethra where the two lateral vaginae joined to form a common urogenital canal. He proposed that the young travelled through these canals at parturition—although we now know they travel through the central medial vagina.

Despite Tyson's careful observation, many subsequent authors throughout the eighteenth and nineteenth centuries remained convinced that the young grew out of the teat, including Franscois Valentyn, who described the Filander or Dusky Pademelon from Ambon in the Moluccas in 1726.[21] Valentyn concluded that the young developed from the teats because bleeding followed their forcible removal—in fact, this occurs because once the young are attached to the nipple, the teat expands inside the mouth and the lips and tongue actually grow around it, making removal difficult.[22]

In 1795 Everard Home dissected a female macropod and recognised that it had the same anatomy as that of the opossum observed by Tyson in 1698, although he seems to have been confused in his interpretation of the parts of the specimen examined because the specimen had an enlarged median vagina filled with semen.[23] Home thought this large organ was a gravid uterus and unsuccessfully attempted to find a foetus within it. Nonetheless he made the astute observation of the small open canal between this chamber and the urogenital sinus, posterior to the bladder, and correctly concluded that this was the route taken by the foetus at birth.

John Morgan was a British surgeon and Fellow of the Linnean Society of London. His enthusiasm for anatomy and natural history led to some important early work on the anatomy of the mammary organs of kangaroos. Morgan was fortunate to have access to captive kangaroos—his papers mention several kangaroos, confined together in an enclosure, that had borne young and which he was keenly studying—however it is evident from his writing on the subject that witnessing a birth was proving difficult:

The development and growth of the foetus in marsupial animals has long afforded an interesting subject of inquiry for the researches of the physiologist; yet, not withstanding the numerous opportunities for observation supplied by the domestication of the most interesting of theses animals, namely, the Kangaroo, it is to be regretted that hardly any information has of late years been obtained upon this important branch of natural science; for although we are acquainted with a few insulated facts relative to this subject, yet we are at present left in total ignorance respecting the principal object of our researches. We know little or nothing of the nature of those changes which must necessarily take place in the young while remaining in the uterus, or of the mode by which it is conveyed from that part to the teat ...[24]

Morgan received his first live female kangaroo, probably an Eastern Grey, in October 1828. He was able to domesticate it so that it would follow either him or his servant like a dog. When it arrived, the animal had a young in its pouch that was 'about equal to that of a small rat' with skin 'entirely destitute of hair' so it had been developing in the pouch for about three months before Morgan could calm the animal sufficiently to allow '... for as long a period as I could wish, and as frequently as I thought proper, the most complete examination of the young one within, and of the teat to which it was adherent'.[25]

Of course, the fact that the kangaroo's young was already in its pouch meant that Morgan was not able to study the actual birth process, as he lamented in his follow-up paper read at a meeting of the Linnean Society of London in 1830:

> As the young one had been already delivered into the pouch, my observations were of course confined to the condition of the pouch and teats during its growth: these may perhaps appear of a nature too trivial for the subject of a communication to the Society; yet, as we are at present so completely in the dark respecting the ultimate object of our researches, namely a knowledge of the mode in which the foetus is passed from the uterus to the teat, and as it is therefore impossible to determine how far a few insulated facts may assist in bringing our inquiries to a satisfactory termination.[26]

Finally, 200 years after Pelsaert's discovery, and about 450 kilometres south of where Pelsaert first described the Tammar Wallaby, Scottish anatomist and surgeon Alexander Collie was the first to describe a macropod birth and the neonate's subsequent solo journey from the urogenital opening to the pouch. By an odd coincidence, the animal under observation was again a Tammar Wallaby. Collie was a keen naturalist, and no stranger to reproduction and birth—he had recently assisted at the birth of the Governor of Western Australia's child on board HMS *Sulphur*, en route to Western Australia. Collie established a medical tent at the new settlement on Garden Island just off the coast of present-day Rockingham, but, like many surgeons of the day, studied natural history in his spare time. He recorded the observation in a letter of 26 January 1830, when he wrote that:

> An officer of H.M.S. *Success* at present here, observed a kangaroo in the act of parturition. When the foetus was expelled ... the mother was lying partly on one side and partly on her back, resting against the side of the cage where she was confined... and the very diminutive young, when brought forth, crept among the fur of the mother towards her belly and towards the opening of the abdominal pouch; whilst she, with her head turned towards her tender offspring, seemed to watch its progress, which was about as expeditious as that of a snail. After it had made some advance, my informant, unconscious of the remarkable economy of generation in this class of quadrupeds, removed the newly born animal before it had reached its destination, which must have been the mouth of the sac.[27]

Nevertheless, this record seems to have been overlooked, or at least treated with suspicion, because uncertainty about how kangaroos were born, and how they came to be in a pouch, continued. In his detailed account 'On the generation of the marsupial animals, with a description of the impregnated uterus of the kangaroo' presented to the Royal Society in 1834, Sir Richard Owen asserted, correctly, that the young did not originate on the teat in the pouch, noting that the idea that young grew out of the nipple had been around for a while:

> The minute size of the young of the American Opossum when found in the marsupium, their pendulous attachment to the nipples, and perhaps the mode in which the latter were developed, gave rise among the earlier observers to a supposition that they were originally formed from those parts, and the gemmiparous theory, which has subsequently often been revived, appears to have been prevalent at the time when TYSON first devoted his attention to the subject.[28]

Owen also received a gravid uterus of a female kangaroo from his good friend George Bennett in New South Wales, who had preserved the specimen in spirits before shipping it to him in London. Owen's minute dissection of this specimen gave him the confidence to conclude 'that the ovulum in the Kangaroo quits the ovisac in a condition corresponding to that of the ordinary *Mammalia*, and increases in a similar manner as it descends to the uterus'.[29] Owen followed this up with some experimentation on live captive animals, but alas, his female kangaroo gave birth in the night and was discovered the following morning with young already in the pouch. Undaunted, Owen detached the young from the nipple four days later, and deposited it back inside the pouch. The female's response to this act led Owen to believe that the young had been carried from the vulva to the pouch in the mother's mouth:

At length she grasped the sides of the orifice of the pouch with her fore paws, and drawing them apart, as in the act of opening a bag, she thrust her head into the cavity as far as the eyes, and could be seen moving it about in different directions … After repeating the above act about a dozen times she lay down, and seemed to be at ease. The freedom with which the mother reached with her mouth the orifices both of the genital passage and pouch, suggested at once a means adequate to the removal of the young from the one to the other; while at the same time her employment of the fore paws indicated that their assistance in the transmission of the foetus need not extend beyond the keeping open the entrance of the pouch while the foetus was being introduced by the mouth, when it is thus probably conducted to, and held over, a nipple until the mother feels that it has grasped the sensitive extremity of the part from which it is to derive its sustenance.[30]

Despite contrary mounting evidence, the surgeon on HMS *Beagle*, Benjamin Bynoe, continued the error in 1840 when he dissected Tammar Wallabies on the Houtman Abrolhos Islands and was convinced that he had discovered the direct connection from the uterus to the pouch when he thought he saw one neonate in the process of passing to the teat in one animal.[31]

It was not until 1881 that the issue was finally resolved scientifically when a major review was undertaken that included the examination of a large series of several species of macropods in which the reproductive status was known.[32] Finally, a year later, in 1882 a neonate was observed to crawl up into the pouch of its recently deceased mother. Joseph Bancroft, President of the Queensland Philosophical

Society, transcribed the following observations made by the Honourable L. Hope:

The dam that I shot had been dead, perhaps, five minutes before I noticed what was going on, but I don't think sufficient time had elapsed for the young one to have made its way so far. It was then within about five inches of the orifice of the pouch, or where that should have been, as on examination this appeared to be closed, being surrounded by folds of shrunken skin (not open, as in Professor Owen's case).

The embryo looked like—and, in fact, at first I took it to be—a piece of raw flesh, which I supposed had been driven out by the bullet; but closer inspection showed it to be working actively with its fore legs—arms, in fact—which were considerably developed, with the claws apparent. It was about one and one-third inches in length, the tail and hind legs undeveloped, and giving the hinder parts of the animal the appearance of a red 'grub.' After watching it a few minutes, and not having much time to remain, I took it from the fur, to which it seemed to adhere pretty firmly, and placed it on the closed orifice of the pouch. It soon left this, however, and commenced travelling though the fur, which was pretty long, with considerable energy: as, however; it began to describe circles, and appeared, as I may say, rather to have lost its way, after a few minutes more I placed it again on the supposed orifice of the pouch, taking care that the head sunk among the folds of the skin I have mentioned. It then seemed to endeavour to burrow in. At this stage I had to leave it, as the day was advancing, and I had an engagement elsewhere. Had I had the means of preserving it I would have removed the skin of the abdomen, including pouch and the embryo, and brought it away; but it appeared to me that, as after death no assistance could come from the dam, no further reliable observations could be made. My theory is that in life the irritation produced by the burrowing of the young one causes the pouch to open for its reception; and this is just what can only be observed in the captivity of the animal. What struck me was the marvellous energy and apparent endurance of the embryo in its course, and the small chance there seemed to be of its falling from the fur, which, while producing adherence, did not seem to impede its progress materially.[33]

Despite the issue being resolved, confusion over the transfer of the young into the pouch continued, as we can see in Dudley Le Souef's rather fanciful account, written in 1900:

When the young one is ready to be born, the mother sits down on the ground, resting on the upper portion of the base of her tail, and with that appendage resting level on the ground in front of her; she then holds her pouch open with her two forepaws, and, as the helpless mite is born, it rests on the soft fur of the under side of the tail. The mother immediately transfers it to her pouch with her lips only, and evidently with great care attaches it to the nipple. The mouth of the young one is apparently only a round hole, and it as yet has no power of suction; but the nipple is of a peculiar shape, with the point hard, and the mother is thereby enabled to insert it into the mouth of the young one.[34]

The issue appears to have been resolved for good by Dudley's brother, Albert, who, together with Harry Burrell, outlines in excellent detail the nature of the macropod birth process and the neonate's attachment to the teat of the mother.

> The young are born in a very immature state. For a long time observers were puzzled as to how such a tiny, naked thing, about an inch in length, could get into the pouch, and when there become firmly attached to the nipple. It was very commonly concluded that it *grew* there. This, however is not so. When the young is born, its forelegs and head are disproportionately large and mobile, and it is able to make its way through the hair (assisted sometimes, perhaps, by the mother's lips), to the pouch, and then fasten itself to the nipple. The nipple at this time is pointed and firm, but when it enters the little one's mouth it softens and enlarges, filling the cavity so that it cannot be detatched without rupturing the parts.[35]

THAT FIRST MOMENTOUS JOURNEY

How does such a tiny, jelly bean-sized creature find its way from the urogenital opening to the pouch unassisted and only moments after being born? In spite of its tiny size, the neonate's lungs are functional, its nostrils are open and the olfactory centre of its brain is well developed, as are its head, shoulders and forearms, in comparison to its minute, paddle-like hind limbs and underdeveloped hips and tail.[36] Sir Richard Owen recognised this when he wrote '... the new-born Kangaroo possesses greater powers of action than the same-sized embryo of a Sheep, and approximately more nearly in this respect, to the new-born young of the Rat.[37] Furthermore, at birth,

the skeleton in the neonate's shoulder region is a single cartilage, providing firm support while the young makes the long
climb to the pouch. Later, this cartilage will differentiate into
the scapula, sternum and associated bones.[38] Newborn kangaroos make alternating left-right movements of their forearms
in conjunction with opening and closing their hands so that
they grab handfuls of the mother's fur on their upward pull
to the pouch. These 'clock-like' movements will occur as long
as the animal is seeking the warmth of the pouch and the nourishment offered by the mother's teat. Experiments have shown
that Tammar Wallabies which are cooled or removed from the

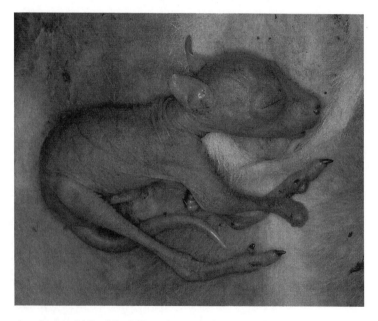

A naked and blind Red Kangaroo pouch young photographed inside
the pouch of its mother. (Photo: Gerhard Körtner)

teat will begin these movements; the movements cease when the animal is warm and reattached to the teat. Simulating proximity to the teat by gently stroking the lips and mouth of a newborn Tammar Wallaby also will cause the clock-like movements to cease.[39]

When the neonate arrives at the teat, its mouth, tongue and digestive system (including the liver and pancreas) are sufficiently developed to cope with a milk diet. In contrast, its eyes, hind limbs and gonads are undifferentiated and the sex can only be determined several days after birth. Marsupials' lungs are functional at birth, but they are extremely small and it is becoming evident that for the first few days after birth, neonates rely on gas exchange through the skin to compensate for the immaturity of their lungs.[40] This fascinating discovery—first made on the Tammar Wallaby—revealed that about 30–40 per cent of gas exchange is through the skin, while in smaller species of macropods and other marsupials the reliance on skin exchange is almost total.[41] Skin is so effective in gas exchange because it has a relatively large surface area compared with the young's body mass, and it allows the neonate to meet its oxygen demands before the lungs are fully functional.[42]

PREDICTABILITY IN AN UNPREDICTABLE ENVIRONMENT

Most macropods mate within a few days of giving birth, in a process known as 'post-partum mating', although the Swamp Wallaby is unusual in having pre-partum mating in the week or so before giving birth.[43] In either pre- or post-partum mating, the resultant embryo develops to the blastocyst stage at which point embryonic diapause is initiated as we discussed earlier.[44] This strategy ensures that a new birth can occur very soon after the first young exits the pouch, taking advantage of good feeding conditions to maximise reproduction. At this stage, a female can have an embryo in diapause, a new young in the pouch and a third young that has left the pouch but periodically puts its head back into the pouch to feed from an elongated teat. Remarkably, the milks that the young in the pouch and the young at foot feed upon are very different in composition, as the female's milk changes gradually throughout the development of the young. Initially, the

Female Red Kangaroo feeding young at foot aged 302 days outside the pouch while a pouch young aged 67 days feeds at another teat. (Taken from Tyndale-Biscoe and Renfree, 1987)

milk is quite dilute and contains more sugars than fats, but by the latter stages of lactation the milk has little sugar but is rich in fats and proteins.[45] Each young has its own supply, because the teat it first attached to at birth is the one that will nourish it through to weaning, even when it is spending extended periods outside the pouch, and nursing only intermittently.

Macropods are beautifully adapted to Australia's range of environments and their fickle climates, and this is in large part due to their reproductive behaviours. Species such as the Red Kangaroo, the Euro and the Agile Wallaby that live in the arid and semi-arid regions where rainfall is unpredictable, utilise what is known as facultative breeding.[46] As long as there is adequate food and water, facultative breeders will breed continuously with young at all three stages of development (i.e., blastocyst, in pouch and at foot). If the pouch young is lost prematurely, the development of the blastocyst is activated and the young that had been 'on hold' is born 31–35 days later, with a subsequent post-partum mating by the female and a new blastocyst placed in embryonic diapause.[47] In drought conditions, the female kangaroo can produce a succession of young that die after about two months of development. While this might seem a wasteful enterprise, the mother's investment in the young is minimal up to that stage, and loss of immature young under drought conditions preserves the mother's health for the good times that will inevitably follow. If the drought is prolonged, that is, it continues for six months or more, the females cease to ovulate and enter a true anoestrous.[48] However, the kangaroos' physical response to drought-breaking rainfall is almost immediate—female kangaroos have been observed to begin ovulating within 14 days.[49]

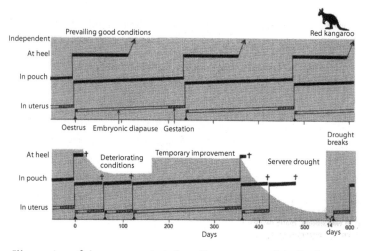

Illustration of the opportunistic breeding strategy of the Red Kangaroo and how females and their young respond to the prevailing conditions as influenced by rainfall (indicated by the grey shading). (Taken from Tyndale-Biscoe, 2005)

This means they can immediately take advantage of the good conditions, and raise their young before the next drought—this is the fundamental advantage of marsupial reproduction over that of placental or eutherian mammals, where mothers have to invest large amounts of energy in gestation even if food and water are in short supply.

In contrast to the macropods from arid regions, the Tammar Wallaby and the Bennett's Wallaby (the Tasmanian subspecies of the Red-necked Wallaby) utilise a very different reproductive strategy. Their reproduction is governed by the summer and winter solstices. Some 70–80 per cent of females give birth and undergo post-partum oestrus in late January to early February and the young leave the pouch in October and are weaned in November.[50] The blastocyst remains in diapause until the summer solstice in late December when growth is triggered and the resulting young is born early the next year.[51] Even sub-adult animals that are weaned in November can mate, and their blastocyst will remain in diapause until after the summer solstice, just like the adults.[52]

When the young joey first begins to leave the pouch, it is at a similar stage of development as a newborn placental mammal. The timing of permanent pouch emergence and weaning varies from species to species but is, typically, about 147 days for the Musky Rat-kangaroo (with weaning unknown); 100–150 days for the potoroids (with weaning at 106–185 days); and 120–310 days for the macropodoids (with weaning at 190–500 days).[53]

So after the different species of macropods are born how long do they live? This is difficult to establish with any certainty for animals in the wild, though it appears that the small species such as the potoroos and bettongs live approximately four to six years, while the larger species typically live 10–15 years. There are records of animals living in captivity for as long as 20 years.[54] The age of many species can be determined by their teeth, because as the animal grows the molars erupt from the gum line and move along the jaw-line, escalator-fashion. Therefore the animal's age can be calculated by measuring the progression of these molars along its upper jaw.[55]

ARE YOU MY MOTHER? CONSERVATION THROUGH REPRODUCTION

Macropods' use of embryonic diapause is being used in the conservation of some species by an ingenious process called 'cross fostering'. This typically involves transferring the joey from a female of a threatened species to the pouch of another female of a common species that has a joey of similar size. The recipient then raises the new joey as its own, while the first young is removed to be hand-reared, or euthanased.[56] This technique has been used successfully to transfer young between different species and even different genera.[57] The technique is useful in the conservation of macropods because it takes advantage of the females' post-partum oestrus and embryonic diapause. The female whose joey is removed will give birth shortly after and then mate again within a few days to produce another blastocyst. By continually fostering out the pouch young, the target species' breeding frequency can be increased dramatically, from one young per year to potentially more than six per year. This technique has been used successfully in Victorian Brush-tailed Rock-wallabies (critically endangered under Victorian legislation), where pouch young were transferred to Tammar Wallabies and to other more common species of rock-wallabies.

Data from pouch young translocation studies indicate that it is, theoretically, possible to transfer very small pouch young from an animal in the wild and highly probable that the young would survive a short period outside the pouch before being reattached to the teat of a captive foster mother. This would allow small pouch young from threatened macropod species to be recruited directly from the wild into captivity; either for captive breeding or to improve genetic diversity in captive colonies. It could also serve to reactivate diapaused embryos in the wild animals and hence accelerate breeding in wild-living mothers.[58]

The evolution of macropod reproductive strategies allows them to not only survive, but indeed thrive in the most hostile environments of arid Australia. Yet in some cases these clever

modifications are not enough to counter the effects of introduced predators such as foxes or cats, while in other cases they
are so successful that the animals become overabundant and
have to be culled. We will explore each of these issues in later
chapters. However, because macropod reproduction is not the
only aspect of the animal that merits a closer investigation, we
will continue the discussion of kangaroo natural history with a
look at behaviour.

5

BOXING KANGAROO

Macropod Behaviour

A male is a clever and determined fighter, and when brought to bay by dogs will put its back against a tree or rock, and be ready for all comers. Woe betide the rash hound that rushes in impetuously to the attack, for the powerful hind-feet, armed with spear-like claws, can be used with deadly effect, and will rip open the flanks of the enemy in a flash ... Many animals have some form of amusement to occupy their spare time. With larger kangaroos this takes the form of 'boxing'. They do this quite naturally and seemingly for fun, and it is indulged in only by the males. The performance consists of grappling and cuffing about the head and shoulders, and vigorously kicking the opponent on the body with the hind limbs. The 'rounds' are fairly regular as regard to time—a three minutes' bout, with a rest of about the same time.[1]

The image of the 'boxing kangaroo', where two big kangaroos face off and try to kick each other while wrestling with their strong forearms, is one that dominates many people's perceptions of kangaroo behaviour. Macropod behaviour, of course, is not limited to these physical encounters; they display a complex variety of behaviours, of which some are unique to them and their relatives. These behaviours are as diverse as the species themselves and their habitats: some species are intensely solitary, others gregarious; some occupy overlapping home ranges, others staunchly defend their individual territories; and some, as in the case of 'boxing kangaroos', fight violently for the right to mate, but others use tact and secrecy in order to secure a mating opportunity. This chapter explores the fascinating and diverse behavioural repertoires seen in the macropods.

GROUP LIVING

There is a strong relationship between size, habitat and gregariousness among the macropods. The smallest species tend to be forest-dwelling and solitary; however, as physical size increases we can see a preference for more open habitats and group living. Dr David Croft from the University of New of Wales identified three types of macropods in terms of their size and behaviour: Type 1 species are solitary except for reproductive associations; Type 2 species are often solitary but aggregate on favoured resource patches; and Type 3 species are gregarious. Type 1 and 2 species are small to medium-sized animals that are nocturnal and forage in or close to cover. Type 3 species tend to be large, exhibit strong sexual dimorphism in their body proportions, are partially active during the day as well as at night and live in more open habitat.[2]

The present-day macropods with their diversity of social structures are thought to have had much humbler ancestral beginnings in the temperate rainforests that once covered continental Australia. These ancient macropods were small, nocturnal and probably solitary, and lived on an omnivorous diet of fruit and insects. As we saw in Chapter 1, as the Australian continent drifted ever northwards during the Miocene and Pliocene (from about 24 million years ago to about 2 million years ago), the continent dried out. Dense, damp forests gave way to open woodland and grasslands, and kangaroos evolved into larger species, becoming increasingly herbivorous and gregarious as they colonised the emerging open habitats.

The solitary nature of the smaller species appears to be reflected in their secretive behaviour. They prefer closed habitats and have very small group sizes. In contrast the increasing sociality of the larger species is perhaps both a response to the increased risk of predation of living in open habitat and the result of a low level of aggression between members of the mob, or group, of kangaroos.[3] The most gregarious species is the Whiptail Wallaby, which can have group sizes of up to 50 individuals of mixed age and sex.[4] Like other open-country species of herbivorous mammals elsewhere in the world, large macropods living in open habitat have evolved a group behaviour because there is safety in numbers. Predation risk is reduced through group vigilance—the more eyes there are looking for danger, the more time each animal can spend engaged in other activities such as feeding and searching for mates.[5] Larger groups of kangaroos typically see dingoes at a greater distance than smaller groups and can therefore respond to the danger more quickly.[6] Though this is the general theory, other studies suggest that vigilance behaviour is not influenced by group size but rather that the most vulnerable members of the group—reproductive females, individuals on the periphery of the group and individuals far from cover—are most vigilant.[7]

In areas where there is a high predation risk, macropods spend more time foraging close to refuge and also tend to have larger group sizes. For example, one study on the Eastern Grey Kangaroo showed that they would form smaller group sizes in sites where foxes have been removed, but only between June and October, when the majority of females had large pouch young. Between November and March, group size decreased in all sites, whether foxes were removed or not, owing to the solitary behaviour of many females with young at foot. However, where foxes were removed, the mean group size of females was smaller than in control sites and females were also more often alone.[8] These results suggest that solitary behaviour increases predation risk, but also highlights that grouping behaviour is risk sensitive—some individuals were willing to accept higher risks of predation to offset the disadvantages of group foraging. Of course, there is also an upper limit to the size of the group beyond which the benefits of group living start to tail off, because each animal has diminished access to available food.

SPACE USE, HOME RANGE AND TERRITORIALITY

Nearly all macropods have a similar spatial organisation, with home ranges varying from only 1 hectare for the smallest species, the Musky Rat-kangaroo, to over 650 hectares for the Red Kangaroo.[9] The male's home range typically is larger than the female's and in most species a male's home range will overlap those of several females.[10] The female's home range typically overlaps with those of several, and often many, other females.[11]

Once weaned, it appears that young males disperse completely from the mother's home range while the young females remain nearby, sometimes inheriting part or all of their mother's home range in a process known as philopatry.[12] The females' continued residence close to their birth-place produces life-long associations among related females. Male dispersal does not appear to be initiated by the older residents of the range or by other environmental factors, but appears to be innate.

While for many species the size of home range increases relative to the animals' body size, recent studies suggest that habitat productivity explains the greatest amount of variation in home range size.[13] The reason for this is that in comparison with eutherian herbivores the macropods inhabit a wider range of climatic variation, resulting in a greater influence of habitat productivity.

Nearly all macropod species for which data are available have promiscuous mating systems where home ranges overlap extensively within and between the sexes.[14] The only macropods known to defend their territories are the two Australian species of tree kangaroo, the Lumholtz Tree Kangaroo and Bennett's Tree Kangaroo, while the Long-footed Potoroo is suspected to utilise territories that are occupied by socially monogamous pairs because the core home ranges of males overlap little with other males, and female ranges are usually exclusive of one another, generally being found within the boundary of their socially paired mate.[15]

Dr Graeme Newell, who worked with Lumholtz Tree Kangaroos in the 1990s on the Atherton Tableland in North Queensland, witnessed first-hand their extreme degree of site fidelity. He originally intended to complete a straightforward study of tree kangaroo home range, but when a 20-hectare block of rainforest that was home to six of his animals was cleared, he was in a position to look at how his population responded to habitat disturbance. The animals remained in their trees right up until just before they were felled, then fled a very short distance (on average about 30 metres), before returning to their home ranges—now clear-felled forest—within 24 hours. Newell caught another nine resident animals after the forest was cleared and attached radio-collars to them. Along with the six original animals, they were tracked for several months. Six females and five males directly affected by clearing continued to use their original home ranges and lived among the 1- to 2-metre tall tangles of woody debris. These animals never relocated to nearby forest blocks and only one animal in the study established a completely new home range. The tree kangaroos' mortality rates rose after clear-felling, with at least four being killed by domestic dogs or dingoes. The survival prospects of the remaining animals were not much better, as the felled debris was eventually burned to create cattle pasture, destroying the already modified habitat and leaving the tree kangaroos vulnerable to predators. The remarkably strong site-tenacity of this species suggests that habitat availability and connectivity strongly limits their distribution, and that the outlook for animals in disturbed areas is poor.[16]

IT'S ALL ABOUT SEX

Interactions between male and female macropods almost always concern reproduction.[17] The male will check a female's oestrous status, attempt to be her close consort, and try to court or mate with her—and the female is free to comply with or to reject the male's advances. Females of the larger species that show sexual dimorphism (that is, the males are larger than the females) do not oppose inspection by males larger than themselves (which means most adult males) but the female usually controls the final outcome, deciding whether or not to mate with a particular male. In contrast the females of some medium-sized species, such as the Swamp Wallaby and Brush-tailed Rock-wallaby, grow to be larger than the adult males and will physically fend off a smaller male's advances with threats, pushes and kicks. The smaller female potoroids show intense aggression to any male even trying to inspect them. A female Rufous Bettong, for example, will throw herself on her back or side when a male approaches and growl. The male approaches the female at an angle, drumming his leading foot, but if he continues to advance, she will lash out at his head with her feet. As both sexes of these small macropods are of similar body size and share a repertoire of aggressive behaviours, a female can significantly injure an approaching male. To gain access to the female the male must see off any other males and move with and be accepted by the female a week or more before oestrus. Only rarely are these interactions non-sexual and involve other behaviours such as the grooming of another individual (known as allogrooming). Dr Lisa Pope studied the mating system of the Northern Bettong at Davies Creek in north-eastern Queensland, and determined that a male will build his nest in close proximity to as many nests as possible of the females that overlap his home range. In order to beat other males to a female nearing oestrus, a male bettong becomes active each evening earlier than the females in his range, and 'does the rounds', checking in on the females and determining their reproductive status.[18]

One of the difficulties associated with determining the social behaviour of macropods, and most species for that matter, is that what researchers see through direct observation may not be what actually occurs. An intriguing example of this is illustrated by two concurrent studies undertaken on the Allied Rock-wallaby at Black Rock, north-west of Townsville, Queensland. One of these studies involved direct behavioural observation of the animals and suggested that their mating system was best described as 'facultative, long-term and monogamous', with females remaining in close contact with their consorts and excluding other males.[19] The behavioural study also suggested that pair members were faithful to small, shared (and highly overlapping) territories on the rock, which they defended against other rock-wallabies and that the pairs foraged together at night. The second study took a different approach, by examining the genetic makeup of the same population through determining relatedness of individuals. The genetic study revealed that covert matings outside the pair relationship were rife: an average of one in three offspring was not fathered by the socially paired mate.[20] Some wallabies were true to the relationship, with the offspring of 11 females being fathered exclusively by their partners, however, five other females had young fathered entirely through extra-pair copulations or 'sneaky breeding'. For a further five females, at least one of their young was fathered by a non-paired male. The females whose young were always fathered by their consort had higher reproductive success than those whose young were always fathered by their non-social partner. But the females with some offspring fathered by their regular consort and others via a non-social partner had the greatest probability of their young reaching adulthood. Furthermore, a female was significantly more likely to have an offspring fathered by a non-social partner if her previous young had failed to survive to pouch emergence. As it turns out, the high degree of extra-pair copulations in rock-wallabies appears to be the best way to maximise the genetic diversity of the population, and that females select their mates so as to maximise their reproductive output. Comparison between the males with which females sought extra-pair mating and the regular consorts revealed that arm length rather than body weight or testes size was a selection criterion used by females. By choosing better-quality fathers irrespective of their social pairing, females can maximise their overall lifetime reproductive success and, presumably, that of their offspring.[21]

The two most important aspects of sexual interaction between male and female macropods are checking the female's reproductive status and mating.[22] The males routinely assess a female's reproductive status, in particular, whether she is ready to mate, by smelling her urine, urogenital area and pouch opening. They do this in a process known as 'flehmen'.[23] The male gently nudges the female's urogenital area with his nose, which stimulates the female to urinate. The male then moves his snout into the stream of urine. As the male removes his head he often licks his lips and shakes his head slightly; he may also make a lateral and upward retraction of his upper lip, which exposes the incisor teeth. If the female is in oestrus, mating behaviour is triggered in the male, whose penis becomes erect.[24] He also begins to make 'clucking' sounds and to lash his tail from side to side. Typically, the female moves away, at which point the male follows her, grasping and stroking her tail near its base. This sequence, the male approaching, sniffing the female, the female leaving and the male grasping her tail, may be repeated

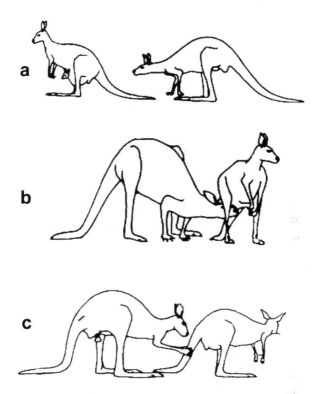

Sexual behaviour of the kangaroos: (a) the male approaches the female; (b) the male sniffs the female's urogenital region; and (c) the male grasps the female's tail. (Taken from Croft, 1981)

several times. The frequency and persistence of these behaviours increases as the female approaches oestrus.[25]

BOXING KANGAROO

To get this far in the mating process, the male kangaroo must invest a significant amount of time and effort in ritualised behaviour with other males in order to reinforce his place in the dominance hierarchy. This is important because although the most dominant males have priority access to females in oestrus, this does not guarantee that the dominant animals will father the young. As we saw above, 'sneaky breeding' can occur. This ritualised behaviour often involves fighting, which has given rise to the famous boxing kangaroo.[26] The importance of fighting in the larger macropods is reflected in the significantly larger body sizes seen in males. For example, male Red Kangaroos and Eastern Grey Kangaroos can weight over 85 kilograms, whereas the females weigh less than 40 kilograms. Male Common Wallaroos can reach 60 kilograms, but females weigh less than 30 kilograms. Most fights are one-sided and therefore very brief because the kangaroo being attacked usually beats a hasty retreat.[27] More significant fights, though relatively rare, typically occur when males are well matched and begin with both animals adopting a high-standing posture. As combat commences, the two males lock their forearms and paw at each other's head, shoulders and chest with their extended paws. Each animal holds his head as far back as possible, to protect his eyes and ears from the raking claws.[28] As the bout continues one animal (or both) will lean back on its tail and kick into its opponent's abdomen. These kicks are of great force, and when used in defence have been known to disembowel and kill predators such as dogs. However, fights between kangaroos rarely result in serious injury or death; although this can happen, most injuries are minor, such as cut lips—and, of course, the sting of defeat. The fight is over when one animal breaks off the fight and retreats, often signalling defeat with a coughing sound; or when the stronger animal is able to push his opponent

Sparring male Red Kangaroos. The animal in the foreground arches its head backwards to avoid the sharp raking claws of its opponent. (Original artwork: Gerhard Körtner)

backwards or down to the ground. The winner is typically the larger animal that initiated the fight. When the two animals are evenly matched, the one that can maintain a greater elevation has the advantage.[29]

Aggressive behaviour is not limited to gaining access to females. The two main types of interactions are supplanting behaviours and fighting behaviours.[30] These aggressive encounters are more common than fights and can be both active and passive. Passive encounters are very brief and end with the approached animal moving away, while an active encounter involves obvious acts of aggression such as threatening postures, pushes, hits and pursuits. The supplanting behaviours are used for a variety of reasons, though the most common appear to be to gain access to a 'lying up' place or to maintain personal space when another animal is too close. In Euros, for example, supplanting behaviour is often seen around good cave sites.

Aggressive behaviour in the potoroids and smaller kangaroos and wallabies such as the forest wallabies, pademelons, rock-wallabies and tree kangaroos is often manifested in the aggressor jumping onto his opponent, either from behind or from the side. Male tree kangaroos have different fighting behaviours because their tails are weaker and therefore unable to support them.[31] Instead they fight by wrestling, hitting with the forepaw and biting, a behavioural repertoire that appears to be less ritualised than the larger kangaroos. This fighting behaviour may reflect their highly territorial and solitary nature.

Antagonistic interactions between females also occur and there seems to be a correlation between decreasing body size and sociality, and increasing aggression.[32] Aggressive interactions between female potoroids, and between female rock-wallabies in captivity, for example, have resulted in deaths. The females of the smaller species of macropods tend to use the same limited repertoire of aggressive behaviours as that used by males. In the larger species, females typically confine their aggressive interactions to non-contact 'threat-states', or 'nose-jabs' that only rarely result in physical contact.[33]

Other complex stylised threat displays include vocalisations and grass-pulling, whereby the male aggressively pulls ends of grass tussocks or occasionally branches towards his chest, to mark the vegetation with scent glands located there. Urination, also a means of scent-marking, can form part of this display. If a subordinate male approaches, the dominant male may also make

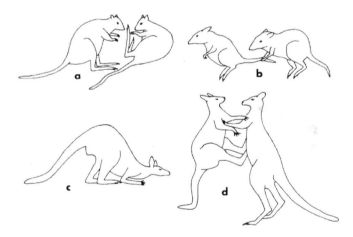

Macropod behaviours: (a) a female bettong lies on its side while kicking at a male attempting to nose her urogenital area; (b) a male potoroo pawing at a female's tail; (c) a male kangaroo rubbing its chest on the ground after pawing at a clump of vegetation; (d) a male kangaroo uses its tail for support as it kicks at an opponent. (Taken from Coulson, 1989)

a short charge towards him but stop short of physical contact, which serves to intimidate but not risk injury.[34]

COMBATING PREDATORS: FIGHT OR FLIGHT

Smaller macropods must evade their predators either by stealth or, if detected, by flight. The larger kangaroos have additional options.[35] One tactic used against dingoes is to back up against a natural barrier, which prevents the kangaroo being attacked from behind and effectively reduces the attack to one dingo at a time.[36] Another option is to take to the water. One observer saw a male kangaroo defend itself during an encounter with a dingo that lasted over 60 minutes. The kangaroo's actions included high-standing, kicking, thumping the tail, and hopping towards the dingo. The encounter involved up to six intense bouts, during which the dingo was within 5 metres of the kangaroo. Most bouts involved the dingo circling and the kangaroo turning to face the dingo, with the kangaroo's degree of reaction depending on the distance between it and the dingo. The response of the kangaroo diminished during later bouts. Another observation of a kangaroo pursued by a dingo revealed the animal taking to water. After swimming to shallow water the kangaroo crouched down until only his head showed. The dingo remained on the bank watching for some time. Both encounters ended with the dingo leaving.[37]

Almost all the macropod species demonstrate alarm behaviour—the Musky Rat-kangaroo is the notable exception—an important component of which is foot-thumping. This behaviour appears to have evolved either with or following the evolution of bipedal locomotion.[38] Foot-thumping produces an audible signal that appears to be used to reduce predation risk. An animal can strike the ground with one or both feet to produce a single or double thump. Macropod foot-thumping links a sender and a recipient that are not necessarily in visual contact, for example nocturnal animals, or animals living in dense cover. There are several theories as to why macropods and other mammals undertake foot-thumping, but it appears to be related to communication with both members of the same species and predators. It is thought that the foot-thump is intended either to startle predators, to alert the predator that their approach has been detected, or as a deterrent to pursuit.[39] A deterrent theory is borne out by the fact that foot-thumping is common in the smaller, solitary macropods that presumably have little interest in alarming other members of the same species that might be nearby.

We can see, therefore, that different macropod species display very different behaviours. In the following chapter, we will see that their diets are similarly varied.

6

TRUFFLES, FRUIT, LEAVES AND GRASS

Kangaroo Diet

The teeth of this animal are so singular that it is impossible from them to say what tribe it is of. There is a faint mixture in them, corresponding to those of different tribes of animals.[1]

The different species of macropods may be considered, broadly, as herbivores, though their diets vary enormously, ranging from grasses and browse for the larger species to insects, fruit and underground fungi for the smaller species. But why do their diets vary so much and what modifications have they evolved in order to consume such a varied diet?

One of the unique features of the macropods is their gut flora that helps them digest food in a different manner to that of domestic animals such as cattle and sheep, a difference that may one day be used in the struggle to fight global warming. In this chapter we investigate the diets of the different species, the physical adaptations they have evolved to cope with these diets, and the potential benefits that these modifications could have for the planet.

In looking at the different groups of macropods and their diets, body size is clearly an important factor. Why? There are two interlinked reasons—the animal's metabolic rate and the rate at which it digests its food. The smaller species have higher metabolic rates and therefore need more easily digestible food sources. Macropod metabolic rates decrease as size increases, so the larger species can feed upon food items that take longer to digest. Body size is in turn linked to the rate at which gut fermentation occurs. This is a slow process that increases in relative efficacy as body size increases. Smaller species, therefore, are restricted to high-energy food items such as insects, fruit seeds and fungi while the larger species are able to utilise more abundant but lower-energy food items such as grass and other vegetation.

The diets of the different groups of macropods are also reflected in their dentition. Ecologist Gordon Sanson classified every macropod species on the basis of their dentition, into one of four different dietary grades. The first grade consists of the smallest macropods including the potoroids and Musky Rat-kangaroo, which feed on invertebrates, seeds, low-fibre plants and underground, or hypogeal, fungi—the latter often referred to as truffles. The next consists of small to medium-sized animals, generalist browsers that consume a low-fibre diet. This group includes the New Guinean forest wallabies, tree kangaroos, pademelons, the Quokka, the Swamp Wallaby and the rock-wallabies. The third group is an intermediate browser/grazer grade that consists of the smaller wallabies in the genus *Macropus* such as the Agile Wallaby, Black-striped Wallaby, Tammar Wallaby, Parma Wallaby, Western Brush Wallaby, Whiptail Wallaby and Red-necked Wallaby. The last grade contains the medium-sized to large macropods, specialist grazers whose diet is comprised mostly of grass. This group includes the nailtail wallabies, Eastern Grey Kangaroo, Western Grey Kangaroo, Antilopine Wallaroo, Common Wallaroo and Red Kangaroo.[2]

SECRETIVE SEED SCATTERERS

What does each of the different groups of macropods eat as part of their diet? The Musky Rat-kangaroo is the most primitive of all the macropods and its diet is different to those of all the other macropod species because it is primarily a frugivore that is known to consume fruit from at least 40 species of trees in the tropical rainforests of North Queensland.[3] In addition to the fruit pulp, they have been observed to feed upon the seeds of about half of those fruits. The Musky Rat-kangaroo supplements its diet with invertebrates that it finds in the leaf litter of the forest floor as well as the fruiting bodies of above-ground, or epigeal, fungi.[4] The Musky-rat Kangaroo eats the lowest-fibre diet of any macropod and as a result has the most unspecialised digestive tract. The Musky Rat-kangaroo is an important seed disperser, because it hoards the seeds it collects in scattered locations in the undergrowth. As not all of these seeds are subsequently eaten, this process protects the seeds from predation by other animals such as White-tailed Rats, and also helps them to germinate, because they have been buried.[5] Another 'scatter-hoarder', the Woylie (or Brush-tailed Bettong), also seems to help the spread and survival of certain tree species, such as Western

Australia's native sandalwood. In places where Woylies are no longer found, few sandalwood seedlings can be found growing; where they still occur, however, the Woylies gather sandalwood seeds while foraging and disperse them tens of metres away from the parent tree, sometimes burying, digging them up and reburying them many times over the course of several nights. The Woylies 'forget' where they have buried some of their seeds, which then germinate undisturbed.[6]

TRUFFLE-EATING EPICUREANS

The somewhat larger potoroids such as the potoroos and bettongs feed upon fruits, seeds, leaves and stems, tubers, rhizomes, fungi and invertebrates. For most species, however, the most important food item is the below-ground fruiting bodies or 'truffles' of particular forest fungi.[7] Many people are aware of the famous French black truffles that fetch enormous prices in markets and restaurants; far fewer realise that truffles are not only common in Australian forests, but that there is a staggering diversity of species. Two of the world's foremost authorities on truffles—Dr Jim Trappe from Oregon State University and Dr Michael Castellano from the United States Department of Agriculture—have estimated that Australia's truffle diversity probably exceeds 2000 species, many of them as yet undiscovered.[8] Furthermore, they believe that this makes Australia a hot-spot for global truffle diversity, which goes some way towards explaining why we have so many mammals that eat truffles.[9] The availability of the different truffles fluctuate throughout the year depending on the species, and natural events such as bushfires. Typically more species are available after heavy rainfall, though some species seemingly proliferate after fire while others become scarcer. Fungi that form truffles are important for the health of the world's forests because they form a symbiotic association with the roots of forest trees which results in 'mycorrhiza' (meaning 'fungus root') that benefits the trees by increasing mineral nutrient uptake, drought-tolerance and disease-resistance. In turn, the fungi receive some of the tree's sugars. Mycorrhizal fungi, by and large, require mammals to excavate and consume their truffles so that their spores can be liberated via the mammal's faeces. It appears that the spores that have passed through the gut of a mammal are a more effective inoculum for the trees than spores taken directly from the truffle itself.[10] This is why the importance of mycophagous (that is, truffle-eating) mammals for the health of forested ecosystems has been recognised worldwide. In Europe and North America, the key mycophagous mammals are rodents, especially squirrels such as the Red Squirrel and Northern Flying Squirrel; in Australia, it is the small macropods that play this vital role in shaping forest health.[11]

Macropods consume fungi because they are easily digestible and nutritious.[12] The fungi can be identified by the structure of the spores contained in the animals' faecal pellets as each fungi's spore morphology is unique. Various studies have investigated the diet of all the living species of potoroos and bettongs and these have revealed that the potoroids consume an extraordinary diversity of underground fungi. It is also apparent that the animals have a well-developed sense of smell to enable them to find the fruiting bodies of the hypogeous fungi hidden underground. These fruiting bodies become increasingly odiferous as they mature, with the odour varying depending on the species. Different varieties have been described as smelling 'nutty', 'fruity', 'cheesy', 'fishy' or 'spicy'. Some species have even been described as smelling like dog faeces! In the 1990s, Rebecca Donaldson and Michael Stoddart performed an elegant experiment to demonstrate the facility with which bettongs find truffles.[13] They first buried whole truffles in sand trays within enclosures containing Tasmanian Bettongs that had been raised in captivity and were unfamiliar with truffles as a food source. The animals rapidly uncovered the truffles, suggesting that their response to truffle odour is an instinctive rather than a learned behaviour. Next, different chemical components of the truffle were extracted on to filter paper. The papers were buried and, again, the bettongs rapidly dug them up. What was particularly interesting is that unlike the female pigs that were traditionally used to detect gourmet truffles in Europe, the bettongs were responding to a whole range of truffle chemicals. Pigs, however, respond only to those chemicals that mimic the pheromones produced by male pigs.

Dr Karl Vernes has spent several years unravelling the diets of mycophagous macropods—first through examining the dietary ecology of the Northern Bettong on the Atherton Tableland in North Queensland and, later, through studying a range of different macropods—a study which revealed that many different species of the smaller macropods consume fungi as part of a varied diet.[14] Vernes's work on the Northern Bettong revealed that the species consumed at least 35 hypogeous taxa. The number of taxa consumed during different seasons was quite similar, but after the habitat had been burned, there was a higher consumption of those fungal species that are known to be fire-adapted, such as truffles from the endemic Australian genus *Mesophellia*. Bettongs clearly preferred these fire-adapted

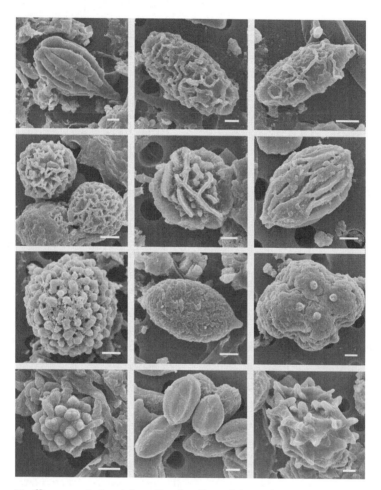

Truffle spores isolated from faecal pellets of Australian macropods. In many cases, the size, shape, and spore ornamentation allow identification of the type of truffle eaten. The scale bar on each image represents 2 micrometres (μm). (Jim Ehrman, Digital Microscopy Facility, Mount Allison University)

truffles, foraging more on the burned ground than on the adjacent unburned ground, despite the fact that the unburned ground retained a greater diversity of truffle species. Bettongs were also able to survive fire very well, and were quick to establish new nests on the burned ground, all of which goes to show that the Northern Bettong itself is wonderfully fire-adapted.

Vernes's results on the Northern Bettong closely matched those of other studies: potoroids from eastern Australia, Long-nosed and Long-footed Potoroos in south-eastern Australia, Gilbert's Potoroo in Western Australia, and the Tasmanian Bettong in Tasmania. The potoroids were shown to have a diet that consists largely of truffles; in some species up to 90 per cent of the diet is fungal, and many species of truffle are consumed by these animals. For example, in a study of Long-nosed Potoroos in south-eastern Australia, the animals were estimated to have consumed at least 58 different species of fungi as part of their diet.[15]

Mycophagy is remarkably widespread in Australian mammals. In the most comprehensive review of mammal mycophagy undertaken to date, Andrew Claridge and Tom May compiled a list of Australian mammals reported to have consumed fungi as a part of their diet. Claridge and May's list includes the rat-kangaroos, bettongs and potoroos—well-documented mycophagous macropods. But the list also includes many native rats and mice, the alpine-dwelling Mountain Pygmy Possum, the typically carnivorous Brush-tailed Phascogale, omnivorous bandicoots such as the Southern Brown Bandicoot, Long-nosed Bandicoot and Bilby, and tree-dwelling possums such as the Yellow-bellied Glider, Common Brushtail Possum and Mountain Brushtail Possum. Notably, however, the list contained few of the larger macropods—only six species out of a total of more than 40 that between them occupy practically every terrestrial habitat across Australia.[16] Puzzled by the apparent lack of mycophagy among the macropods— particularly the medium-sized browsers—Karl Vernes set about examining the diet of as many medium-sized macropods from which he could obtain samples. What appeared to be a lack of mycophagy among the kangaroos and wallabies turned out to have been a lack of awareness that these species ate truffles. Vernes' investigations revealed that all the pademelons eat truffles, as do the New Guinea forest wallabies (*Dorcopsis* and *Dorcopsulus*), several rock-wallaby species, and some of the smaller wallabies such as the Parma Wallaby. Forest-dwelling wallabies such as the Red-necked Pademelon and the Swamp Wallaby were also established as regular truffle consumers, whose faecal pellets contained the spores of many different kinds of truffles. What's more, several macropod species from the same area were shown to eat different types of truffles, so a diverse community of macropods may help to maintain a diverse fungal community.[17]

So important are mycophagous mammals that various authors have suggested that there is a tripartite symbiotic relationship between the underground truffle-forming fungi, mycophagous mammals and vascular plants.[18] Furthermore, the fact that bettongs, the Swamp Wallaby and perhaps other mycophagous mammals seem to show a preference for foraging on burned ground and for fire-adapted fungi genera such as *Mesophellia*, means that fire, fungi and macropods probably share a coevolutionary relationship that is vital to the regenerative health of Australian forests and woodlands.

HAVING THE GUTS TO GO THE DISTANCE

The macropod stomach, with the exception of that of the Musky Rat-kangaroo, is quite complex and is divided into three primary regions: the sacciform portion of the forestomach (the region adjacent to the oesophagus' entry point); the tubiform portion of the forestomach (the main tubular body); and the hind stomach (the gastric pouch and the adjacent region terminating at a pylorus).[19] The size of the sacciform and tubiform regions of the forestomach reflect the type of diet utilised.[20]

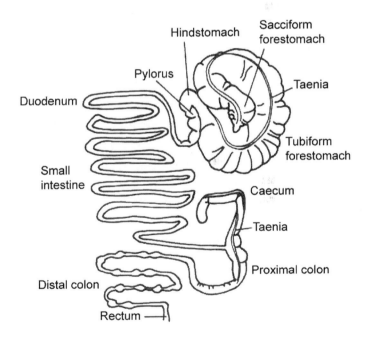

Digestive tract of the Eastern Grey Kangaroo. (Taken from Hume, 1982)

In the smaller macropods such as the potoroids, their volumous sacciform forestomach is able to digest their diet of grass seeds, rhizomes, tubers, hypogeous fungi and invertebrates.[21] As their diet is more nutritious and less fibrous, the potoroids do not have the adapted dentition such as molar progression or high crowned teeth found in the larger macropods.[22]

Forest herbivores such as the pademelons possess a large sacciform forestomach similar to that of the potoroids but have a slightly enlarged tubiform forestomach that appears to aid in the passage of less digestible plant material.[23] The pademelons' molars have elongated cusps which form narrow ridges that are suitable for chewing softer, less abrasive food.[24] Macropod species that occur on the forest edge and feed on both browse and grass, such as the Swamp Wallaby and the rock-wallabies, have an enlarged tubiform forestomach, which may increase the flow of the less digestible but more abundant grasses in their diet.[25] These macropods also have intermediate dentition that includes molars capable of both shearing and crushing.[26] Macropods that are specialist grazers such as the Red Kangaroo, Eastern Grey Kangaroo and Tammar Wallaby have the most reduced sacciform forestomach and a greatly enlarged tubiform forestomach.[27] As the grasses they feed upon are not only highly fibrous but also covered in silica, which makes them very abrasive, these kangaroos have specially adapted dentition with molars more able to sustain this additional wear. Their teeth are high-crowned, or hypsodont, ideal for shearing through grasses. Other modifications include a curved tooth row and serial replacement of teeth through a process known as 'molar progression' where the teeth move forward along the gum line escalator-fashion.[28]

The kangaroos' complex forestomach is essentially a large digestion vat in which plant material is partially digested by micro-organisms. These organisms' most important role is to extract energy from the complex plant carbohydrates contained within the structural components of the plant cell walls—more commonly known as fibre.[29]

The structure of the macropod stomach is somewhat similar to that of ruminants such as cattle and sheep, which have four stomachs—the rumen, reticulum, omasum and abomasum. There are also similarities in that ruminants chew the cud or 'ruminate' while kangaroos practise an analogous process known as 'merycism' (from the Greek for chewing the cud).[30] Merycism is a much more active process than rumination, however, in that it involves vigorous heaving movements of the chest and abdomen through which the contents of the stomach are moved up into the mouth and then re-swallowed, apparently without chewing. On occasion these heaving movements can be violent enough to result in what looks like projectile vomiting. There appears to be no particular requirement for merycism in macropods as they chew their food more thoroughly than ruminants, so it would appear that its primary reason is to facilitate the digestion process by adding additional saliva to the food.[31]

There has been a lot of debate over the years about the potential competition between the larger macropods such as the Eastern Grey Kangaroo, Western Grey Kangaroo, Red Kangaroo and Wallaroo, and livestock such as sheep and cattle. Pastoralists have argued that these kangaroos compete with the livestock and use up valuable food resources that could have been used by the livestock. Studies on Red Kangaroos and cattle, however, suggest there is no evidence that one species attracts or repels the other spatially and there appears to be little overlap in diet, so the two species could readily coexist if cattle numbers were reasonably controlled.[32] The dietary overlap between kangaroos and sheep is more complicated as their diets are broadly similar. However when we take a closer look, it is difficult to assess the actual level of competition because it appears that they often eat different species of grass.[33] It would seem, therefore, that competition is likely to be greatest during periods of drought when the availability and diversity of grasses is reduced.[34]

COULD KANGAROOS SAVE THE PLANET?

Although the basic fermentation process in both macropods and ruminants such as sheep and cattle is superficially similar, the digestive products are very different. The differences were first recorded way back in 1976, when an investigation of the diets of Eastern Grey Kangaroos and sheep demonstrated that macropods did not produce waste products such as methane, while sheep excreted 80–90 per cent of hind gut methane via the lungs.[35]

Ruminant livestock can produce 250 to over 500 litres of methane per animal per day, which is mostly (about 96–97 per cent) produced by burping gas produced in the rumen. Many factors influence methane emissions: the level of feed intake; the type of carbohydrates in the diet; feed processing; addition of lipids or ionophores to the diet; and alterations in the ruminal microflora.[36] Methane is a by-product in the digestion of plant material in cattle and sheep and is effectively wasted feed material and energy.[37]

More recently the difference in fermentation between traditional livestock and macropods has been identified as critically important because of methane gas's significant contribution to the Earth's current greenhouse crisis. The 'greenhouse' effect is the sum of all interactions between the heat that is trying to escape from the Earth's surface and the molecules of various gases that trap this heat, redirecting it within the atmosphere, and preventing its loss into space.[38] Although the Earth would not be habitable without the greenhouse effect, the atmospheric blanket that keeps us warm is now too thick. Indeed the levels of greenhouse gases from anthropogenic (that is, caused by humans) origins are greater than at any time in the past 160,000 years, and we are already experiencing significant climatic consequences.[39]

The quantities of methane in the atmosphere are second only to carbon dioxide, and methane is 21 times as effective in trapping heat than carbon dioxide—so it's a significant contributor to global warming.[40] Livestock are estimated to produce between 300 and 450 million tonnes of methane per year, which is about 20 per cent of the total anthropogenic sources of this gas, measured as carbon dioxide equivalents—more than that produced by all the cars and trucks in the world.[41]

Cattle produce almost three-quarters—about 70 per cent— of animal emissions. Affluent countries produce more carbon dioxide; developing countries which have greater numbers of domestic animals produce greater amounts of methane.[42] As far as Australia is concerned, it is estimated that 97 per cent of greenhouse gas emissions from the livestock industry are the result of methane-producing enteric fermentation. In 1999, this equalled some 62.6 megatonnes of carbon dioxide equivalents, making it the largest source of agricultural greenhouse gas emissions.[43] In 2008 it was estimated that ruminant livestock contribute 11 per cent of Australia's total greenhouse gases, which is equivalent to two-thirds of the total emissions produced by the Australian transport sector.[44] It has been proposed that Australia could reach an interim greenhouse gas emissions reduction target of greater than 30 per cent below 1990 levels, but only through concerted actions in the energy, industry and land-use sectors.[45] Theoretically, removing large numbers of cattle and sheep and replacing them with kangaroos could contribute as much as one-third of this reduction, though from a practical viewpoint it is unlikely.[46] Current emissions trajectories suggest that livestock methane emissions will increase by 7 per cent on the 1990 values and that by 2010 total Australian emissions are expected to be 28–43 per cent higher than the 1990 values.[47] Therefore quick and significant action is required, and as livestock emissions are the second largest source of greenhouse emissions this area of the agricultural industry will face increasing pressure to reduce its emissions to meet global targets.[48]

It has been estimated that as much as 10 per cent of Australia's total greenhouse gas emissions could be eliminated—permanently—if the gut flora of kangaroos was able to replace that of livestock. To this end, research into a probiotic approach through manipulating the rumen's microbial ecosystem—by replacing one group of microbes with another—is being actively pursued by Dr Athol Klieve from the Queensland Department of Primary Industries. When grass ferments in the stomach of animals such as sheep and cattle, excess hydrogen is produced, which is then expelled by burping and farting. Dr Klieve's team has revealed that Australian macropod stomachs contain a microbial ecosystem with a novel bacterial biodiversity comprising a high percentage of previously unrecognised species. Kangaroos use these bacteria to convert the excess hydrogen into organic compounds known as acetates, which are akin to vinegar. These acetates are a valuable energy resource for kangaroos, with the result that kangaroos produce very little methane.[49] Dr Klieve and his team have been endeavouring to identify these bacteria, with the ultimate aim of transferring them across to cattle and sheep.[50] Another benefit of macropod digestion is that it is more efficient than that of ruminants, so livestock inoculated with kangaroo bacteria would require less food and therefore be cheaper to maintain.[51]

There are an estimated 1.5 billion head of cattle and 7 billion sheep on Earth, which together are thought to produce the equivalent of 2 billion tonnes of carbon dioxide every year. Given that the Earth's population will continue to grow rapidly, these numbers—and methane output—are only going to increase unless we can utilise the kangaroos' clever bacteria. Kangaroos could literally help save the planet.[52]

7

HIGH JUMPERS

Locomotion in the Kangaroo

The Kanguroo ... moves altogether on its hind legs, making successive bounds of ten or twelve feet, with such rapidity as to outstrip the fleetest greyhound. In hopping forward, the whole weight of the hinder parts is supported by the tail. It springs from rock to rock, and leaps over bushes seven or eight feet high, with great ease.[1]

The sight of a big Red Kangaroo making great bounds of many metres at a time over the red plains of central Australia is an extraordinary one. As we have already seen, all but one species of macropod hops in a bounding motion on their two powerful hind legs. Indeed, the word 'macropod' literally means 'big foot' in Latin. But why and how do they hop? In some ways, the mechanics of hopping are very complex, in others extraordinarily simple, but most of all it is effective. Kangaroos can travel for many kilometres more efficiently by hopping than can other mammals by running on all four legs. Here in this chapter we explore how kangaroos hop, and examine the advantages of this unusual form of locomotion over quadrupedal locomotion used in mammals of a similar size.

WHO ELSE HOPS?

The macropods are not the only mammals to hop, although they are by far the largest to do so. At least four families of rodents hop, whose members range in size from less than ten grams up to some three kilograms. Indeed, hopping seems to be the standard mode of locomotion for granivorous desert rodents the world

An example of a hopping rodent—the Spinifex Hopping Mouse (*Notomys alexis*)—native to the deserts of central Australia. (Photo: Gerhard Körtner)

over, having evolved independently in the Family Heteromyidae (21 species of kangaroo rats and mice, all weighing less than 200 grams) from the deserts of North and Central America;[2] the Family Dipodidae (more than 40 species of jerboas and jumping mice, weighing from 40 to 400 grams) that occur throughout northern Africa, south-western and central Asia, and North America;[3] the Family Muridae (ten species of the diminutive—between 20 and 100 grams—Australian hopping mice) that occur in the deserts of Australia;[4] and the Family Pedetidae (two species of southern African springhares) which are the biggest of the hopping rodents, weighing over 3 kilograms.[5]

The first European explorers were already familiar with some of these small rodents when they first saw the kangaroos of Australia, so we can understand their astonishment and disbelief at the sight of these giant hopping 'mice'. Indeed the first macropod to be described—the Eastern Grey Kangaroo—was given the name *Jerboa gigantea*, or Giant Jerboa, in 1777.[6] This was later revised to *Macropus giganteus* when it was realised that the animals were in fact marsupials with big feet rather than outsized hopping rodents.

THE MECHANICS OF HOPPING

So what happens when a kangaroo hops? Although this seems a relatively easy question, breaking it down into the specific components of hopping is actually a bit tricky. High-speed film of hopping kangaroos has revealed that when an imaginary line is drawn from the hip joint to the top of the head, the animal's head moves back and forth by 10° in synchrony with its hind legs throughout the hop.[7] This movement is necessary because if the body were rigid, at high speeds the animal's head would

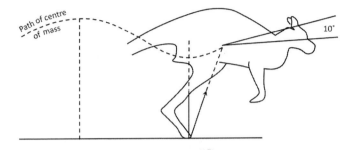

The location of the centre of mass of a hopping kangaroo showing the change in head position during hopping. (Redrawn from Baudinette, 1994)

be whipping back and forth at about double this rate. The tail compensates somewhat for the movement of the head and legs; as the limbs move backwards, the tail rotates downwards, thus countering the body's pitching motion. In large kangaroos, the weight of their tail, together with their increased muscularity and conical body shape mean that the animal's centre of mass is displaced posteriorly.[8]

When a kangaroo hops, energy is stored in the limbs' tendons when it lands.[9] Macropods' elastic tendons can capture up to 70 per cent of the potential energy invested in a leap, compared with up to only 25 per cent in animals such as dogs, stump-tailed macaques and spring hares.[10] By contrast, in the much smaller, lighter hopping rodents such as the kangaroo rats, the energy recovery from elastic storage is much less important and their hopping appears to be much less efficient.[11]

Let's take a closer look at the structure of a macropod's hind limbs. The powerful muscles that work with the energy-storing tendons are the ankle extensor muscles (the plantaris, medial gastrocnemius, lateral gastrocnemius and small soleus).[12] The gastrocnemius are the largest and most important muscles. They begin on the underside of the femur (or thigh bone) and swell into two large muscle masses before narrowing at the ankle where they connect to the powerful Achilles tendon that, in turn, is attached to the heel. The gastrocnemius extends the foot and in doing so lifts the body off the ground. The smaller plantaris is also attached to the femur but its tendon passes round the heel and attaches to the sole of the foot, towards the largest fourth toe, that is used to push off during a hop.[13] As these muscles' tendons stretch, they store the potential energy that is then released when they shorten to produce the explosive movement of the next hop.[14]

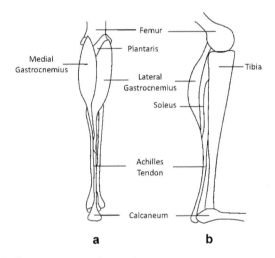

Anatomical arrangement of the ankle extensor muscles of the macropod lower leg showing the muscles that are important in hopping: (a) posterior view; (b) lateral view. (Redrawn from Dennington and Baldwin, 1988)

If we compare the tendon design and acceleration capacity of hopping rodents (~0.10 kilograms) with that of wallabies (~10 kilograms), the hopping rodents' ankle extensor muscles are proportionally more robust than those of the wallabies. This is perhaps because they have to accelerate so rapidly to escape predators.[15] If macropods were to accelerate at the same rate as kangaroo rats they would probably rupture their tendons. Hopping rodents might hop faster, but macropods hop smarter, as their hopping is much more energy-efficient than that of the hopping rodents.[16]

The larger kangaroos and wallabies appear to be unique among hopping mammals in having the ability to harness the energetic cost of bipedal hopping locomotion over a certain range of speeds, making hopping a highly economical gait.[17] When a macropod hops, kinetic energy lost from the body is stored during the first half of the ground-contact phase as elastic strain energy, predominantly in the hind limbs.[18] In the second part of the ground-contact phase the subsequent recoil returns kinetic and potential energy to the body, allowing the kangaroo to hop into the air.[19]

IS HOPPING ENERGETICALLY EFFICIENT?

So how efficient is kangaroo hopping in terms of energy consumption? One of the ways to establish this is through the animal's consumption of oxygen. Laboratory trials have shown that quadrupeds' oxygen consumption increases proportionally with their speed and that this increase generally varies proportionally with an animal's body mass, regardless of its taxonomic group.[20] Macropods, however, especially those weighing more than 5 kilograms, do not follow this simple linear progression.

Professor Terry Dawson from the University of New South Wales was a pioneer of macropod research. In the early 1970s, he trained several Red Kangaroos to hop on a treadmill and fitted them with a mask to measure their oxygen consumption.[21] This fascinating research showed that the cost of locomotion increased sharply as the speed increased when using all four limbs, and their tail as a fifth limb, in what is known as 'slow progression' or 'pentapedal' locomotion. This is a rather clumsy and relatively energy-costly gait, when compared to other mammals that use

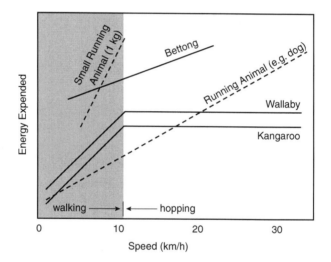

A comparison of the energetics of walking and hopping in the 18-kilogram Red Kangaroo, 5-kilogram Tammar Wallaby and 1-kilogram Brush-tailed Bettong. In the two larger species, oxygen consumption (i.e. energy expended) does not increase at speeds between 11 and 30 kilometres per hour compared to similar-sized quadrupeds; even the smaller bettong is more economical than the 1-kilogram quadruped. (Adapted from Tyndale-Biscoe, 2005, after Dawson and Taylor, 1973; Baudinette *et al.*, 1992; and Webster and Dawson, 2003).

all four limbs, in which the weight of the body is supported alternately by the hind legs and then the small front legs in combination with the tail. The heavier the animal, the higher the energy cost of pentapedal locomotion and the more energy expensive it is compared to similar sized animals that always use quadrupedal locomotion. Macropods weighing more than 5 kilograms use pentapedal locomotion at low speeds because it would be even more energy expensive to hop.[22]

At low speeds the larger macropods, weighing more than about 5 kilograms, use more oxygen than animals of similar body mass that use quadrupedal locomotion. However, once the macropod begins to hop at approximately 10 kilometres per hour, their oxygen consumption plateaus until approximately 35 kilometres per hour. This appears to be the most economical hopping speed as the energy cost is about half that of running in similar sized animals. As hopping speed increases further, hopping continues to have a considerable advantage over running.[23] The increase in speed is achieved by increasing the length of the hop rather than increasing hopping frequency. For example the Brush-tailed Bettong hop frequency at all speeds has been recorded at 3.5 hops per second and the stride length ranged from 0.3 metres to a maximum of 1.8 metres, whereas the Red Kangaroo has a hopping frequency of 2.5 hops per second and a hop length of 0.8 to 4.0 metres. The Tammar Wallaby has intermediate hopping lengths of 0.8–2.4 metres and a hop frequency of 3.5 hops per second.[24] The larger kangaroos can often reach speeds of approximately 50 kilometres per hour with speeds of up to 65–70 kilometres per hour having been recorded. At these extreme speeds the kangaroos increase both stride frequency and hop length.[25]

Studies on the energetic efficiency of macropods weighing less than 5 kilograms suggest that the advantage seen in the larger macropods, where oxygen consumption is uncoupled from the speed of locomotion, does not occur in these smaller species. Instead oxygen consumption increases linearly with speed. Some researchers consider that smaller macropods, such as the potoroos and bettongs, behave more like true running animals than their larger hopping relatives—although their acceleration is slower than in quadrupeds of the same size.[26] These small species often utilise all four limbs at lower speeds and only truly hop at high speeds, so when small macropods hop they are still saving energy.[27] Research on the hopping of Brush-tailed Bettongs found them to have a metabolic rate of up to 50 per cent less than that of quadrupedal running by a mammal of the same mass. Therefore there is still a distinct energy saving when small macropods hop because they can travel as fast as quadrupedal runners but have only half the oxygen comsumption.[28]

The changing gaits of kangaroos from pentapedal locomotion (top) to high-speed hopping in excess of 40 kilometres per hour (bottom). (Taken from Dawson, 1977)

As we discussed above, macropods increase speed during hopping through increases in stride length, with stride frequency remaining constant.[29] This contrasts with quadrupeds that typically increase their speed by increasing both stride frequency and stride length, although increases in stride frequency are small during galloping.[30] In contrast to all other macropods that are capable of bipedal hopping, the Musky Rat-kangaroo is a quadrupedal bounder even when travelling at speed.[31]

During hopping, the macropod takes one breath per hop.[32] The movement in abdominal mass necessary to alter the abdominal pressures and induce respiratory gas flow has been referred to as a 'visceral piston'. The breathing cycle is synchronised with the animal's hopping frequency. The kangaroo breathes in as it leaves the ground. Its diaphragm moves backwards and its tail rises into the air so that the kangaroo's lungs are at their fullest just before it reaches the highest point in its hop. As the kangaroo lands, it breathes out. Its tail lowers and the diaphragm moves forwards so its lungs are at their emptiest when its feet are on the ground.[33] In order to keep cool during this vigorous exercise macropods could use one or more of three evaporative cooling behaviours: panting, sweating and spreading saliva over the forelimbs.[34] Studies on the Red Kangaroo have revealed, however, that during exercise they cool down only by sweating. In contrast, resting kangaroos pant and spread saliva when under temperature stress during hot weather.

As well as the low-speed pentapedal locomotion and hopping, the tree kangaroos have developed a bipedal walking gait, taking alternate left and right 'steps' much like you and I do—and they will even walk backwards. Dr Udo Ganslosser undertook detailed studies on captive New Guinean tree kangaroos in

German zoos, concluding that walking was common in some species as a means of slow locomotion on the ground. Hopping was used when moving faster along the ground, while quadrupedal locomotion was used on most branches, although animals were seen hopping on some of the larger boughs. The authors have observed similar behaviour in Peter Johnson's colony of captive Lumholtz Tree Kangaroos at Pallarenda in North Queensland, and Roger Martin, who has studied tree kangaroos for many years in North Queensland, has even seen them walk backwards![35]

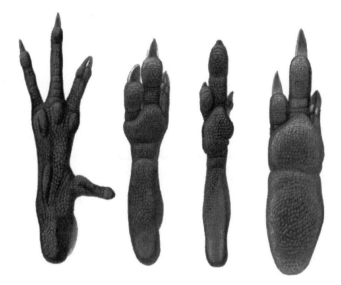

All-terrain footwear. The hind-foot shape of some macropods, from left to right, are: Musky-rat Kangaroo, Black Dorcopsis, Black-footed Rock-wallaby and Bennett's Tree Kangaroo. (Paintings by Peter Schouten from the collection of Tim Flannery. Reproduced with the kind permission of Peter Schouten and Tim Flannery.)

Young male Eastern Grey Kangaroos sparring. Younger animals will often engage in this ritualised fighting in preparation for the 'title fights' that establish the dominance hierarchy among adult males. (Photo: Gerhard Körtner)

A large male Common Wallaroo, showing the thickset features and coarser coat that easily distinguish wallaroos from kangaroos. (Photo: Gerhard Körtner)

Portrait of a Western Grey Kangaroo, showing the rich chocolate-brown colour of the Kangaroo Island sub-species. (Photo: Gerhard Körtner)

While now rare on the mainland, quokkas are common on Rottnest Island, as they were in the seventeenth century when the Dutch named the Western Australian island in recognition of its 'giant rats'. (Photo: Stephen Jackson)

If tree kangaroos can 'walk', why isn't this mode of locomotion seen in the other macropods? Nobody has ever seen other macropods use bipedal walking, so we can safely assume they simply do not do it. Curiously, it would seem that there is no physiological barrier to kangaroos moving their hind limbs independently. Kangaroos are good swimmers, and when in the water they paddle their hind legs alternately much like a dog does. The moment their feet touch *terra firma*, however, the legs once again move in unison. A partial answer may be that tree kangaroos have shorter, broader feet than other macropods, so perhaps it is the length of their hind feet that makes it difficult for a kangaroo to walk.

COULD THE MEGAFAUNA HOP?

The 'safety factor' is a term used in biomechanics and engineering alike and is calculated by dividing the load or force that will cause a device to fail by the maximum load or force that device was designed to withstand.[36] If you've ever ruptured a tendon or broken a bone, for example, you've exceeded its safety factor, and the consequences are painful and debilitating. Engineers like to have large safety factors—for example, elevators usually have a safety factor of about ten; that is, they can withstand a load of ten times the recommended load before things start getting interesting. Within hopping mammals, locomotor performance in relation to body size has been linked to a trade-off between the tendons' capacity for elastic energy storage and their safety factor—the force under which tendons will fail and be torn from the bone. To store and recover elastic strain energy inflicts high stresses on the tendons, therefore it seems that this capacity is traded off against a lower safety factor. The ratio of muscle and tendon cross-sectional area observed in macropods of different body masses indicates that the larger species are better able to utilise elastic energy recovery, but operate with lower tendon safety factors. The largest living species of kangaroo, the male Red Kangaroo, which weighs about 85 kilograms, operates with a safety factor possibly as low as 1.1. It appears that hopping kangaroos could reach a size of about 140 kilograms before the tendon safety factor would fall below one.[37] This figure is considerably higher and probably more realistic than the 35–40 kilograms that has been proposed by some researchers.[38] Other comparative studies of the limbs of kangaroos suggest that the optimal mass for a macropod is 50–60 kilograms, with larger animals at risk of tendon breakage during hopping.[39]

Given that this is the case, could the extinct kangaroos have been able to hop? As we saw in Chapter 1, several species of giant kangaroo reached 150 kilograms or more, with the largest, *Procoptodon goliah*, estimated to have weighed as much as 240 kilograms.[40] The morphology of the limbs of these fossils shows that all these species had the same skeletal morphology associated with bipedal hopping in extant species.[41] However, the issue of whether or not they hopped is hotly debated. One study suggested that *P. goliah* was the largest hopping mammal to have ever existed.[42] In contrast, another study suggested that despite its morphology, *P. goliah* had a tendon safety factor of approximately 0.89 so was unlikely to have been able to hop, even at moderate speeds.[43] It also appears that these large fossil forms would also have been severely limited in their ability to accelerate.

Nearly all large (>45 kilograms) Australian mammal species, including the largest kangaroos, disappeared shortly after humans arrived in Australia.[44] If these giant kangaroos were limited in their locomotor performance, they would have been easily hunted down by the early Aborigines.[45] It is possible, however, that the tendons of the large extinct kangaroos were not in the same thickness proportion as those of most modern species. For example, the Yellow-footed Rock-wallabies have significantly thicker tendons than similarly sized Tammar Wallabies, to enable them to withstand the high forces associated with negotiating steep, rocky habitat.[46] It is certainly possible then that the extinct giant kangaroos had much thicker tendons than their modern cousins, which would have allowed them to exert the higher force needed to accelerate and hop at their large size.[47] This hypothesis is supported by the fact that tree kangaroos can withstand enormous forces on their hind limbs when they make their spectacular emergency exits from the rainforest canopy to the ground. Humans are the main predators of tree kangaroos; when a tree kangaroo spots a hunter, it takes the survival option of crashing to the forest floor and making good its escape through the undergrowth. While branches and subcanopy shrubs undoubtedly slow the descent of a plummeting tree kangaroo, its landing must exert tremendous forces on its muscles, ligaments and bones. Nevertheless, the authors have witnessed tree kangaroos 'falling' more than a dozen metres on several occasions. In each case, the animal has bounded off seemingly unharmed.

HOW AND WHY DID HOPPING EVOLVE?

It is unclear what evolutionary pressures or constraints led to the development of hopping in the macropods in contrast to the typically quadrupedal gaits of most other mammals.[48]

We do know that hopping evolved before the kangaroos and wallabies separated from the potoroos, bettongs and rat-kangaroos (that is, some 30 millions years ago), but after these two groups separated from the ancestors of the Musky Rat-kangaroo (see Chapter 1).[49] It is possible that hopping evolved from the bounding or semi-bounding gaits common in the smaller potoroos and bettongs, and possibly an inheritance from their possum forebears. Brushtail possums will sometimes adopt a bounding gait when running on the ground or on broad logs and branches, and this sort of locomotion might represent the precursor of the kangaroo hop. Some bipedal mammals can make brief vertical jumps to avoid predators, but these require a considerable amount of energy. Could the macropod ancestors have developed hopping to avoid predators and, in so doing, started along the evolutionary path to bipedal locomotion? As the later macropods evolved and increased in size, their bipedal inheritance may have became more advantageous or pre-adapted for travelling long distances. Therefore it may be no coincidence that most of the modern macropods are at or above the 5-kilogram threshold at which the greatest energetic benefit of hopping occurs.[50]

In his early work on the subject, Dawson suggested that hopping may have evolved as a response to the low metabolic rate characteristic of marsupials. Having a low metabolic rate limits an animal's maximum energy output and, consequently, reduces its potential speed of locomotion. Hopping is a more energy-efficient means of locomotion for kangaroos, which allows them to reach higher speeds than quadrupedal marsupials of a similar size.[51] Hopping allows kangaroos to increase speed by increasing their stride length at a comparatively low energy cost. This reduction in metabolic cost appears to be due to the animal's high proportion of muscle mass around its pelvis, which maximises the storage of elastic energy and limits increases in stride frequency.[52]

So despite hopping's disadvantages, such as reduced acceleration and reduced manoeuvrability at slow speeds, this form of locomotion has significant advantages over running on four limbs at higher speeds, including lower energy costs, greater efficiency on uneven and rocky substrate, and greater energy efficiency at sustained high speeds. It appears that the widespread use of hopping by mammals in the hot, arid zone may be related to the benefits of fast locomotion and the increased opportunities it provides to exploit an open habitat with patchily distributed food resources.[53] At any rate, the kangaroos' effective, energy-efficient form of locomotion ensures their unique status among the world's large grazing mammals.

8

KANGAROO COMMODITY

Hunting a National Icon

A man went out to hunt kangaroos, and having started a large male, the pursued animal took refuge in a water-hole, sufficiently shallow to enable him to keep his head and fore-paws above water, and here awaited the attack of the dog, which he soused fairly under water, when he came within reach. Pat (for the gentleman was from the sister kingdom), in a great rage at the threatened death of the dog, would have shot the kangaroo, but the gun missed fire; he then entered the water-hole 'to bate the brains of the baste out' with the butt-end of the gun; but the 'baste,' not fancying to be thus treated, turned from the soused and now senseless dog to his more formidable adversary, and a struggle took place, in which the man was often thrust under water, and victory was promising much in favour of the kangaroo, when some of Pat's companions fortunately coming to his assistance, attacked and killed the animal with clubs, and rescued him in almost an insensible condition; on recovery he vowed not to hunt the 'big bastes again' ... [1]

As we have seen in earlier chapters, macropods have been hunted by humans since they first arrived in Australia, over 40,000 years ago. Macropods are often considered a nuisance by the agricultural community, and enormous numbers of animals have been killed as pests. More recently, recognition of their commercial potential has led to many more animals being 'harvested', despite protests from animal rights groups who argue that this process is cruel and unethical. In this chapter we explore the history of kangaroos as a commodity, and discuss how commercial harvesting, which developed out of a response to these 'pest' marsupials' impact on the grazing industry, has become a significant commercial industry.

CARRIED TO SUCCESS ON THE KANGAROO'S BACK

It has often been remarked that Australia rode to early prosperity upon the sheep's back, however, it could be argued that early Australian exploration and settlement by Europeans was reliant, in part, on that of the kangaroo. The first ever encounter between a European and a macropod, that of Captain Don Diego de Prado y Tovar and a Dusky Pademelon in New Guinea, ended in the consumption of the wallaby, although unfortunately there is no mention whether Don Diego and his men enjoyed this historic dish.[2] Well before Australia was settled by Europeans, macropods were a welcome addition to the ship's menu for explorers and traders passing along the coast of Western Australia. In October 1629, following the wreck of the *Batavia*, and before setting sail on his rescue mission to Java, Francisco Pelsaert wrote: 'I had ordered to burn away the Thickets on the High Islands ... in order to catch better the

Cats that were on that'. Presumably the intention was to obtain wallabies that could be eaten fresh and possibly salted down for the voyage.[3] In 1699, William Dampier described the Banded Hare-wallabies he encountered on Dirk Hartog Island as being 'very good meat'[4] and when delayed at the Endeavour River, Cook's crew also ate kangaroo, with Joseph Banks remarking in his journal that it 'provd excellent meat'.[5]

In the very earliest days of settlement at Sydney Cove, kangaroo meat sustained the population. Frequent food shortages during the first few years meant that the new arrivals were forced to augment their rations with local foods, often drawing parallels between this new fare and the more familiar foods they had left behind. Watkin Tench provided some culinary notes in his description of the natural history of the kangaroo, astutely observing that 'When young the kangaroo eats tender and well flavoured, tasting like veal, but the old ones are more tough and stringy than bull-beef'.[6] Kangaroo so quickly entered the diet of the colony that it featured on the menu of a dinner party thrown by Governor Phillip in honour of the King's birthday on 4 June 1788. George Worgan described the feast thus:

> [At] about 2 o'clock We sat down to a very good Entertainment, considering how far we are from Leaden-Hall Market, it consisted of Mutton, Pork Ducks, Fowls, Fish, Kanguroo, Sallads, Pies & preserved Fruits, The Potables consisted of Port, Lisbon, Madeira, Teneriffe and good old English Porter, these went merrily round in Bumpers.[7]

John White, the Principal Surgeon aboard the First Fleet, evidently did not share the enthusiasm for kangaroo meat:

Here, where no other animal nourishment is to be procured, the Kangaroo is considered as a dainty; but in any other country I am sure that such food would be thrown to the dogs, for it has very little or no fat about it, and, when skinned, the flesh bears some likeness to that of a fox or lean dog.[8]

A letter dated November 1788 and believed to have been written by a female convict was published in London's *Whitehall Evening Post* in 1789, and reads, in part:

I take the first opportunity that has been given us, to acquaint you with our disconsolate situation in this solitary waste of the creation ... Our passage, you may have heard by the first ships was tolerably favourable, but the inconveniences since suffered ... are not to be imagined by any stranger ... Our Kangaroo cats are like mutton, but much leaner; and here is a kind of chickweed so much in taste like our spinach that no difference can be discerned ...[9]

When the supply vessel *Sirius* was wrecked en route to Port Jackson, the colony's rations were drastically reduced. In addition to detailing all available hands to catching fish in the harbour, the best marksmen were sent off into the surrounding forests to hunt for kangaroo. Despite the loss of the *Sirius*, it would appear that fresh kangaroo meat would have been over-whelmingly preferred to the traditional salted pork, even if the latter had been available in abundance. Tench provides a rich description of the meagre rations:

When the age of this provision is recollected, its inadequacy will more strikingly appear. The pork and rice were brought with us from England. The pork had been salted between three and four years, and every grain of rice was a moving body, from the inhabitants lodged within it. We soon left off boiling the pork, as it had become so old and dry, that it shrunk one half in its dimensions when so dressed. Our usual method of cooking it was to cut off the daily morsel, and toast it on a fork before the fire, catching the drops which fell on a slice of bread, or in a saucer of rice.[10]

So important was the kangaroo to the early Australian colonists that its meat quickly became a tradeable commodity on the open market and contributed significantly to the local economy. In the early 1800s, the fledgling colony at Van Diemen's Land (now Tasmania) was suffering a high incidence of death from malnourishment as a result of the meagre rationing of food imported from England of the type so richly described by Tench. In September 1804, the inaugural Lieutenant Governor David Collins decided to order the government purchase of kangaroo: 'The number of Scorbutic [scurvy-afflicted] Patients increasing daily the Commissary is directed to receive Kangaroo at 6d. per lb. from any person who may deliver such at the Public Stores'.[11] Collins immediately set about turning around the health of the population with the acquired fresh kangaroo: 'The Lt. Governor having directed that a quantity of Kangaroo should be boiled into soup at the General Hospital one quart thereof will be issued daily at the hour of twelve to such persons as choose to apply for the same and until further orders'.[12]

In his thorough contemporary account of the early days of Van Diemen's Land, James Boyce asserts that Collins's decision to acquire kangaroo meat immediately created a large cash market for kangaroo, and this in turn laid the very foundations for a new society.[13] In *The History of Tasmania*, John West described how lucrative kangaroo hunting could be:

> The kangaroo hunters were the chief purveyors of food. The officers allowed servants, sent them to the woods, and sold their spoil to government. Considerable profits were made by the more successful ... and the foundation of some fortunes were laid by persons whose servants were faithful and expert. A marine, assisted by two convicts, delivered to the king's stores, 1000lbs. of kangaroo per month, and continued this occupation for several years.[14]

KANGAROO HUNTING.

'Illustration of kangaroo hunting in Queensland', which appeared in the *Town and Country Journal*, 1871. (John Oxley Library, State Library of Queensland)

The 'kangaroo economy' had such an enduring impact on the society of Van Diemen's Land because hunters were forced (and encouraged) to move further and further afield as sustained hunting pressure around the settlements meant that kangaroo numbers inevitably decreased.[15] On their travels, the hunters—mostly convicts—encountered rich new grazing country that would form the basis of the future sheep-grazing industry. The quest for kangaroo set in motion the European invasion of large parts of Tasmania, which destroyed the local Aboriginal cultures and permanently changed the island's society and economy.

> In what was the most dramatic expansion of British settlement anywhere in Australia since 1788, in just two years the convict kangaroo-hunters of Van Diemen's Land successfully occupied the whole midlands region, stretching about 200 kilometres from the northern to the southern settlements.[16]

So successful was the expansion into these regions that by 1813, just nine years after Collins's original order for kangaroo meat to feed the colony's ailing inhabitants, sheep and cattle numbers had increased to such a degree that the government could stop buying kangaroo.[17] The kangaroo economy had run its course, and had set Tasmania upon the road to prosperity.

THE ROLE OF KANGAROOS IN THE EXPLORATION OF AUSTRALIA

Despite the abundance of fish and other marine life in the oceans, seafarers have always looked to the land for providing fresh meat, especially on long journeys. During his circumnavigation of Australia between 1801 and 1803 on board the *Investigator*,

Captain Matthew Flinders stopped at what is now Kangaroo Island on 21 March 1802. While there he made various observations of the Western Grey Kangaroo, but in the time-honoured tradition of mariners encountering a ready supply of fresh meat, set about capturing as many of these animals he could to supplement the ship's stores.

> Several black lumps, like rocks, were pretended to have been in motion by some of the young gentlemen, which caused the force of the imaginations to be much admired; next morning, however, on going towards the shore, a number of dark-brown kangaroos were seen feeding upon a grass plat by the side of the wood; and our landing gave them no disturbance. I had with me a double-barrelled gun, fitted with a bayonet, and the gentlemen my companions had muskets. It would be difficult to guess how many kangaroos were seen; but I killed ten, and the rest of the party made up the number to thirty-one, taken on board in the course of the day …
>
> The whole ship's company was employed this afternoon, in skinning and cleaning the kangaroos; and a delightful regale they afforded, after four months privation from almost any fresh provisions. Half a hundred weight of heads, fore-quarters, and tails were stewed down into soup for dinner on this and the succeeding days; and as much steaks given, moreover, to both officers and men, as they could consume by day and by night. In gratitude for so seasonable a supply, I named this southern land Kangaroo Island.[18]

French explorer Nicolas Baudin visited Australia between 1801 and 1803 with his two ships, *Le Géographe* and *Le Naturaliste*.

Although the expedition was interested in the natural history of the continent, the explorers made good use of fresh meat when it was encountered, and after discovering how Banded Hare-wallabies constructed and used their runs through the vegetation on Bernier Island off the coast of Western Australia, François Péron, one of the naturalists on board, noted:

> From the moment this discovery was made, their destruction was certain; our sportsmen collected themselves together, and while some beat the bushes with long sticks, others were on the watch at the entrance of each little path and the animals flying through the usual places of retreat, thus became the victims of the enemies inevitable. The flesh of this animal much resembles that of the wild rabbit, as Dampier remarked before us, but more aromatic, which is probably occasioned by the peculiar property of the plants it feeds on, and which are almost all odoriferous. It was by much the finest flavoured flesh of the kangaroo that we ever tasted, and therefore this species would be valuable to European countries.[19]

Baudin himself puts the hunt in simpler terms, remarking that 'During the day, our huntsmen waged a deadly war on the kangaroos and killed nearly thirty of them'.[20]

The diaries of the early explorers are littered with references to kangaroos and wallabies—occasionally because of scientific curiosity at the discovery of a previously unknown species, but mostly as game. When the early explorers of the continent set out to uncover what lay beyond the fertile margins, they often did so poorly prepared and provisioned for what lay ahead. Food and water were at times scarce, with explorers often finding

'Nouvelle-Hollande, Ile Bernier, kangarou a bandes' (The Banded kangaroo of Bernier Island, New Holland) from François Péron's *Voyage de decouvertes aux terres australes*. (National Library of Australia, nla.pic-an7573688)

themselves on the edge of thirst and starvation. This situation was perhaps no more richly illustrated than by Ernest Giles' second expedition into central Australia, where, on 29 April 1874, nine months into the trip and being 'in such a miserable state of mind and body', Giles happened upon an abandoned baby kangaroo:

> Just as I got clear of the bank of the creek, I heard a faint squeak, and looking about I saw, and immediately caught, a small dying wallaby, whose marsupial mother had evidently

161

thrown it from her pouch. It only weighed about two ounces, and was scarcely furnished yet with fur. The instant I saw it, like an eagle I pounced upon it and ate it, living, raw, dying—fur, skin, bones, skull, and all. The delicious taste of that creature I shall never forget.[21]

Kangaroos were by no means ubiquitous in the landscape, and when they were seen, they were not always easily acquired, as Giles' enthusiasm for the orphaned joey clearly attests. Another reason for the multitude of references to kangaroos in the diaries of the early explorers is because their presence or absence was as important to record as an unexpected rainfall event, or a navigation landmark observed en route. The presence of kangaroos, and the visible health of these large grazing animals, was indicative of good grazing country, something in which the financiers of expeditions were often extremely interested.

Ludwig Leichhardt's journal of his overland expedition from Moreton Bay to Port Essington contains more than 50 references to kangaroos.[22] Most of these entries are factual; whether kangaroos had, or had not been present that day: 'At night, a thunder-storm from south-west. Our dogs caught a female kangaroo with a young one in its pouch, and a kangaroo rat'; and 'Kangaroos seemed to be very rare; but kangaroo rats were numerous'; but also 'We did not see any kangaroos'.

However, when provisions were in short supply and Leichhardt's party acquired a kangaroo, the diary entry conveys the importance of the capture. Nothing was wasted. Leichhardt 'made it an invariable practice to dry the meat which remained after the consumption of the day's allowance' as it 'served considerably to save our stock of dried beef'. Well into the expedition, Leichhardt praises the value of these provisions, saying that 'The dried kangaroo meat, one of our luxuries, differed very little in flavour from the dried beef, and both, after long stewing, afforded us an excellent broth'. Leichhardt is careful though to temper this comment on the luxurious quality of dried kangaroo meat, by noting that 'It is remarkable how soon man becomes indifferent to the niceties of food; and, when all the artificial wants of society have dropped off, the bare necessities of life form the only object of his desires'. Nevertheless, on 14 October 1845—more than a year into the expedition—Leichhardt's enthusiasm for kangaroo leaps from his diary, as he convey the sheer culinary delight of eating roast kangaroo:

> I had promised my companions that, whenever a kangaroo was caught again, it should be roasted whole, whatever its size might be. We had consequently a roasted Red Forester for supper, and we never rolled ourselves up in our blankets more satisfied with a repast.

Like Leichhardt, Eyre also appreciated the importance of fresh meat in lifting the spirits of his party. In his *Journals of Expeditions of Discovery into Central Australia*, he writes:

> 'Before sunset, I got a shot at a kangaroo with my rifle, which, though severely wounded, gave me a long chase before I could capture it; this furnished us with a welcome and luxurious repast. We had been so long living upon nothing but the bush baked bread ... that we were delighted to obtain a

supply of animal food for a change; and the boy, to shew how he appreciated our good luck, ate several pounds of it for his supper.[23]

Similarly, John Forrest, during his 1869 expedition in the footsteps of Ludwig Leichhardt, also talks of the pleasures of eating fresh kangaroo, noting it '... was a great treat, after living so long on salt pork'. Like Leichhardt, Forrest saw the value in salting and drying kangaroo when it could be obtained, noting that the kangaroo rats he captured in the spinifex grasslands formed a valuable addition to his stores.[24] John Oxley frequently mentions kangaroos during his expedition into outback New South Wales, noting in his diary whether or not kangaroos had been seen, and showing obvious excitement when a kill was made:

> Kangaroos of a very large size abound in every direction around us: our dogs killed one weighing seventy or eighty pounds, which proved a great and refreshing acquisition to us.[25]

The explorer George Grey, who as Governor of New Zealand would introduce many different macropod species to that country (see Chapter 9), gives over an entire chapter of his journal to the food habits of the Aborigines he encountered. He provides what is perhaps the earliest published recipe for preparing and cooking a whole kangaroo:

> Two modes of cooking the kangaroo are common; the first is to make an oven by digging a hole in the sand, in which a fire is lighted; when the sand is well heated and a large

heap of ashes is collected the hole is scraped out and the kangaroo is placed in it, skin and all; it is then covered over with ashes, and a slow fire is kept up above it; when sufficiently baked it is taken out and laid upon its back; the first incision is made directly down from between the forearms to the bottom of the abdomen, the intestines are then removed, and the whole of the juice or gravy is left in the body of the animal. This is carefully taken out and the body is then cut up and eaten.

The other mode is simply to kill the kangaroo and then to broil the different portions of it on the fire: certain parts are considered great delicacies, and these the young men are forbidden to eat; such are the blood, the entrails, and the marrow. The blood is always carefully collected in one of the intestines so as to form a long sausage and is afterwards eaten by the most influential man present.[26]

Grey adds with obvious relish '… to the taste of a native the skinning a small animal would be an abomination, and I must really confess that a kangaroo-rat, nicely singed and cooked by them, is not a bad dish for a hungry traveller'.[27]

By the mid-1800s, the kangaroo had become firmly entrenched in the colonial diet. George Bennett, an English surgeon and good friend of Sir Richard Owen, visited Australia in the 1830s, and described how native and colonial Australians preferred their kangaroo:

The part of the kangaroo most esteemed for eating is the loins; and the tail, which abounds in gelatine, furnishes an excellent and nourishing soup; the hind legs are coarse, and usually fall to the share of the dogs. The natives (if they can be said to have a choice) give a preference to the head. The flesh of the full-grown animal may be compared to lean beef, and that of the young to veal; they are destitute of fat, if we except a little being occasionally seen between the muscles and integuments of the tail. The colonial dish called a steamer, consists of the flesh of this animal dressed, with slices of ham. The liver, when cooked, is crisp and dry, and is considered a substitute for bread; but I cannot coincide in this opinion.[28]

FROM CULINARY DELIGHT TO AGRICULTURAL PEST

Desperate for meat, the first Europeans hunted kangaroo with muskets, on horseback and with hounds. Beaters drove them towards lines of guns or they were herded into corrals and clubbed.[29] Despite the value of the macropod as a source of meat, the early settlers still preferred to eat the flesh of animals they were familiar with, such as sheep and cattle, and were therefore eager to introduce these livestock to Australia.[30] As the farming community expanded and more and more land was allocated to introduced livestock and the growing of crops, public opinion of kangaroos changed. They were no longer considered a valuable food resource in their own right, but were seen increasingly as a significant pest to livestock enterprises because they ate grass that could otherwise feed livestock. The kangaroo industry grew out of this need to mitigate damage to grazing lands, but now exists in its own right to support a sustainable industry in kangaroo products, providing, of course, that kangaroo conservation is not compromised.

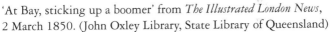

AT BAY,—" STICKING UP A BOOMER."

'At Bay, sticking up a boomer' from *The Illustrated London News*,
2 March 1850. (John Oxley Library, State Library of Queensland)

In 1889, the Norwegian explorer Carl Lumholtz was staying
at Peak Downs, about 300 kilometres west of Rockhampton:

> I was surprised at the great number of marsupials that had their
> abode there. They had proved to be so trouble-some that several
> of the squatters had found it necessary to surround their large
> pastures with fences so high that the animals could not jump

over them and consume the grass. One of the sheep-owners told me that in the course of eighteen months he had killed 64,000 of these animals, especially wallabies [Black-striped Wallabies] and kangaroo-rats [Spectacled Hare-wallabies], and also many thousands of the larger kangaroo [Eastern Grey Kangaroos]. The bodies of these animals are left to lie and rot, for none but the natives will eat the flesh; and although the skin of the large kangaroo can be tanned into excellent leather, still it does not pay to skin the animal so far away from the coast. The only part that is used occasionally is the tail, from which a fine soup is produced ...

Near Springsure I stopped a day at the station, where I was invited to take part in a kangaroo hunt...The kangaroo jumps as quickly as a galloping horse, but usually gets tired soon, especially if it is an 'old man', as the colonists say. He then places himself with his back against the trunk of a tree and sees to protect himself from the dogs to the last. Woe be the dog who comes within reach of his paw! He seizes it with his arms, and rips its belly open with his strong big toe. The dog therefore takes good care not to come near. Sometimes the kangaroo takes refuge in a pool of water, and if the dog is too intrusive the kangaroo ducks it instantly under water, and holds it there till it is dead. The hunt proceeded as rapidly as our horses could gallop, but it did not take long before the kangaroo turned on the dogs in the manner I have described. One of the hunters came up, dismounted, and one or two powerful blows from his club put an end to the animal. We killed six of them in this manner.[31]

As farms expanded to provide grazing for livestock they also improved conditions for the large species of macropods by clearing forest and creating grasslands that fed kangaroos, persecuting dingoes, and increasing the number of watering points. Increased availability of water meant that more macropods were able to breed during extended drought conditions rather than self-regulate their population either by females going into anoestrus or high mortality rates of pouch young (as we discussed in Chapter 4). Aborigines were being moved off grazing lands and stockowners shot dingoes on sight, which meant that the macropods' traditional predators were decreasing in number. By the mid-to-late nineteenth century, some kangaroos were considered to be more numerous in some regions than when Europeans first arrived, though it is unknown whether this actually was the case.[32]

Many began to consider that macropods were a threat to the livelihoods of the rural community. By the 1880s, legislation had been passed in all the eastern colonies to encourage stockowners to destroy kangaroos and wallabies as well as rabbits and dingoes.[33] In New South Wales, for example, by the late 1870s, some 90 years after settlement, complaints were being made to the NSW Legislative Assembly about the large numbers of marsupials, particularly macropods.[34] These complaints led to the *Pasture and Stock Protection Act 1880*, which encouraged graziers to kill the macropods which were considered to be competing with their livestock and destroying the fences. Encouragement was in the form of 'bounties', managed by the establishment of Pasture Protection Boards in specific districts. Initially the bounties were mostly paid on kangaroos such as the Eastern Grey Kangaroo, wallabies such as the Red-necked Wallaby and Swamp Wallaby, and the dingo. Large numbers of macropods were killed—260,780 in 1884 in the Tamworth district alone.[35]

The macropods' pest status was not restricted to the larger kangaroos, as in some areas even the small potoroos and bettongs were considered pests. For example, in the mid-1800s, John Gould reported that Burrowing Bettongs were the most destructive animals to the garden of the settlers in Western Australia as they attacked almost every kind of vegetable, especially peas and beans. As late as 1924 Burrowing Bettongs were considered extremely bold and observed to enter a homestead in search of food.[36] In north-east New South Wales in the 1880s and 1890s, the Rufous Bettong and other 'rat kangaroos' were considered to be in plague proportions and were heavily hunted.[37] Close to a million bounties were paid for 'Rat Kangaroo' scalps on the New England Tableland between 1888 and 1914, with more than 100,000 bounties paid in 1892 alone. Kangaroos and wallabies were also targeted. In the early 1880s, the Tamworth Pasture Protection Board regularly paid bounties on more than 100,000 kangaroo scalps annually. In 1884 alone, more than 250,000 bounties were paid for kangaroo scalps, and more than 86,000 bounties were paid for 'scrub wallaby' (Red-necked Wallaby) scalps.[38]

There are three major reasons why Europeans have killed macropods since they arrived in Australia. The first is hunting, undertaken for food production or government-sanctioned bounties; the second is culling that is typically undertaken to remove or reduce localised overabundant macropod populations; and the third is harvesting, where the animals are killed commercially for their meat and skin under a sanctioned government harvest with restrictions set to ensure the take is sustainable. The number of macropods killed by government sanction was, and still is, enormous. For example, in Queensland between 1877 and 1987 over 65 million kangaroos were destroyed and a greater number of species were killed compared with the few that are harvested today.[39] It is estimated that between 1883 and 1920 approximately 3 million potoroos and bettongs were killed under bounty schemes, while between 1884 and 1914 over 640,000 bounties were paid for the Brush-tailed Rock-wallaby alone, which is today a 'near threatened' species in most of its range due to fox predation.[40]

A secondary result of the destruction of macropods as pests was the development of an industry selling kangaroo products, although this is more likely to have arisen from the abundance of kangaroo hides, rather than any idea of exploiting kangaroos as a renewable resource.[41] The primary product of this industry was the trade in skins which were exported as leather to be used as fashion garments, floor rugs and souvenirs.[42] Commercial use of kangaroo meat began in the mid 1950s, after the collapse of the rabbit meat industry—due to the release of myxomatosis—freed up chillers and refrigerated trucks for storing and transporting kangaroo carcasses.[43]

Initially, kangaroo meat was only allowed to be used as pet food in Australia, though it was exported to the Federal Republic of Germany as game meat for human consumption from 1958. This market was subsequently lost in 1964 due to poor quality product, poor handling and packaging techniques, and a lack of government supervision at the time, but it was restarted later under tighter regulation. The export of kangaroo products from Australia was suspended by the Customs Minister in 1973 but was relaxed in early 1975, allowing them to be exported to over 40 countries. The United States implemented its own ban in December 1974 as

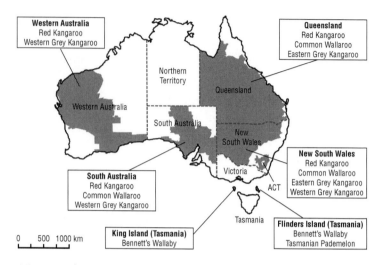

The area of the Australian rangelands in which commercial harvesting of macropods is practised, and the species harvested in each state. (Redrawn from Wilson and Edwards, 2008, and an updated map provided by Tony Pople)

a result of misguided concerns over the impact of harvesting on macropod populations, which was not lifted until 1981 by the Reagan administration, though some US states still have a ban in place.[44]

A ban on the sale of kangaroo meat for human consumption also occurred in most states of Australia around this time, except Tasmania. Perhaps it was at least in part due to livestock producers' fears that traditional meats such as beef and lamb might lose ground to the new competitor. Kangaroo meat was cleared for human consumption in South Australia in 1980, and in 1993, when mutual recognition legislation came into force, it was available in all states.[45] The market for kangaroo meat for human consumption has grown considerably in the past 20 years but although fresh kangaroo can now be purchased in Australia's major supermarket chains, it will always be a small player compared to traditional meats. Even if the full culling quota were filled (which rarely happens), kangaroo would only represent about 2% of lamb and beef production. Nonetheless the industry is now worth some A$100 million per year.[46]

Sheep Replacement Therapy

Australia's commercial kangaroo harvesting zone is largely restricted to the sheep rangelands, much of which occur within semi-arid and arid regions. Australia's soils are sensitive to erosion and compaction, and the impact of millions of hard hooves and decades of overgrazing have contributed to land degradation becoming Australia's worst rural problem.[47] The philosophy of rangeland management underwent an important change in 1987, when Professor Gordon Grigg suggested that Australia needed new ideas to solve the land degradation dilemma.[48] His ideas were supported by studies suggesting that over 1.85 of the 3.5 million square kilometres of the continent is degraded from overgrazing by domestic stock, particularly sheep, with one-quarter of this area being at risk of becoming permanent desert.[49] At a pivotal scientific forum on kangaroo harvesting convened in 1988, Professor Grigg said 'My proposed solution is that the best way to counter desertification on our marginal sheep grazing land is by a market drive for kangaroo products, raising prices to the extent that will encourage graziers to reduce their traditional hard-footed stock in favour of free-range kangaroos'. He added, '… we should be striving for a solution that leaves kangaroos as widespread and abundant as they are now'.

There are important differences between macropods and traditional livestock that make this a persuasive argument. First, kangaroo feet are softer than those of livestock and so cause less compaction and erosion of the soil. Second, macropods are better adapted to arid environments because of their ability to reduce breeding during periods of prolonged drought (as discussed in Chapter 4); kangaroos also die during prolonged drought, which further reduces grazing pressure on the land. Third, the digestive system of kangaroos also operates more efficiently on poor-quality forage than does the ruminant digestive system of cattle and sheep. These differences prompted Grigg to propose that traditional high stocking densities of sheep in the fragile rangelands could be reduced by graziers profiting from a commercial macropod harvest. The loss of income from fewer sheep could be offset by the value of harvested kangaroos, with a net benefit to the ecology of the rangelands. Grigg called this 'sheep replacement therapy for the rangelands'. In a thorough review of the harvesting debate, Dr Daniel Lunney states: 'There is no doubt that Gordon Grigg's ability to speak up and, particularly, to publish, have moved the debate into the public spotlight for the good of the land and the fauna.'[50]

Traditionally, the harvesting of macropods was undertaken as a measure of pest control or to mitigate damage to crops, pasture and fences; however, kangaroos are now recognised as a valuable resource whose commercial uses are in tune with modern ecological ideas about gaining conservation benefit from the use of wildlife.[51] Professor Grigg suggested that if sustainable commercial harvesting of macropods could be achieved, it would revitalise Australia's overgrazed semi-arid lands, result in less killing or wounding of kangaroos by amateur shooters and, in the long term, actually conserve kangaroos by protecting their prime habitat. Since Professor Grigg first proposed 'sheep replacement therapy', the development and application of survey methodology has provided a scientific basis to kangaroo harvesting, which has allowed it to develop into a significant industry and become an important contributor to the economy of a number of rural towns. However, despite all the positives that can be gained by harvesting kangaroos, Professor Grigg concedes that kangaroo meat has still not found the place it deserves on the international game meat market. This, he says, 'is a major impediment to implementing "sheep replacement therapy for rangelands", and only when prices rise significantly will landholders choose to reduce sheep numbers and invest their hopes in kangaroos'.[52]

But what species of macropods are involved in a kangaroo harvesting industry? Six are currently the subjects of management programmes where the products are approved for export: the Red Kangaroo, Eastern Grey Kangaroo, Western Grey Kangaroo, Common Wallaroo, Bennett's Wallaby and Tasmanian Pademelon. The first three species are the most widespread and abundant macropods, and they make up over 95 per cent of the commercial harvest. In addition to the species that are exported, several other species are harvested but not exported by individual states, including the Whiptail Wallaby in Queensland, and the Tammar Wallaby on Kangaroo Island, South Australia.[53]

HOW ARE QUOTAS SET?
To regulate the commercial harvest of macropods, each state that has a commercial industry sets and regulates yearly quotas as

part of its respective macropod management plans. The quotas are revised and set each January with the goal of maintaining viable populations of macropods throughout their ranges, in accordance with the principles of ecologically sustainable harvesting.[54]

Quotas are derived primarily from estimates of population size from aerial and ground surveys, but also from a variety of sources including population trends, climatic conditions (particularly rainfall) and changes in harvest statistics (e.g. sex ratio and carcass weight). The aerial surveys are undertaken with the use of fixed-wing aircraft and, in Queensland and New South Wales, also with helicopters.[55] The fixed-wing aircraft technique is known as strip transect sampling. Two trained observers, travelling at 185 kilometres per hour at about 76 metres (250 feet) above the ground, count the animals within a 100- or 200-metre wide area on the ground that is delineated

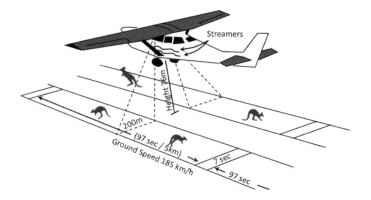

Strip transect sampling from fixed-wing aircraft. (Redrawn from Pople and Grigg, 1999)

by streamers or fibreglass rods attached to the wing struts on either side of the aircraft and trailing parallel to the fuselage. The observers count in 97-second units, with a seven-second break in between counts, giving a sampling unit of half or one square kilometre.[56] The quotas are also based on modelling which indicates the sustained yield and corresponding population depression for a given harvest rate. A harvest rate of 15 per cent corresponds to a depression of a Red Kangaroo population to between 60 and 70 per cent of its unharvested mean density.[57]

So how large are the quotas for each species? Between 1980 and 2001 the national annual quotas have ranged from 700,000 to 2.4 million for Red Kangaroos, 1.3 to 2.2 million for Eastern Grey Kangaroos, 150,000 to 545,000 for Western Grey Kangaroos, 77,000 to 526,000 for Common Wallaroos and 25,000 to 75,000 for Whiptail Wallabies. In Tasmania some 140,000 to 175,000 Red-necked Wallabies (Bennett's Wallabies) and 110,000 to 125,000 Tasmanian Pademelons are taken.[58]

In recent years the overall quotas have totalled approximately four million animals per annum or, typically, 15 per cent of the estimated population size. This figure can range between 10 and 20 per cent of the conservatively estimated total population.[59] Some states have allowed slightly higher quotas, which allows greater suppression of population size from a sustained yield closer to the maximum sustained yield.[60] To date, these quotas have typically not been achieved nationally, although the proportion of the national quota taken has increased in recent years to the point where they have been achieved in the last few years in Queensland and New South Wales. Between 2001 and 2006, for example, the harvests took between 6 and 13 per cent of the population or 51–81 per cent of the total available

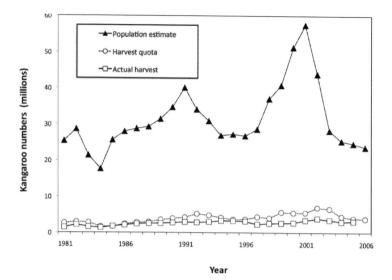

Kangaroo population estimates, quotas and harvests for commercial zones between 1982 and 2006. (Derived from Wilson and Edwards, 2008)

quota.[61] Many rural industries complain that harvesting is not doing enough to reduce macropod numbers, but the states' respective management programmes have been consistently endorsed by professional ecologists and wildlife managers and their associations.[62]

THE PROBLEM OF 'PROBLEM KANGAROOS'

The culling of macropods becomes most controversial when it occurs in reserves and parklands near urban areas.[63] Macropods, usually Eastern Grey Kangaroos, become overabundant in these places because they are usually confined within fenced areas where there are no predators and they have no opportunity to disperse elsewhere, or because of the high quality of food available due to irrigation. Under these circumstances overpopulation often raises valid animal welfare concerns due to the animals starving during periods of drought, or because they can cause adverse environmental impacts such as soil erosion, or the loss of vegetation that can in turn impact upon threatened species. Overabundance can also have adverse impacts on agriculture or other human activities, including frequent collisions between kangaroos and vehicles.[64]

One example of the impact of overpopulation occurred at the Woodlands Historic Park (also known as Gellibrand Hill Wildlife Nature Reserve) on the outskirts of Melbourne.[65] This reserve held the largest population of Eastern Barred Bandicoots on mainland Australia, an estimated 600 animals, and cost an enormous amount of money to establish through captive breeding and reintroduction programmes. This population ultimately went extinct in the late 1990s because the vegetation cover was so decimated by drought, rabbits and the overabundant Eastern Grey Kangaroos that the responsible government agencies were reluctant to cull.

The culling of macropods in overpopulated reserves and parklands in urban areas is highly visible and invariably attracts significant media attention and protests from animal activists. A recent example of this was the overpopulation of Eastern Grey Kangaroos in a northern suburb of Canberra in 2008. The population had reached some 650 animals resulting in a proposal for the animals to be culled rather than translocated.[66] Another population at Majura Army Base in Canberra was approaching 9000 when 7000 were culled in 2009. Decisions to cull these populations generated significant media coverage both within

Australia and overseas—Sir Paul McCartney publicly objected to the culls, and the Japanese media accused Australia of hypocrisy for culling kangaroos while simultaneously opposing Japan's hunting of whales.[67] Despite these protests, the culls proceeded as planned because the animals were thought to be near starvation, and translocation was not considered a humane option because there was no identified release site and the potential for injury and stress that could result, chief among which is 'capture myopathy', a stress-related condition suffered by the larger macropods that manifests as irreversible muscle damage, often leading to death.

Culling is the most immediate response to a need to reduce population numbers, but there are other options. Translocation has been used with some success in the past, but researchers and conservationists are becoming increasingly aware of the adverse effects and stress experienced by translocated animals. Surgical sterilisation can also be successful for relatively small populations, and completed in as little 15 minutes, with the animals left to recover overnight.[68] At this point in time, there is no practical alternative to culling; however, the use of contraceptive implants, surgically placed under the skin, have been trialled and might one day make a useful contribution to the problem of overabundance.[69]

HARVESTING CONTROVERSIES

The hunting of macropods is an issue that has long attracted controversy. As early as the 1920s, Frederick Wood Jones expressed his concerns over the possible impact of hunting on macropod populations when he noted that between 1919 and 1921 no less than 1,763,826 pelts entered the fur market alone.[70] In more recent times public debate over the commercial use of macropods has increased in intensity, particularly since the 1970s.[71]

The arguments against harvesting are often highly emotive and sometimes irrational, and can include considerable misinformation. Because many of these arguments are based upon personally held beliefs and value judgements, they cannot be debated logically.[72] The harvesting of macropods has been opposed on three grounds: conservation, animal welfare and animal rights.

With regard to the first point, that the survival of macropods is under threat from harvesting, the anti-harvest lobby raises a number of issues: that the macropod industry is threatening species with extinction; that there is a bias in the age and sex of animals taken towards adult males; that the quotas are being exceeded; and that the quotas themselves are based only on guesstimates of total population size.[73] So, what is the conservation status of the macropods that are harvested and is there any real risk of these species being hunted to extinction? As it turns out none of the kangaroo species being harvested are considered to be under any threat of extinction, as all of them are considered abundant in the states in which they are harvested.[74] Animal rights groups have also claimed that harvesting macropods affects the species' fitness and therefore their evolutionary potential because the harvest is selective for larger individuals, usually older adult males which have the greatest breeding success, and so there is supposedly selection for smaller body size in males.[75] Despite these fears it appears that species numbers are healthy enough that the likelihood of the commercial kangaroo industry as it is currently practised having a long-term genetic impact on kangaroo populations is negligible.[76]

The second point raised by the anti-harvest lobby of the animal rights movement is inevitably far more emotionally laden, and often heated. They question the morality of harvesting macropods on the grounds that they are native—that is, non-domesticated—wildlife, with the question 'how can we kill and eat our coat of arms' often forming part of this argument.[77] Harvesting is seen as a fundamental violation of the animals' rights.[78]

The third point raised by animal welfare groups claims that harvesting is cruel; that many shot animals suffer protracted pain before dying, that young joeys starve or are killed inappropriately, and that it is inherently cruel to kill mothers with pouch young.[79] Others claim that codes of practice for safeguarding the welfare of macropods are voluntary and that even if they are adhered to, they do not safeguard juvenile macropods such as young at foot that are incapable of surviving if their mother is killed.[80] Some anti-harvesting lobbyists also raise public health concerns, claiming that kangaroos carry internal parasites and diseases dangerous to humans, and that inadequate hygiene controls and refrigeration of meat immediately after harvesting puts consumers at further risk.[81]

While it is widely recognised that a small number of kangaroos are wounded or not killed outright during harvesting, this must be weighed up against the various benefits of harvesting to the agricultural community, to the Australian landscape, to the Australian economy and to the animals themselves.[82] Indeed, the RSPCA argues that the potential animal welfare benefits of harvesting kangaroos at the expense of traditional livestock are significant.[83] First, wild animals are unaware of their impending death so, unlike domestic animals, they do not suffer the stress of being mustered, transported and

penned before being killed. Second, highly trained professional shooters achieve a high rate of head shots during the
harvest, which means that the animals die instantly and do not
suffer. Finally, a government-sanctioned harvest is thought
to reduce various forms of illegal killing such as poisoning,
snaring or locally organised 'drives', and the fact that there
is a kangaroo 'industry' goes some way towards removing the
'pest' label from macropods, because they are perceived as a
valuable resource.

To ensure that the harvesting process is as humane as
possible, the *National Code of Practice for Humane Shooting of
Kangaroos and Wallabies for Commercial Purposes* ('the Code') was
developed in 1985 by the Federal Government. The Code
has been regularly updated over the past 25 years.[84] The aim of
the Code is to ensure that all persons intending to shoot free-
living kangaroos are aware of the welfare aspects of that activity.
The RSPCA undertook an assessment of the effects of the Code
in 2002, which not only explored the extent of compliance with
the requirements for the humane shooting of kangaroos but also
compared the results obtained with those of its previous report
prepared in 1985. The 2002 assessment showed that an average
of 96 per cent of carcasses were killed by a single head shot,
compared with 86 per cent in the 1985 survey. It was recognised that the survey only included carcasses taken to processors
and did not include animals that were shot and injured, but not
taken in for processing, nor dependent young whose mother had
been killed. While accurate figures on injury rates are difficult
to obtain, independent observers have accompanied shooters
and found that only 1 per cent of kangaroos are injured but not
killed outright by the shooter.[85] It does appear that there has

been a significant improvement in the head shot rate, which can be attributed to the Code, a requirement that only headshot kangaroos will be accepted by processors, and a generally higher level of professionalism in the industry. If there was no commercial harvest, non-commercial destruction—with its higher rate of inhumane killing—would be unchecked.

It might also be argued that the protests by animal rights groups that focus on these non-threatened, larger macropods take away valuable attention and resources from the smaller threatened macropods and other species that desperately need our help if they are to survive. Efforts should therefore be made to provide the public with a broader understanding of the kangaroo industry, the humaneness of the methods used and the benefits it can bring. The time, money and effort spent arguing over the protection of overabundant species should really be diverted to true conservation efforts.

SAVE THE PLANET—EAT A KANGAROO

In Chapter 6 we discussed how kangaroos' gut flora could significantly reduce the methane output of domestic livestock, but did you know that by putting a 'roo' on the barbie, you could also be doing your bit to save the planet?[86] The increased consumption of non-methane-producing macropods at the expense of methane-producing cattle and sheep would have significant benefits for Australia, and the planet.[87] In his report on the impact of climate change on the Australian economy, Professor Ross Garnaut made the controversial suggestion that the consumption of macropods at the expense of traditional livestock could be a source of international comparative advantage for Australia, though he recognised that there are significant barriers to such a change including livestock and farm management issues, consumer resistance and the slow rate at which the public's food tastes change.[88]

Gordon Grigg has long argued that the fragile rangelands could be greatly assisted by partial replacement of cattle and sheep with kangaroos. The *Garnaut Review* also discussed the potential for the kangaroo industry to assist in the management of Australia's rangelands. Modelling has shown that by 2020 sheep and beef cattle numbers could be reduced by 36 million and 7 million respectively, which would create the opportunity for kangaroo numbers to increase by over 200 million by 2020. However, some (including Gordon Grigg) have argued that the practicality of that many kangaroos in the landscape—and harvesting them—is dubious.[89] It has also been estimated that meat production of 175 million kangaroos would be sufficient to replace the reduction in lamb and beef production, and that meat production from kangaroos would become more profitable than cattle and sheep when emissions permit prices exceed A\$40 per tonne of carbon dioxide equivalents. On the modelled figures, the net reduction in Australia's greenhouse gas emissions would be about 16 megatonnes of carbon dioxide equivalents per year, or 3 per cent of its annual emissions.

The response to this proposal was mixed: some opposition that at times bordered on farcical, but also support, of course, from the kangaroo industry.[90] The industry's suggestions were that farming could work together with an emissions trading scheme and that more work was needed to encourage Australians to eat kangaroo. The kangaroo industry also acknowledged that the idea of reducing sheep numbers in the rangelands and off-setting the loss of profit with kangaroos has been around for a long time, that it has a great deal of support, and that it makes environmental and economic sense for Australians to produce food from the animals that truly belong to the Australian landscape. In response, the National Farmers Federation (NFF) said that the future of Australia's red meat industry should be decided by market forces, not climate change. The NFF reaffirmed that they were not prepared to see the cattle and sheep industries being put out of business because of a carbon trading scheme, and that it would be extremely unlikely that the sheep and cattle industries could be replaced completely by the kangaroo industry, but they did concede that increasing the market for kangaroo meat in some areas could be a good thing.[91]

Despite the concerns of some sectors of the farming community there are very good arguments for landholders to be involved in kangaroo production including reduced greenhouse gas emissions, better management of total grazing pressure, reduced land degradation, improved vegetation coverage and biodiversity outcomes, and greater valuation of kangaroos by landholders. One of the greatest impediments to landholders becoming involved in kangaroo harvest and production appears to be misconceptions of what is required, as there is an apparent widespread belief that it would involve domestication, fencing, mustering and trucking of live animals. There are different options for landholders to be involved in managing and harvesting wild kangaroos, of which one assessment suggests collaboration with harvesters and the establishment of a management, processing and marketing co-operative.[92]

With all this talk about harvesting macropods for human consumption, is the meat actually any good? Promoting 'roo' to the human palate has always been a challenge. Even the earliest European culinary reviews were mixed. Watkin Tench wrote that 'of the flesh we always eat with avidity; but in Europe it would not be reckoned a delicacy: a rank flavour forms the principle objection to it...'[93] In contrast, Surgeon Cunningham of the Royal Navy noted that 'our largest animals are the kangaroos, all of which are fine eating, being clear of fat except about the tail, tasting much like venison, and making the most delicious stews and steaks'.[94] The fact that early descriptions of kangaroo meat as tasting like veal, mutton, venison and beef demonstrates how difficult it was, and still is, for the consumer to compare the taste to that of more familiar meat products. People who have never tried kangaroo often ask, 'What does it taste like?', to which the most appropriate response is, of course, 'Kangaroo!'. First Fleet surgeon George Worgan perhaps summed it up best when he remarked that 'the Flesh, when the Animal is young eats something like Veal, as some think, but for my own part I am puzzled to know what it eats like'.[95]

As it turns out there are also significant health benefits to eating kangaroo. The meat is consistently very lean—less than 2 per cent fat—and has a relatively high proportion of poly-unsaturated 'structural' fats, making it perfect for low-fat diets designed to reduce risk factors for cardiovascular diseases.[96] Indeed macropod meat could play an important role in choles-terol-lowering diets—research has found that people of both Aboriginal and European origin showed decreases of 19–24 per cent in their plasma cholesterol levels following two weeks on a diet that included 500 grams per day of macropod meat.[97] Despite concerns that macropod meat is unfit for human consumption because it contains parasites or pathogens, it actually presents little or no danger to human health as com-pared to other forms of meat. Therefore there is no reason why it should not be considered a viable alternative to meat from domestic livestock.[98]

The meat's high quality and current limited supply has created a high-quality niche game market, which appears to be slowly expanding as more households are consuming it. Many of the kangaroos shot commercially each year enter the petfood market, so meat production for human consumption could be increased without more kangaroos being harvested or quotas being raised.[99] A recent survey suggests that although there is still a way to go in converting the Australian public to kangaroo, the market has great potential. Fifty-eight per cent of the survey's respondents had at least tried kangaroo; 14 per cent had eaten kangaroo at least four times per year; and 44 per cent had eaten it at least once. Of the 42 per cent that had not eaten kangaroo, just over half were willing to try it but as yet had not given it much thought, with the remainder either not willing to try it or convinced it was unhealthy. Intriguingly, the consumption of kangaroo varies considerably between the states with 21 per cent of South Australians and 19 per cent of Western Australians being medium- to high users, as opposed to 9.2 per cent of Queenslanders. New South Wales has the highest number of objectors. Most consumers were aware that kangaroo meat was low in fat and contained less cholesterol than beef or lamb, but the most common reasons given for not eating kangaroo meat were that people were unsure how to prepare it and that half the consumers surveyed prefer their meat cooked medium- to well-done, whereas the general recommendation is that due to its very low fat content kangaroo meat should be served rare to medium-rare. Many of the survey's correspondents were under the mistaken impression that kangaroo populations are managed in fenced farms (36 per cent) or free-ranged on properties like cattle stations (36 per cent), with only 27 per cent knowing they were harvested as wild animals.[100]

KANGAROO FARMING?

This brings us to one of the most common misconceptions of the kangaroo industry—that kangaroos can be 'farmed' in a traditional sense, where stock is fenced and managed. No such enterprise has yet been attempted, although its potential has been explored.[101] This type of farming would require the domestication and active management of a captive population of kangaroos—something that would be very difficult to do—and a major investment in land, stock, farm equipment and labour.

Farming of kangaroos might take one of two forms, each with its own implications. Intensive, high-production farming based on small landholdings would involve regular inspection of domesticated and selectively bred stock, grazed on improved pasture in small paddocks. Alternatively, low-production farms based on large landholdings in the semi-arid zone would involve more free-ranging stock that graze on native vegetation in large open paddocks, and that are not inspected regularly. Because there would be relatively little investment in the livestock, selective breeding would not be a feature of such an enterprise.

However, even if one ignores the fact that macropod 'farming' is simply not economically viable because the set-up and maintenance costs of new equipment and high fences would likely exceed profits, any dreams of a kangaroo farming industry are fanciful because they ignore some basic biological facts about macropods. Chiefly, macropods are impossible to muster, yard or transport, and they die easily from post-capture myopathy.

189

In addition, although female kangaroos can have two or more young at various stages of development at the same time, kangaroos have lower rates of reproduction and slower growth rates than domesticated livestock.[102]

So far we have discussed the 'direct-use' value that kangaroos offer in the form of meat and skins. But there is another way of assigning value to such a unique, aesthetically pleasing and wholly remarkable animal—and that is the topic of the next chapter.

9

FLYING KANGAROOS

Ethnotramps and Public Fascination

The Wonderful Kangaroo from Botany Bay
(The only one ever brought alive to Europe)

Removed from the Hay Market, and now exhibited at the Lyceum, in the Strand, from 8 o'clock in the morning, till 8 in the evening.

This amazing, beautiful, and tame animal, is about five feet in height, of a fawn colour, and distinguished itself in shape, make, and true symmetry of parts, different from all other Quadrupeds. Its swiftness, when pursued, is superior to the greyhound: to enumerate its extraordinary qualities would far exceed the common limits of a Public Notice. Let us suffice to observe, that the public in general are pleased, and bestow their plaudits; the ingenious are delighted; the virtuous, and Connoisseur, are taught to admire! Impressing the beholder with wonder and astonishment, at the sight of this unparalleled animal from

191

the southern hemisphere, that almost surpasses belief; therefore
ocular demonstration will exceed all that words can describe, or
pencil delineate ... Admittance, One Shilling each.[1]

Kangaroos (and, by extension, wallabies) are considered to be true symbols of Australia; 'the kangaroo' either as a living, breathing mammal, or in any of its various artistic depictions, is recognised the world over as Australian—notwithstanding the fact that macropods also play an important role in the societies of New Guinea and its surrounding islands. Macropods' modern popularity has seen them used in everything from the Australian coat of arms to children's cartoons and slick advertising campaigns; they have been transported to various locations as both pets and pet food and, more recently, they have had a starring role on the dinner plate as a native dish in the finest restaurants. In this chapter we explore the cultural impact of the kangaroos, and examine their place in human society both within Australia and throughout the world. In doing so we also explore the concept of macropods as 'ethnotramps', transported by humans within Australasia for thousands of years and, more recently, to far-off destinations around the globe.

KANGAROOS IN POPULAR CULTURE

Such is the status of the kangaroo that it features on the Australian coat of arms, granted by King George V in 1912. The shield in the middle depicts the badges of the federation of six states that occurred in 1901, with the seven-pointed Commonwealth Star or Federation Star above the shield. The coat of arms' defining features, of course, are the Red Kangaroo and Emu supporting the shield. Underneath and behind are many branches and flowers of that quintessentially Australian floral symbol, the Golden Wattle. The Red Kangaroo and Emu were chosen not just because they are iconic native animals, but also because, as it is believed that they cannot walk backwards, they represent progress.[2]

In recognition of their place on the Australian coat of arms the menu of some Australian restaurants features a dish of the same name, with slices of kangaroo meat and emu meat arranged either side of a serving of vegetables in the middle. Australia may be the only country in the world where it is possible to eat—legally—the national faunal symbols.

One of the earliest depictions of a kangaroo on official government-issued currency was the one-penny 'Kangaroo and Map' stamp, the winning entry in a stamp design competition

The Australian coat of arms, adopted in 1912. (Reproduced with permission of the Department of Prime Minister and Cabinet)

The first Australian stamp—the 'Kangaroo and Map' that caused
such controversy when it was released in 1914.

that attracted over 1000 entries. The stamp entered circulation on 2 January 1913. The decision to put a kangaroo on the
first stamp issued by the Commonwealth of Australia might
appear innocent enough, but in fact had strong pro-republican
overtones that deeply offended Britain and King George V.
One penny was precisely the cost of mailing a letter or postcard
within the British Empire at the time, and the expectation of
'Mother England' was that the new Commonwealth of Australia
would honour the King on its first stamp series. However, the
government of the day, led by Prime Minister Andrew Fisher,
had among its ranks a number of 'anti-royalists' that included
the Postmaster-General, Charles Frazer. The Fisher Government strenuously opposed the standard design of the monarch's
profile, and showed its hand by choosing the kangaroo design.
All returned to order later that same year when the newly elected

Cook Government immediately issued a new one-penny stamp with the King's profile at its centre.[3]

The one-penny stamp was only one of the kangaroo's many early appearances in Australian popular culture. The kangaroo appeared (as part of the coat of arms) on the threepence, sixpence, shilling and florin coins when minted in 1910. The kangaroo was subsequently shown by itself on the half-penny and one-penny coins when introduced in 1938 and 1939, and remained in circulation until decimal currency was introduced in 1966. The coat of arms turned up again on the 50-cent coin introduced in 1966, and the kangaroo again appeared in 1984 when the new one-dollar coin was minted. The kangaroo design on the half-penny and penny coins was the inspiration for QANTAS in 1944 when it painted a kangaroo beneath the cockpit of the airline's first aircraft following the decision to name their Indian Ocean passage the 'Kangaroo Service'.[4]

The first appearance of the boxing kangaroo was in 1891, in a cartoon entitled 'Jack, the fighting kangaroo with Professor Lendermann' which celebrated a live boxing kangaroo show that toured the east coast of Australia at the time. 'Fighting Jack' the 'Marsupial Warrior' attracted big crowds, and visitors found his performance both 'instructive' and 'entertaining', adding that the kangaroo 'evidently feels pleased at the applause he receives'.[5] Only four years later a German silent movie, *Das boxende Känguruh*, was first presented in Berlin on 21 November 1895. A British silent movie with the same title, *The Boxing Kangaroo*, was released a year later, and was another take on this theme in the United States in 1920. These early works were followed by a number of cartoons featuring boxing kangaroos— first the Disney cartoon *Mickey's Kangaroo* (1935), and then a

'Jack, the fighting kangaroo with Professor Lendermann'. This cartoon appeared in the Melbourne *Punch* of 16 April 1891, to celebrate a boxing kangaroo show that toured eastern Australia at the time, attracting large crowds.

The famous 'boxing kangaroo' mascot of the Australian Olympic Team. (Reproduced with permission of the Australian Olympic Committee)

series of 'Looney Tunes' cartoons featuring 'Hippety Hopper', the baby kangaroo that is mistaken for a giant mouse, beginning in 1948 and running for 16 years. These cartoons helped to establish the concept of a boxing kangaroo in popular culture.

The boxing kangaroo became the Royal Australian Air Force's national symbol, with the design being inspired by the travelling boxing shows that featured bouts between kangaroos and men. In 1941 boxing kangaroos were stencilled on the Australian fighters of the No. 21 Squadron RAAF based in Singapore and Malaya.[6] The boxing kangaroo landed its biggest punch in 1983 when it was used during the successful Australian challenge for the America's Cup. It was during this

Cover of the first edition of the much-loved children's story
Dot and the Kangaroo by Ethel Pedley, published in 1899.

campaign that the red-gloved golden kangaroo on a green background first appeared; the image was owned by Alan Bond, the businessman who also owned the winning yacht, *Australia II*. Bond allowed the image to be licensed for mass production and ever since, the boxing kangaroo has accompanied Australian supporters to sporting events around the world. The image was subsequently bought by the Australian Olympic Committee, and the Australian Olympic Team carried a boxing kangaroo toy at the opening ceremony of the 2000 Sydney Olympics. At the 2010 Winter Olympics in Vancouver, the boxing kangaroo flag caused controversy when it was draped from the balcony of the athletes' village. The International Olympic Committee initially considered that the flag was a commercial product and demanded that it be removed—but this was challenged successfully by the Australian team, and the flag was allowed to stay.[7]

One of the earliest literary appearances of a kangaroo was in Ethel Pedley's children's book, *Dot and the Kangaroo*, which was written in 1899.[8] Dot is an adventurous little girl who gets lost in the Australian outback and is befriended by a Red Kangaroo and several other marsupials. The book was adapted into a stage production in 1924 and a film in 1977. The first animated cartoon kangaroo, the nine-minute-long *Mickey's Kangaroo* (1935) in which Mickey Mouse received a decidedly mouse-headed kangaroo named 'Hoppy' from a friend in Australia, also paints the kangaroo as hero, with Mickey teaching the kangaroo and her pouch young to be champion boxers.[9] Another cartoon that celebrated the famed boxing abilities of kangaroos was *Kiko the Kangaroo*, created by Terrytoons, and released in 1936 in the United States.[10] Kiko was a happy-go-lucky kangaroo who could transform himself into a champion boxer to defend his owner and friend, Farmer Al Falfa.

Much more recently, in March 2010, a contentious 'Rocky Show Circus' act at a cultural festival in Texas involved a Red Kangaroo fitted with boxing gloves sparring with a clown. The clown baited the kangaroo by poking it and placing it in a head lock while a second person controlled the animal from behind by a harness that was strapped around its chest.[11] The show was cancelled after protests from animal rights activists and the Australian public, including the Australian Prime Minister. The festival was supposed to celebrate Australia, and was sponsored by Kraft, the US owners of Vegemite!

A less controversial treatment was *Captain Kangaroo*.[12] This show's central character, played by Bob Keshan, was so named because he always wore an overcoat with large, kangaroo-like pouches. *Captain Kangaroo* was the longest-running network children's show of the time, running from 1955 until 1984 on CBS, then from 1986 to 1993 on public television when the American Service (now American Public Television, Boston) distributed the programme with some newly produced segments edited into re-runs of past episodes.[13] When the show was first introduced television was a relatively new addition to most American homes, and the series was designed to give kids a gentle alternative to the frenetic nature of most children's shows of the day.

Skippy the Bush Kangaroo was a much-loved Australian television series about a talented female Eastern Grey Kangaroo named 'Skippy' and her companion 'Sonny', the young son of the Ranger of 'Waratah National Park'.[14] This series initially ran between 1966 and 1968, with a total of 91 episodes. Due to its popularity it was syndicated between 1969 and 1972 and screened in over 80 countries including the United States, the United Kingdom and Canada. A real 'Waratah Park', in operation on the site of the television series from the 1960s until 2003, held Eastern Grey Kangaroos, including one that of course was called 'Skippy'. More recently, the movie *Kangaroo Jack* (2003) followed the misadventures of two misfits from Brooklyn, forced to deliver mob money to Australia.[15] After hitting a wild kangaroo with their car, they dress the stunned animal in a jacket for a photo stunt. The kangaroo comes to and bounds away with the mob's money in the jacket pocket, so the hapless pair is thus forced to give chase through the Australian outback.

The immediate appeal of the archetypical 'kangaroo' is most visible, however, not in literature nor on-screen, but as a sporting emblem and industry logo. North Melbourne's Australian Rules footballers are 'The Kangaroos' as are Australia's national rugby league team. The national rugby union team is known as 'The Wallabies'. Australia's national soccer team are 'The Socceroos', the national hockey team 'The Hockeyroos', the national ice hockey team the 'Mighty Roos', the national basketball team 'The Boomers' (a nickname for the Red Kangaroo), and the national under-17s football team 'The Joeys'. Australia's national airline

The logo of the University of Missouri-Kansas City 'Roos', which has evolved from the first kangaroo mascot drawn for the university by Walt Disney. (Reproduced with permission of UMKC)

carrier QANTAS famously sports a Red Kangaroo alongside its nickname, 'The Flying Kangaroo', and many other companies, large and small, have adopted the kangaroo logo as an immediately recognisable symbol of Australia.

Surprisingly, several American schools and universities have adopted the kangaroo as their mascot too, including the University of Missouri-Kansas City (Kansas City, Missouri), The University of Akron (Akron, Ohio), the State University of New York at Canton (Canton, New York), Austin College (Sherman, Texas), Terryville High School (Terryville, Connecticut), Lake Washington High School (Kirkland, Washington) and Wilmington Friends School (Wilmington, Delaware). How is it that colleges and universities half a world away have kangaroos as mascots? Each emblem has its own unique story, but the basic reason is the same—people are fascinated by kangaroos. In the case of the University of Missouri, the arrival of two young kangaroos at the Kansas Zoo in 1936 sparked such excitement in Kansas City that 'Kasey (as in KC, or Kansas City) the kangaroo' became the university's official mascot—with the first incarnation drawn by Missouri native Walt Disney.[16]

These are just a few examples of the long-standing fascination people have for macropods. Although the status of 'the kangaroo' is such that it holds a special place in Australian hearts, the national symbol and the animal itself have in fact travelled widely around the world.

ETHNOTRAMPS

Macropods have been travelling or 'translocating' around the world for many, many years (see Appendix 2). Dr Tom Heinsohn's studies of marsupial translocations by humans in Australasia led him to coin the term 'ethnotramp' for any species of wild animal that, due to its economic value to humans, has its geographic range either deliberately or accidentally expanded.[17] These animals are culturally and economically significant wild animals that are captured alive and then transferred to locations outside their natural distribution as either pets, food, trade, animal products or for ceremonial purposes. The people of New Guinea and its surrounding islands have been transferring different species of macropods between the islands for thousands of years.[18] For example, the occurrence of the New Guinean pademelons on several islands off New Guinea is probably entirely the result of human translocations dating to at least 7000 years ago.[19] Other New Guinean translocations include the Huon Tree Kangaroo to Umboi Island; the Brown Dorcopsis to Halmahera and Gebe Islands; and Brown's Pademelon to New Britain.[20] Most of these translocations were from the main island of New Guinea to smaller offshore islands, and the animals would have been carried as food and for trade during inter-island expeditions.

Kangaroos and Wallabies: European Ethnotramps

Very soon after the European settlement of Australia in 1788, live kangaroos were making the long journey to England aboard ships returning from the colony. The first live kangaroos to reach England were a gift from Governor Arthur Phillip to King George III, and shortly after their arrival 'the kangaroo from Botany Bay' could be seen in the Haymarket in London on payment of a shilling.[21] The *Morning Post and Daily Advertiser* of 9 December 1791 was understandably effusive in its encouragement of the public to come and see this 'singular native of the southern hemisphere':

There certainly was never seen in this Country, or any country in Europe, such a prodigious Creature of the Wild Animal Species as that Wonderful animated and uncommonly astonishing Animal, the KANGAROO from Botany Bay, now exhibiting at No. 31, top of the Haymarket. The concourse of people of all ranks, and of both Sexes that daily report to see it, their wonder and surprise at that peculiarity of attitude and uncommon proportions of parts, which so strikingly distinguish the KANGAROO from all other Quadrupeds, is a fair instance of the truth of this assertion, and it may be presumed that few who possess a taste for science, or a laudable curiosity of inspecting the wonders of Nature, will omit embracing the only opportunity hitherto offered in Europe of viewing this singular Native of the Southern Hemisphere, in its natural state of vigour and activity.[22]

Soon after, there were several animals in the Park of Kew (probably Richmond Park), where a birth was recorded in December 1793.[23] More than ten years after the first public viewing of the 'Kangaroo from Botany Bay', kangaroos were still a fascinating novelty in London, getting top billing in Pidcock's Royal Menagerie, which excited the public with exotic animals from all corners of the world, as reported in *The Morning Chronicle* of 7 August 1802:

Every effort has lately been exerted to continue the well-earned reputation of Pidcock's Royal Menagerie, Exeter Change, by adding every curious animal from abroad that could be procured from the fleets lately arrived; and we must confess we never saw a more beautiful animal than the Nyl-Ghaw or

Horned Horse, from Surat, to be seen there with two handsome Tiger Cats from America… but what exceeds all other curiosities is the young Kangaroo, daily seen entering and leaving the pouch in the body of the female at pleasure, to the no small satisfaction of numerous and fashionable visitants.[24]

The macropods that endured the long boat journey back to England not only survived, but thrived to the point that, as early as 1805 the Reverend W. Bingley of Surrey in England declared:

The Kanguroo may now be considered as in a great degree naturalised in England; several having been kept for some years in the royal domains at Richmond, which, during their residence there, have produced young, and apparently promise to render this most elegant animal a permanent acquisition to our country; though it must, no doubt, lose, by confinement and alteration of food, several of its natural habits, and exhibit somewhat less of that bounding vivacity which so much distinguishes it in its native wilds of New Holland.[25]

By the 1820s mobs of macropods and flocks of emus had been established at several English estates, including Windsor Great Park, where kangaroos formed part of a menagerie that included elk, wildebeast, llamas, zebras, a range of foreign deer, sheep and goats, and various other exotic mammals and birds.[26] However, when William IV came to the throne in 1830 the kangaroos, along with many of the other exotics that roamed the Great Park, were sent off to the London Zoological Garden (now known as London Zoo).[27] Although, inevitably, animals escaped

KANGAROO

Escaped kangaroo from Regent's Park {London Zoo} by R. Cruikshanks
c. 1840. The inscription below, reads in part 'laughing at the bustle
and alarm occasioned amongst the visitors by the escape of a kangaroo'.
(iStockphoto/Getty Images)

from captivity, few of the species of kangaroos and wallabies
brought to Britain have survived in the wild outside of zoos
—although one, as we shall see, is a decidedly well-travelled
and successful Aussie ethnotramp.

In his three-volume *The Mammals of Australia*, John Gould
declares his interest in seeing Eastern Grey Kangaroos roaming
free in the forests and parks of Europe:

> Such is the earliest notice to be found relative to this fine
> species, of which living examples were a few years afterwards
> brought to Europe, and have from time to time formed an
> interesting addition to our menageries. It is however remark-
> able, that though it has now been introduced for so long a

period, all attempts at naturalizing it have hitherto proved futile; still, from my own observations of the animal in a state of nature, I am led to believe that a small degree of perseverance is alone requisite to effect so desirable an object. Should I be so fortunate as to interest any who have the means, as well as the inclination, in the furtherance of this object, we may yet hope to see our large parks and forests graced with the presence of this highly ornamental and singular animal. That it would bear the severities of our winters is almost beyond a doubt, since in Van Diemen's Land, among other places, it resorts to the bleak, wet, and frequently snow-capped summit of Mount Wellington. The kind of country which appears most suitable to its nature, consists of low grassy hills and plains, skirted by thin open forests of brush-wood, to the latter of which, especially on the continent of Australia, it resorts for shelter from the oppressive heat of the mid-day sun.[28]

While macropods did not establish themselves in the 'large parks and forests' of England, Gould would have been pleased to have followed the successes of that most well-travelled of macropods, the Red-necked Wallaby. A feral species in New Zealand, where it has achieved notorious pest status, the Red-necked Wallaby has had a more favourable reception in Europe, where it has been released or has escaped into the wilds of Czechoslovakia, Germany, Hungary, France, Ukraine, England, Scotland, the Isle of Man and Ireland. Its success is related to the fact that Red-necked Wallabies—or, in Tasmania, Bennett's Wallabies—often occur naturally in cold and sometimes snowy conditions both in Tasmania and on the mainland, so they are pre-adapted to the often cold and dreary European climate. Some of these introductions were unsuccessful, possibly because of the small numbers introduced, though several releases (intentional or otherwise) have led to the establishment of self-sustaining wild populations. Until very recently, one of the strongest populations lived on Inchconnachan, an island in Loch Lomond near Glasgow, Scotland. The wallabies there were introduced by Lady Arran Colquhoun in the 1940s, and recent estimates put the population at about 60 strong. However, in June 2009, the National Parks Service suggested culling the wallabies in order to protect the island's vegetation and the rare Capercaillie grouse.[29] The impending cull caused outrage among local animal protection groups, and questions were asked in the Scottish Parliament later that year as to whether a cull could be avoided.[30] Some of the wallabies are known to have even swum (or, in winter, traversed the sometimes frozen loch) the short 800 or so metres to the mainland, and occasionally end up as road-kill—much to the bewilderment of motorists and insurance companies alike.[31]

A semi-captive population of Red-necked Wallabies was established at Whipsnade Zoo (north-west of London) when the zoo first opened in the 1930s.[32] The original animals came from Tasmania, via the Duke of Bedford's estate. The colony was founded with approximately 90 individuals and reached a maximum population of about 900 animals in 1978, but the extremely harsh winter that year caused the population to crash to about 400 animals, of which around 25 pairs were caught and sold to zoos around the world.

Captain Henry Courtney Brocklehurst established a population of Red-necked Wallabies in the 1930s on the grounds of

Roaches House, near Leek, in the Staffordshire moorlands. At the start of World War II, five of these animals escaped to the surrounding countryside and established a population in the Peak District in nearly Derbyshire.[33] The Leek population stabilised at an estimated 50 animals in the 1950s, but when the once private estate became open to the public after the owner died in 1977, the wallaby habitat patches became smaller in size which resulted in many animals apparently being killed by cars. In 1990 this population was recorded as consisting of fewer than 15 animals, and it continued its decline until the last male died in 1996, leaving an elderly female and her female young.[34] In early 2009 that young female was 13 years old so the population was due for imminent extinction as the animal is approaching its maximum longevity. However, in late 2009, wallabies were still being seen on the moorlands near Leek, which suggests that the original Staffordshire population still persists.[35]

A healthy population of over 100 wallabies on the Isle of Man is descended from a pair that escaped from a local wildlife park, while a population on Lambay Island, Ireland, is the result of a deliberate translocation in the 1980s to relieve overcrowding at the Dublin Zoo. Other populations in the United Kingdom include one near Teignmouth, in Devon, and another in the Ashdown Forest in East Sussex, both of which are small and apparently dwindling, although present-day sightings still occur and are routinely reported in the 'odd spot' sections of local newspapers. Many deliberate introductions, however, such as those on Lundy Island off the coast of Devon, and the Isle of Bute off Scotland's west coast, failed to establish. One of the smaller Channel Islands, Herm, supported a population of Red-necked wallabies during the early 1900s, but these were eaten to extinction by the English soldiers stationed on the island during World War II.[36]

However, Britons need not fear that their wild Red-necked Wallabies are on the way out due to natural population decline or feral animal control. Wallabies, it would seem, are the new exotic pet for landowners wanting to keep their lawns well clipped. The *Telegraph* of 11 May 2009 reported that Red-necked Wallabies are being sold as a 'cuter, friendlier and more exotic alternative' to sheep. The *Australian*'s coverage of the same story ran under the headline 'Poms replacing lawn mowers with wallabies'. A pair of wallabies can fetch £800, and demand seems to be outstripping supply—one breeder suggested that he could easily find homes for 100 animals.[37] So it would seem likely that escaped wallabies will continue to establish new populations across Britain for some time to come.

Red-necked Wallabies also invaded continental Europe. In Germany, two males and three females were introduced into a 500-hectare private forest reserve in 1887, and numbers quickly increased to around 40 wallabies. In 1893, however, the gamekeeper looking after them died, and poachers had hunted out the population by 1895.[38] Another German introduction of Red-necked Wallabies in the early 1900s was initially successful, resulting in a population of more than 70 animals by the outbreak of World War I. Following the war however, only a few animals remained, and these were taken into captivity. In his extensive analysis of the introduced mammals of the world John Long also notes that deliberate introductions of Red-necked Wallabies were attempted in Czechoslovakia, Hungary and the Ukraine, but none of these populations survived very long.[39]

One European population, however, is still thriving, just one hour's drive from Paris. Red-necked Wallabies descended from 25 or so animals that escaped from the Parc Zoologique de Sauvage in Émancé in the 1970s roam wild in the ancient forest of Rambouillet. Moreover, in recent years, the population has been shown to be expanding its range outside of the forest reserve.[40] These animals appear to be having an unwanted impact—literally—on the local people. Every few months a French provincial motorist submits a claim for vehicle damage as a result of a collision with a wallaby in the Rambouillet forest. The scepticism of insurance companies has forced the Mayor of Émancé to write numerous letters vouching for the wallabies' presence there.[41]

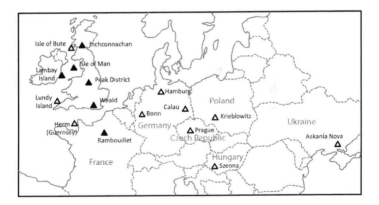

Australian ethnotramps. Red-necked Wallabies escaped or were intentionally introduced to wild or semi-wild conditions in Europe periodically throughout the 1800s and 1900s. The solid triangles are believed to be extant populations, open triangles are populations that died out.

Wallabies in the United States of America

The Brush-tailed Rock-wallaby was introduced to Hawaii by a Mr R.H. Trent, who purchased a male, and a female with a pouch young from the crew of an Australian ship passing through Honolulu in 1916.[42] The animals were initially housed in a tent on the island of Oahu, but after an attack by a pack of dogs (during which the pouch young was killed) the adults escaped and established a wild population. In 1981 the population was estimated to be about 250 animals, though this had declined to about 100 by 1987.[43] Mark Eldridge and Teena Browning analysed the genetics of the Hawaiian rock-wallabies following claims that they were rapidly evolving into a 'new' species of rock-wallaby. Their results indicated, however, that these animals were not genetically novel, but shared genetic characteristics with the south-eastern Queensland rock-wallabies from which they were probably descended.[44]

Mainland North Americans periodically report sightings of 'phantom kangaroos'. Some are legitimate sightings of escaped animals from zoos or private collections, as was the case when a Red-necked Wallaby escaped from a zoo in Ottawa, Canada, and was estimated (via numerous reported sightings) to have covered a distance of more than 80 kilometres before being found dead a few weeks later.[45] Most tales from North America, however, are of the tall variety. For example, in 1934 in South Pittsburg, Tennessee, several witnesses (including, apparently, a Reverend W.J. Hancock) claimed to have seen a 'large kangaroo' running and leaping across a field. Credible enough, except that the witnesses also claimed that the creature was responsible for a rash of mysterious killings that included an Alsatian dog and several chickens, all of which were partly devoured. The reason the kangaroo was implicated in the killing spree is because it was observed fleeing the scene 'carrying a sheep'. The sighting sparked a 15-hour hunt that ended in the killing of the 'kangaroo'—a lynx, whose long legs and leaping strides had befuddled witnesses of the incident. Another kangaroo incident—equally strange but this time involving a real kangaroo (presumably a zoo escapee)—took place in the early hours of the morning of 14 October 1974 in Chicago. Two police officers were called to a report of a kangaroo on the front porch of a house, but by the time the officers arrived the kangaroo had escaped to a nearby blind alley. Unsure of how to apprehend the animal, the officers attempted to 'hand-cuff' it—only to be kicked and scratched, and to have the animal disappear into the night.[46]

Translocations in Australia and New Zealand

Several Australian species of macropods have also been transferred to islands off the coast of Australia for reasons other than conservation efforts (see Appendix 2), including Tasmanian Bettongs, Agile Wallabies, Western Grey Kangaroos, Eastern Grey Kangaroos, Northern Nailtail Wallabies, Whiptail Wallabies, Common Wallaroos and Red-necked Wallabies.[47] The motivations behind these transfers are unclear, though it appears that in most cases it was just a simple desire to have the animals present. Some macropod species have, with a little human help, crossed 'the ditch' to establish themselves in nearby New Zealand. Long-nosed Potoroos, Black-striped Wallabies, Tammar Wallabies, Brush-tailed Rock-wallabies, Parma Wallabies, Red-necked Wallabies and Swamp Wallabies have all been introduced to New Zealand, mostly by the Auckland Acclimatisation Society between 1867 and 1870. Several notable releases were at the hand of Sir George Grey, two-time Governor of New Zealand.

Before taking up the governorship of New Zealand, the adventurous Grey had explored parts of northern Australia where he was shipwrecked (and very nearly drowned) on one expedition, and rescued by Aborigines on another.[48] He then served as Governor of South Australia, and it was perhaps this posting, along with his other Australian exploits, which gave him an interest in macropods. By 1862, during his second stint as Governor of New Zealand, Grey had assembled on his private estate on Kawau Island, near Auckland, populations of no less than five species—the Parma Wallaby, Tammar Wallaby, Swamp Wallaby, Black-striped Wallaby and Brush-tailed Rock-wallaby.[49] All except the Black-striped Wallaby thrived—indeed, they went on to become environmental pests by browsing down the island's vegetation and making life hard for endangered birds such as Kiwis and Wekas. The four remaining macropod species are the subject of vigorous control and eradication programmes. In 2004, the descendants of some of those wallabies came full circle, Kawau Island Tammar Wallabies being repatriated to their ancestral home on South Australia's Yorke Peninsula. Mainland Tammar Wallabies had been extinct there since 1925, but as part of a joint Australia–New Zealand conservation initiative, the New Zealand wallabies were released into a predator-controlled site at Innes National Park.[50]

Wherever macropods have gone in the world, they have created a stir, whether it's the excitement felt by a hiker on the Staffordshire moors on seeing a wild Red-necked Wallaby, the chant of an American collegiate basketball crowd cheering on 'their' kangaroos, or the frustration felt by a New Zealand conservation officer trying to control feral Tammar Wallabies. The humble macropods of Australia and New Guinea are a world phenomenon. The sad irony, however, is that while macropods were fascinating those who came into contact with them elsewhere in the world, in their own native habitats many species were dwindling to the point of no return. In the next chapter, we explore the grim history of macropod extinctions.

10

EXTINCT?

The Disappearance of Australia's Macropods

Until recently, this decline was accepted as an inevitable cost of 'progress', an economic necessity in the process of creating jobs and developing the nation. Now after 200 years of intensive grazing, forestry and mining, with little regard for their effects on our wildlife, fundamental attitudes are at last changing. We—and nations worldwide—are beginning to understand just what the extinction of our animals represents.

Many people argue that the vanished species, although interesting and attractive, were useless, and that the loss of a few rats and wallabies has no effect upon humans. Nothing could be further from the truth. We are learning to our cost that the human animal cannot exist in isolation. Destroy the environment that supports other creatures and we put ourselves under threat....Vanishing wildlife is a first obvious sign of a serious environmental malaise, one that will deepen as extinctions continue, so that eventually human existence itself is placed in jeopardy.[1]

The term 'to go the way of the Dodo' refers to the infamous extinction of the large, flightless bird endemic to the island of Mauritius in the Indian Ocean which was probably wiped out in 1681 at the hands of seafarers, eager for easily procured fresh meat, and the pigs and macaques they introduced.[2] Australia has one of the worst records of modern extinctions (that is, since 1800) of any country on Earth many of which, like the Dodo, can be directly attributed to human activity. One could just as easily use the term 'dead as a Toolache, Crescent Nailtail or Eastern Hare-wallaby' to refer to something irretrievably lost. Since European settlement the macropods have suffered more than most other Australian groups, with many species experiencing significant range reductions and others extinction. In this chapter we explore how it came to be that so many species have disappeared from Australia, and what can be done to prevent further extinctions.

The list of Australian mammals that have become extinct since the continent's colonisation by Europeans in 1788 is long and sobering. Of the 70-odd species of mammals that have become extinct worldwide since 1500, 26 were from Australia and its surrounding islands, and a quarter of these (seven species) were macropods.[3] A further nine species, more than half of them (five species) macropods, have become extinct on the Australian mainland and now only occur on offshore islands. Five additional subspecies of macropod are also extinct, with subspecies of the Tasmanian Bettong, Burrowing Bettong, Brush-tailed Bettong, Banded Hare-wallaby and Rufous Bettong now extinct on the mainland.[4] In addition there are many more Australian mammals that are considered 'vulnerable', 'endangered' or 'critically endangered', so are at serious risk of extinction in the future (we will explore these further in the next chapter). New Guinean macropods have fared somewhat better, with no species driven to extinction, although overhunting of some species means that they face a real risk of extinction in the foreseeable future.

Did these extinct species share a common factor that made them particularly susceptible to extinction? The primary factor that links most of the extinct species is their size. They generally fall within what is known as the 'critical weight range', that is, between 35 grams and 5.5 kilograms.[5] This holds true for all the extinct macropods except the Toolache Wallaby, which appears to have become extinct due to loss of habitat and overhunting. The second common factor is that the extinct species tended to occur in drier, semi-arid and arid regions of the southern half of Australia and, third, the animals were all ground-dwelling or resided in rock-piles. To date, no mammal from Australia's forested regions has become extinct.[6]

In an excellent analysis of the trends of Australian mammal extinctions Professor Chris Johnson showed that the smallest species tended to disappear first.[7] Professor Johnson suggests there were four major extinction pulses after the arrival of Europeans to Australia that affected different components of the Australian mammal fauna, including the macropods:

- During the 1840s and 1850s five species of rodents from south-east and south-west Australia were lost.
- Between 1880 and 1920 there were five further rodent extinctions as well as the Broad-faced Potoroo and Eastern Hare-wallaby.
- In the 1930s, the Thylacine, Toolache Wallaby and Lesser Stick-nest Rat disappeared, with many other bandicoots and wallabies decreasing greatly in range.

- After 1939, there was the demise of a very distinct group that included rat-kangaroos, bandicoots and small wallabies of arid Australia.

THE EXTINCT MACROPODS

The Nullarbor Dwarf Bettong may have been the first modern extinction of a macropod in Australia—but if so, it disappeared

Extinct macropods. Clockwise from top left: Desert Rat-kangaroo, Eastern Hare-wallaby, Crescent Nailtail Wallaby, Toolache Wallaby, Broad-faced Potoroo. (From Gould, 1845–1863, National Library of Australia)

Australian mammal species that have become extinct since 1788 (derived from Johnson, 2006, and Van Dyck and Strahan, 2008). Note that Australia includes the mainland and all surrounding islands including Christmas Island.

Common Name	Scientific Name	Last Record
Carnivorous Marsupials		
Thylacine	*Thylacinus cynocephalus*	1936
Bandicoots and Bilbies		
Pig-footed Bandicoot	*Chaeropus ecaudatus*	1950s
Desert Bandicoot	*Perameles eremiana*	1960s
Lesser Bilby	*Macrotis leucura*	1960s
Wallabies and rat-kangaroos		
Nullarbor Dwarf Bettong	*Bettongia pusilla*	Early 1800s?
Desert Rat-kangaroo	*Caloprymnus campestris*	1950s?
Broad-faced Potoroo	*Potorous platyops*	1875
Central Hare-wallaby	*Lagorchestes asomatus*	1940s
Eastern Hare-wallaby	*Lagorchestes leporides*	1889
Toolache Wallaby	*Macropus greyi*	1939
Crescent Nailtail Wallaby	*Onychogalea lunata*	1956
Shrews		
Christmas Island Shrew	*Crocidura attenata trichura*	1985?
Bats		
Percy Island Flying-fox	*Pteropus brunneus*	1874?
Lord Howe Long-eared Bat	*Nyctophilus howensis*	1920s
Rats and Mice		
White-footed Rabbit-rat	*Conilurus albipes*	1845
Lesser Stick-nest Rat	*Leporillus apicalis*	1933

Common Name	Scientific Name	Last Record
Short-tailed Hopping Mouse	*Notomys amplus*	1896
Long-tailed Hopping Mouse	*Notomys longicaudatus*	1901
Big-eared Hopping Mouse	*Notomys macrotis*	1843
Darling Downs Hopping Mouse	*Notomys mordax*	1840s
Broad-cheeked Hopping Mouse	*Notomys robustus*	1850?
Long-eared Mouse	*Pseudomys auritus*	1850s
Blue-grey Mouse	*Pseudomys glaucus*	1956
Gould's Mouse	*Pseudomys gouldi*	1857
Maclear's Rat	*Rattus macleari*	1904?
Bulldog Rat	*Rattus nativitatis*	1904?

so soon after European arrival that no living record of the animal was made, and the animal is described and known only from various sub-fossil remains in the Nullarbor region of South Australia and Western Australia.[8] As a result nothing is known of the ecology of this species and we do not even know what it looked like.

Of the macropod species that are now extinct, the first confirmed to have been lost was the Broad-faced Potoroo, last recorded in 1875. Regrettably, very little was learned about this species before its demise other than it lived in south-west Western Australia. Sub-fossil remains have also been found in south-western Australia and near coastal South Australia suggesting that the Broad-faced Potoroo's range had already contracted considerably before the arrival of Europeans.[9]

The Eastern Hare-wallaby once had a wide distribution within western New South Wales, north-western Victoria and south-eastern South Australia before its extinction in 1889. The naturalist John Gould recalled that it usually sought shelter in a well-formed seat under a tuft of grass on the open plains. Its fleetness of foot was wonderful:

> Its powers of leaping are also equally extraordinary, in proof of which I may mention an incident connected with the chase of the animal which occurred by myself. While out on the plains of South Australia I started a Hare Kangaroo before two fleet dogs; after running to the distance of a quarter of a mile, it suddenly doubled and came back upon me, the dogs following close at its heels; I stood perfectly still until the animal had arrived within twenty feet before it observed me, when to my astonishment, instead of branching off to the right or to the left, it bounded clear over my head, and on descending to the ground I was enabled to make a successful shot, by which it was procured.[10]

The Toolache Wallaby was thought to be perhaps the most beautiful, elegant and swift of all the macropods. It appears that its numbers began to decline as a result of land clearing in southeastern South Australia between the 1860s and 1900s. Hunting further decreased populations under strain from habitat loss. Unfortunately, this gregarious species remained loyal to a particular location so animals that remained in their partially cleared habitats were easy targets for sportsmen, hunters or pastoralists.[11] The Toolache Wallaby remained relatively common until 1910, but by 1923 it was becoming exceedingly rare and the last known group was found on Konetta sheep run near Robe on the South Australian coast. Efforts to translocate them to Kangaroo Island failed and hunting continued to take its toll until the group's last animal, a female, was captured in 1927.

That animal lived for 12 more years in captivity. With her death, the species finally became extinct in 1939. Despite anecdotal reports of further sightings since this time, no animals have been found.

The extinct macropod about which we know the least is the Central Hare-wallaby. This species is known only from one unsexed adult skull that was extracted from a fresh carcass by the explorer and geologist Michael Terry, during a 1932 prospecting expedition in the Tanami Desert (Northern Territory), somewhere along a 130-kilometre strip of country between Mount Farewell and Lake Mackay.[12] Though it was well known to the Aboriginal people of this region who suggest that it was widespread, we do not even know what the animal looked like. Described in 1943 from that solitary skull, the animal slipped away sometime in the late 1940s before any further collections or observations had been made.

The Desert Rat-kangaroo, which was known in the local Aboriginal language as *Oolacunta*, occurred in one of the hottest, driest and remotest parts of Australia; the gibber plains in north-eastern South Australia and south-west Queensland. The story of the Desert Rat-kangaroo flip-flopped between lost and found for over 100 years before it was finally pronounced extinct. It was first discovered and recorded in 1841 by George Grey (Governor of South Australia) and described as a new species by John Gould in 1843. In the late 1870s Ralph Tate remarked that it was one of the 'commonest mammals in the oasis; and though exceedingly timid in the day time, exhibits little fear of man at night, and is a daring thief. The flesh much resembles rabbit'.[13] However, it is unknown whether any specimens were collected at that time to prove the Desert Rat-kangaroo's identification, so the existence of the species was put in question, and Tate's observations were thought by many to have been of either the Burrowing or Brush-tailed Bettong. If the Desert Rat-kangaroo did still exist, it seemed to have gone and was considered a 'lost' species until 1931, when Lou Reese of Appamunna Station in the Diamantina region of north-eastern South Australia sent a skin and skull to Hedley Herbert Finlayson, the honorary curator of mammals at the South Australian Museum.[14] The reception of a specimen of this highly distinct species, 90 years after its description, prompted Finlayson to make a collecting trip. The specimens Finlayson procured in 1935 were the last ever to be collected.[15] Finlayson subsequently declared the species had been 'resurrected' but, sadly, despite unsubstantiated sightings in 1956–57 and again in 1974–75 in north-eastern South Australia and south-western Queensland, Finlayson is believed to have been the last person actually to have seen the Desert Rat-kangaroo.[16]

Finlayson recorded his excitement at rediscovering the Desert Rat-kangaroo:

Seldom do the things one keenly desires come easily. But on our very first cast we got a prize. The six of us rode east in the early morning, and on a sand-hill picked up fresh *oola-cunta* tracks crossing to a flat on the far side. We followed them out till we lost them in the gibbers; then we opened out to a half-mile front and rode slowly south, each man scanning every lump and tussock for a possible nest. We had ridden less than half an hour when there came a shrill excited *'Yuchai'* from the horse-boy farthest out, and the chase was on. The pre-arranged plan was for each of us to take up the galloping in turn, the rat being headed whenever possible and turned in towards the rest of the party who remained in a group. When the first horse showed signs of losing heart, the next man took the first opportunity of replacing him, and so on.

Following the yell, Tommy came heading back down the line towards the sand-hill, but it was only after much straining of eyes that the *oolacunta* could be distinguished—a mere speck, thirty or forty yards ahead. At that distance it seemed scarcely to touch the ground; it almost floated ahead in an eerie, effortless way that made the thundering horse behind seem, by comparison, like a coal hulk wallowing in a heavy sea.

They were great moments as it came nearer; moments filled with curiosity and excitement, but with a steady undercurrent of relief and satisfaction. It was here! *Caloprymnus* bears a strong external resemblance to five or six other related species and from a distance there was little to distinguish that which was approaching from either of two other marsupials known to occur in adjoining tracts. But as it came down the flat toward me, a little pale ghost from the 1840s, all doubt fled. The thing was holding itself very different from the bettongs. As I watched it through the shimmering heat haze, some sense of the incongruence brought back a vivid memory of a very different scene, two years before, when I sought the nearest living relative of *Caloprymnus*, above the snowline of a Tasmanian range.

Imagine a little animal about the bulk of a rabbit, but built like a kangaroo, with long spindly hind legs, tiny fore-legs folded tight on its chest, and a tail half as long again as the body but not much thicker than a lead pencil, and you have it in the rough. But its head, short and blunt and wide, is very different from that of any kangaroo or wallaby, and its coat is uniformly coloured a clear pale yellowish ochre—exactly like the great clay-pans and flood plains.

As it came up to us I galloped alongside to keep it under observation as long as possible. Its speed, for such an atom, was wonderful, and its endurance amazing. We had considerable difficulty in heading it with fresh horses. When we finally got it, it had taken the starch out of three mounts and run us twelve miles; all under such adverse conditions of heat and rough going, as to make it almost incredible that so small a frame should be capable of such an immense output of energy. All examples obtained subsequently by this method behaved similarly; they persisted to the very limit of their strength, and quite literally, they paused only to die ...[17]

There was much debate among Finlayson's party about the best method of capture for the Desert Rat-kangaroo. One of the party's Aboriginal trackers, Butcher, 'created a sensation by announcing that he could catch *oolacunta* by hand'. Although this was considered a boast, even by the other Aboriginal members of the party, Butcher, it would seem, had spoken truthfully:

... they had been gone no more than half an hour when Butcher rode back into camp alone. With impassive face and in dignified silence, he handed over a bag tied at the mouth. Very cautious investigation showed it to contain a beautiful fully-adult *oolacunta* and a half-grown joey—both alive and undamaged ... [he] had, while riding with the others, spotted a nest and noted the head of the occupant in the opening, watching the party. He rode on without pause for a quarter of a mile, then, leaving his horse, made a rapid stalk up the wind and grabbed both mother and babe from behind. The laying on of hands was no myth![18]

The Crescent Nailtail Wallaby was the last—and perhaps most beautiful—macropod to vanish forever. It was considered plentiful in the agricultural districts of south-western Western Australia until just after 1900, common enough for G.C. Shortridge to collect some 23 specimens for the British Museum between 1904 and 1907.[19] Thereafter they declined rapidly and hung on only in isolated regions until the mid-1950s. This species also occurred in central Australia, eastern South Australia and south-western New South Wales. As with some other extinct Australian mammals, we must rely on John Gould's writings and paintings to form a picture of the animal:

Although assimilating in form and markings to the *Onychogalea fraenata* [the Bridled Nailtail Wallaby], the present species is certainly less ornamental, and is also much smaller in all its dimensions. The habits and economy of the two species are very similar; both exhibit a remarkable degree of shyness and timidity, and seek safety in flight upon the slightest alarm. I had no opportunity of observing it in a state of nature myself, but Mr Gilbert's notes inform me that 'the *Waurong*' by which name it is known to the natives, 'is found in the gum forests of the interior of Western Australia, where there are patches of thick scrub and dense thickets, in the open glades intervening between which it is occasionally seen sunning itself, but at the slightest alarm immediately betakes itself to the shelter of the thick scrub; the dogs sometimes succeed in driving it out to the open spots, when, like the Kangaroo rats, it runs to the nearest hollow log, and is then easily captured. I remarked, that when sitting quietly cleaning itself, there was a constant twitching of the tail in an upward direction; an action which I have never seen performed by any other Kangaroo. I was not sufficiently near to ascertain whether this motion of the tail had any connection with the claw or nail at its extremity, but I think it not improbable. The *Waurong* makes no nest, but forms a hollow in the soft ground beneath a thick brush in which it lies during the heat of the day.[20]

BACK FROM THE BRINK

The International Union for the Conservation of Nature (IUCN) considers a species to be extinct 'when there is no reasonable doubt that the last individual has died', and presumes extinction when 'exhaustive surveys ... have failed to record an individual'.[21] Though most species that are either presumed to be or declared to be extinct are never seen again, there always exists in the mind of the optimistic naturalist the possibility that a lost species may be rediscovered—and such optimism has, at times, been well founded. So it was with the Parma Wallaby that was thought to have been lost from the wild in the early 1930s, despite having been plentiful in the wet forests of eastern New South Wales up to this point.[22] Until the mid-1960s, Parma Wallabies were known from only 12 specimens in the world's museums. Then, in 1966, a feral population was discovered in New Zealand.[23] The New Zealand population was discovered on Kawau Island, north of Auckland. As we saw in the previous chapter, the Parma Wallaby was among the Australian macropod species introduced into New Zealand in the 1860s. Sir George Grey's estate on Kawau Island was home to several macropod species (see page 214), and the existence of the Parma Wallaby among them was first noted in 1958, when zoologist Dr David Ride suggested that several wallaby skins from Kawau Island that had been identified as Black-striped Wallabies were possibly Parma Wallabies. Five Parma Wallabies were collected in May 1966 and over the four years that followed some 384 Parma Wallabies were exported from the island to zoos in Australia and overseas.[24] Several years after these animals were discovered and plans for their reintroduction to Australia were being developed, it was revealed that Mr Eric Worrel of the Australian Reptile Park in Gosford, north of Sydney, had a Parma Wallaby that had been collected locally. Dr Gerry Maynes from Macquarie University subsequently conducted a number of surveys, both near Gosford and further afield, discovering, quite to everyone's surprise, that the secretive Parma Wallaby was alive and well, and living in dense forests in populations scattered across an area from just north of Sydney to the Queensland border.[25]

Like its relative, the Crescent Nailtail Wallaby, the Bridled Nailtail Wallaby is a beautiful animal. This species was once 'common in the thick patches of scrub which are dispersed over all parts of the Darling Downs' but was exceeding difficult to procure.[26] It was also considered to have been one of 'the most common of all the small species of the kangaroo' in the area near the junction of the Murray and Darling Rivers.[27] Unfortunately, by the 1900s it was in such rapid decline that by 1923 it was considered to be in danger of extinction.[28] In 1931 it was observed only twice during a fauna survey of the Dawson Valley in central Queensland.[29] After that time it was considered extinct until 1973 when a fencing contractor, Mr Daryl

Challacombe, discovered a population near the town of Dingo in central Queensland. Remarkably, Mr Challacombe identified the species from its similarity to one of John Gould's colour plates that had been reproduced in an article on rare fauna in a recent issue of the *Woman's Day* magazine.

The most recent macropod to be resurrected is Gilbert's Potoroo. This species was initially described from a specimen collected in 1840 by John Gilbert near Albany in south-western Western Australia. Around this time the animal was thought to be common, with John Gould remarking that 'natives will often kill them in immense number of both species [the other being the Quokka, of which they were a 'constant companion'] in a few hours'.[30] Other specimens were collected until 1879, after which the species was thought to have declined rapidly to extinction. Gilbert's Potoroo carried the 'extinct' label for 115 years until it was rediscovered by University of Western Australia PhD student Elizabeth Sinclair at Two Peoples Bay Nature Reserve, east of Albany, during a trapping programme aimed at catching the Quokka. The first animal Sinclair caught in December 1994 was thought to be a juvenile Quokka and routinely released. The following day, however, she caught two more animals, one of them a large female that did not look like a Quokka, or anything else she could call to mind. Scientists flocked to the site, including staff from the Western Australian Museum armed with 115-year-old specimens with which to compare the living animal. Soon after, the announcement was made that Gilbert's Potoroo had been rediscovered.[31] Since then, the population has been estimated at less than 50 animals, making it one of the most endangered mammals in the

world. Today an active conservation programme is underway, including the translocation of individuals to a nearby offshore island, in an attempt to bring this species back from the edge of extinction.

Macropods are not the only Australian mammals to have returned from the brink; in 1896, the fossil remains of an enigmatic species of Australian mammal were found in Wombeyan Caves in New South Wales by Robert Broom.[32] It was first described, with some hesitation, as a species of macropod allied to the potoroos and bettongs because of its distinctive serrated premolars. It was not until 1964 that it was redescribed as a species of possum.[33] Shortly after, in August 1966, the 15,000-year-old 'relict' Mountain Pygmy Possum was found alive and well, and living in the oven inside the Melbourne University ski hut at Mount Hotham, Victoria![34] Since its (re)discovery, this species is only known to occur within alpine regions between 1300 and 2228 metres' elevation in Victoria and New South Wales. Due to its highly restricted alpine habitat which totals less than 6 square kilometres, a population of only 1700 animals, competition for its habitat with ski resorts and the effects of global warming, the Mountain Pygmy Possum is one of Australia's most endangered animals.[35]

Several other species of Australian fauna thought to have been extinct have been found alive, including carnivorous marsupials, possums and gliders, rodents, reptiles, birds and even insects. In total, some 18 species including the macropods have been rediscovered, each with its own extraordinary story of how it was brought back from near oblivion.

Australian fauna once thought to have been extinct but then rediscovered

Common Name	Scientific Name	Last Record	Rediscovery
Carnivorous Marsupials			
Dibbler	*Parantechinus apicalis*	1884	1967
Long-tailed Dunnart	*Sminthopsis longicaudata*	1940	1975
Sandhill Dunnart	*Sminthopsis psammophila*	1894	1969
Possums			
Mountain Pygmy Possum	*Burramys parvus*	1896 (Fossil)	1966
Leadbeater's Possum	*Gymnobelideus leadbeateri*	1909	1961
Mahogany Glider	*Petaurus gracilis*	1896	1989
Macropods			
Gilbert's Potoroo	*Potorous gilberti*	1879	1994
Parma Wallaby	*Macropus parma*	1932	1965
Bridled Nailtail Wallaby	*Onychogalea fraenata*	1930s	1973

Common Name	Scientific Name	Last Record	Rediscovery
Rodents			
New Holland Mouse	*Pseudomys novaehollandiae*	1887	1967
Central Rock-rat	*Zyzomys pedunculatus*	1960	1996
Reptiles			
Western Swamp Tortoise	*Pseudemydura umbrina*	1901	1953
Adelaide Blue Tongue	*Tiliqua adelaidensis*	1959	1992
Inland Taipan	*Oxyuranus microlepidotus*	1879	1972
Birds			
Night Parrot	*Pezoporus occidentalis*	1912	1979/1990
Noisy Scrub Bird	*Atrichornis clamosus*	1889	1961
Eyrean Grasswren	*Amytornis goyderi*	1874	1976
Insects			
Lord Howe Island Stick-insect	*Dryococelus australis*	1920s	1960s/2001

Macropods that were thought be extinct but subsequently rediscovered. Clockwise from top left: Gilbert's Potoroo, Parma Wallaby and Bridled Nailtail Wallaby. (From Gould, 1845–1863, National Library of Australia)

PREDATORS

There are various potential causes for the extinction of Australia's mammal fauna: the introduction of herbivores such as cattle, sheep and rabbits; predation by introduced mammals such as foxes and cats; loss of habitat; hunting by Europeans; disease; changes to fire regimes; and destructive agricultural practices.

Professor Chris Johnson argues that with only a few exceptions, most of these extinctions are the direct result of the introduced fox and cat. The fox was first introduced into Victoria in 1871 to provide 'sport for gentlemen' and then spread west and northwards to occupy the lower three-quarters of the Australian

continent. It seems that the foxes spread slowly at first but the rate of dispersal increased after 1900, until the animals were extending their distribution by up to 140 kilometres per year.[36] Recently, almost 150 years after they were introduced into Australia, foxes invaded Tasmania which may have tragic consequences for Tasmanian mammals. A fox was reported to have walked off a container ship in 1998, but it is more likely that their current presence is due to a deliberate act of environmental vandalism in 1999 when foxes were illegally and intentionally introduced.[37] If the invaders establish a population, many small mammals that were either on the brink of extinction or greatly reduced in range on the mainland are likely to disappear completely. Macropods that will be impacted include the Long-nosed Potoroo, Tasmanian Bettong and Tasmanian Pademelon, along with other threatened marsupials such as the Southern Brown Bandicoot and Eastern Barred Bandicoot, to name a few.

Several prominent naturalists of the day, including Charles Hoy and Frederic Wood Jones, had identified the fox as a threat to native mammals in the early 1900s. Jones declared strongly:

> Men who are engaged in various agricultural or pastoral enterprises may differ in the estimation of the fox, but zoologists have no difference of opinion; to the student of the Australian fauna the fox represents nothing but calamity ... From a zoological point of view the fox probably represents the most baneful disturbing influence brought about by the human folly of introducing animals into a new country.

As early as 1938, Ellis Troughton suggested that the way to ensure the continued existence of native mammal species 'appears to be the establishing of reserves from which the fox is excluded', but sadly this call was unheeded.[38] Today the only fox-free places where small to medium-sized mammals occur in Australia are either islands that do not include foxes or cats; fenced reserves (perhaps of the kind imagined by Troughton) that exclude these animals; or areas where fox numbers are kept under control by heavy baiting with 1080 (see Chapter 11).

History demonstrates that the appearance of large numbers of foxes and cats in a region rapidly led to native mammal declines. For example, in Western Australia, Guy Shortridge was collecting for the British Museum of Natural History between 1904 and 1907 and noticed significant declines in native species and proposed several factors including cats, disease, house mice and fire. Given that foxes had not yet arrived when he was collecting and his other possible reasons for the decline have been largely discounted, it appears that cats were the primary cause of the mammal declines he observed.[39] To the east in New South Wales, bounties paid for foxes and rat-kangaroos (including Burrowing Bettongs, Rufous Bettongs, Woylies and, possibly, Tasmanian Bettongs and Long-nosed Potoroos) reveal that the rat-kangaroos disappeared within ten years of the foxes' arrival.[40] The pattern of small macropods disappearing only a few years after the arrival of foxes was repeated in various areas throughout Australia. For example the Tammar Wallaby went extinct on the Eyre Peninsula between 1915 and 1918, barely ten years after the fox arrived.[41] Foxes became established in the Tamworth region in about 1910. Records suggest that before that time the district was literally overrun by Bridled Nailtail Wallabies, Brush-tailed Rock-wallabies and 'Rat-kangaroos' (which encompassed several species of potoroids). Soon after the foxes arrived, however, all these species disappeared from the district.[42]

The cat was introduced into Australia through multiple coastal introductions between 1824 and 1886, and by 1890 nearly the whole continent had been colonised.[43] Cats appear to concentrate on smaller species, which correlates with the disappearance in the drier regions of Australia of rodents and bandicoots weighing less than 1000 grams prior to the arrival of the fox.[44] There is clear evidence that cats are responsible for the disappearance of some mammals on offshore islands, just as there is for foxes on the mainland.[45] Cats have also been identified as significant predators for reintroduction or translocation programmes. One example of this was the introduction of Mala or Rufous Hare-wallabies into two different sites in the Tanami Desert. The first site was at Yinapaka in the southern Tanami where 11 animals were introduced into a 100-hectare fenced area in August 1990. Subsequent monitoring revealed the released animals were doing well until December 1990 when five of the animals were found dead. Three more were killed in January 1991. In July and September 1991 a further 20 hare-wallabies were released, but these too were killed. Most of the dead animals found showed clear signs of being eaten by cats. Cats which were subsequently trapped and euthanased were found to have Rufous Hare-wallaby fur within their stomachs. At the second introduction site at Lungkarta in the western Tanami, a further 23 Rufous Hare-wallabies were introduced in a series of releases. Again, the population did well initially (growing to 30 animals) but it too had collapsed by the end of 1991 as a result of predation by cats.[46]

A study on the Allied Rock-wallaby at 'Black Rock', north-west of Townsville, demonstrates how even a single cat can have a big impact on a macropod population. At this site a lone cat was observed many times over a five-year period on or near the rock pile occupied by the rock-wallabies. The cat was often observed basking in the region of the main rock platform, where the wallabies displayed in the early morning and late after-noon. Although adult wallabies were invariably alarmed by the presence of the cat, they were probably too big for the predator. On one occasion adult wallabies were observed grooming for 20 minutes within 3 metres of the resting cat. However, the decline in the population over the five-year period was related to a lack of recruitment—the cat, it seems, was eating out the juvenile and sub-adult animals, which meant that the popu-lation was ageing without young animals coming through to replace the older ones. On two occasions the cat was observed feeding upon juvenile rock-wallabies, and a further six carcasses (three juveniles, one sub-adult and two 4-kilogram adult males) were believed to have been killed by the cat.[47] The decline in the population might not have been halted were it not for the fact that the cat, like the adult rock-wallabies, was growing long in the tooth. In 1990 Dr Peter Spencer led a field trip to Black Rock with the intention of ridding the site of the cat once and for all. Armed with traps, baits and other cat-extermi-nating devices the group arrived to find the cat already dead, apparently from natural causes. With the cat gone, the young rock-wallabies were able to grow to maturity and the popula-tion bounced back.

The impact of predation by foxes and cats appears to have been compounded by the arrival of introduced herbivores, particularly rabbits and sheep.[48] After their introduction onto a property near Geelong in Victoria in 1860 the rabbits, moving slowly at first, took 16 years to reach the New South Wales border.[49] Once they became established, however, rabbits spread quickly, reaching Queensland 15 years later. By 1900 they were well into Western Australia and the Northern Territory. These figures give them a rate of spread across Australia of 10–15 kilometres a year in forested country and 100 kilometres a year over the rangelands, the second fastest expansion rate of any colonising species anywhere in the world behind the introduction the fox into Australia.[50] Such was the density of the rabbit plagues that they turned productive, well-vegetated land into deserts. In addition the rabbits appeared to take over the burrows of native mammals such as bilbies and Burrowing Bettongs, leaving them exposed at the surface.

The sheep population grew similarly rapidly. For example, in western New South Wales under a million sheep in 1860 had become 13 million sheep by 1894, although by 1902 this total had collapsed to less than 4 million. Inadequate management of stocking rates meant that vast areas of marginal lands in the semi-arid zone were badly overgrazed. The combination of overgrazing by sheep and immense plagues of rabbits must have placed extreme pressure on all small ground-dwelling mammals by dramatically decreasing the amount of food available and greatly increasing their exposure to predation.[51]

Another critical issue is that rabbits are, of course, the preferred prey of foxes, to such an extent that their distributions largely overlap. When rabbit populations decline due to disease or drought, after a short lag in time fox populations show a similar decline. When rabbits increase in number, so too do foxes.[52] As a result, the presence of rabbits means an increased number of foxes, which increases the impact of foxes on prey other than rabbits, a phenomenon known as 'hyperpredation'.[53] Similarly, cat numbers may be kept artificially high by the presence of young rabbits, a preferred prey. Periodic plagues of house mice also provided a superabundant food source for cats and foxes.[54]

So how do these 'super predators' interact with Australia's largest introduced predator, the dingo? Unfortunately dingoes were quickly viewed with loathing by pastoralists because of their predation on livestock, especially sheep. They were actively hunted under a bounty system, which was replaced by extensive government-funded baiting programmes which continue today. The world's second longest fence, known as the Dingo Fence, was built in the 1880s and spans an incredible 3374 kilometres, which is bettered only by the Great Wall of China (estimated to be over 6900 kilometres long).[55] This fence runs from Dalby on the Darling Downs, west of Brisbane, to the Eyre Peninsula in South Australia, but is only partially successful as dingoes occur on both sides of the fence, although there are large areas where they either do not occur or occur at low levels.[56] The unfortunate result of the suppression of dingoes is that they have been rendered ineffective as an ecological predator, allowing medium-sized predators such as the introduced fox and cat to increase in number—a phenomenon known as mesopredator release. These mesopredators are then further elevated in numbers by the availability of rabbits, as we discussed earlier, to produce hyperpredators.

So, where to from here in the protection of Australia's native biodiversity? This is Professor Johnson's proposal for the way forward in the protection of native fauna, including macropods:

to allow dingo numbers to increase as these are the most effective biological control for both foxes and cats. The trouble is, of course, that farmers still have significant concerns about the presence of wild dingo populations, particularly in sheep-farming areas. Some level of dingo control would always be necessary, but as foxes are significant predators of newborn lambs, the presence of dingoes within sheep-farming areas could be beneficial. Domesticated animals such as the Pyrenean Mountain dog and the Maremma dog, alpacas and even donkeys have proven effective in reducing predation on livestock, but farmers are sceptical about their usefulness for very large herds. In the final chapter we will look at conservation ideas and approaches other than the protection of the dingo—some less controversial, others much more so.

11

KANGAROO CONSERVATION

Saving Australia's Macropods

Species recovery is a new and important science. Current management efforts focus on broad scale baiting of foxes, translocation of endangered species to offshore predator-free islands, and their protection in predator enclosures. A national and more corporate approach to species conservation has arisen from national species recovery teams ... History tells us that disturbance of one component of the ecosystem will often provoke changes in other areas. The current intensive focus on foxes demands careful monitoring of the general system as an early warning of developing problems. Study of the interactions between foxes, dingoes, feral cats and rabbits are needed to discover the likely outcomes of control programs, particularly in the more arid regions where all four species coexist.[1]

No group of animals, with the possible exception of the koala, causes as much controversy as the macropods when it comes to their conservation and management. As we discussed in Chapter 8, a handful of species are overabundant and are culled annually in their millions, while many others are listed as 'vulnerable' or 'endangered'. In order to manage the threatened species, intensive efforts have been made to halt their decline and bring them back from the edge of extinction. Untimely extinction is an all too common fate for macropods, and for the species still clinging to existence, conservation action is often urgently required.

THREATENED KANGAROOS

As discussed in the previous chapter, European settlement has been a disaster for macropod biodiversity: of the 57 species that occurred within Australia when the First Fleet landed at Port Jackson in 1788, seven species have been sent to extinction, another 10 species are now listed as threatened with extinction, and a further 10 species are considered 'near threatened'. Many macropod species that are not considered threatened from a national point of view have mainland subspecies or populations that are either extinct or threatened. In comparison, New Guinean macropods have fared somewhat better, but while there have been no recent extinctions, that is not to say they are immune to threat. Of the 22 species that occur within the New Guinea region, eight are listed as 'endangered' or 'critically endangered', seven are 'vulnerable to extinction' and two species have a 'near threatened' conservation status.

We explored in the last chapter the causes of the extinctions of different macropod species. Not surprisingly, introduced predators such as the fox and the cat that were responsible for most of the extinctions we discussed are also responsible for the fact that many species are now sliding towards extinction.

KANGAROO

Australian and New Guinean Macropods that are threatened (or near threatened) with extinction

Common Name	Scientific Name	Status
Australian Species		
Tasmanian Bettong	*Bettongia gaimardi*	Near Threatened
Burrowing Bettong	*Bettongia lesueur*	Near Threatened
Brush-tailed Bettong	*Bettongia penicillata*	Critically Endangered
Northern Bettong	*Bettongia tropica*	Endangered
Gilbert's Potoroo	*Potorous gilberti*	Critically Endangered
Long-footed Potoroo	*Potorous longipes*	Endangered
Bennett's Tree Kangaroo	*Dendrolagus bennettianus*	Near Threatened
Rufous Hare-wallaby	*Lagorchestes hirsutus*	Vulnerable
Monjon	*Petrogale burbidgei*	Near Threatened
Cape York Rock Wallaby	*Petrogale coenensis*	Near Threatened
Black-footed Rock-wallaby	*Petrogale lateralis*	Near Threatened
Brush-tailed Rock Wallaby	*Petrogale penicillata*	Near Threatened
Proserpine Rock-wallaby	*Petrogale persephone*	Endangered
Sharman's Rock Wallaby	*Petrogale sharmani*	Near Threatened
Yellow-footed Rock Wallaby	*Petrogale xanthopus*	Near Threatened
Bridled Nailtail Wallaby	*Onychogalea fraenata*	Endangered
Quokka	*Setonix brachyurus*	Vulnerable
Banded Hare-wallaby	*Lagostrophus fasciatus*	Endangered
Black Wallaroo	*Macropus bernardus*	Near Threatened
Parma Wallaby	*Macropus parma*	Near Threatened
New Guinean Species		
Doria's Tree Kangaroo*	*Dendrolagus dorianus*	Vulnerable
Goodfellow's Tree Kangaroo	*Dendrolagus goodfellowi*	Endangered
Grizzled Tree Kangaroo	*Dendrolagus inustus*	Vulnerable
Huon Tree Kangaroo	*Dendrolagus matschiei*	Endangered
Dingiso	*Dendrolagus mbaiso*	Critically Endangered
Golden-mantled Tree Kangaroo	*Dendrolagus pucherrimus*	Critically Endangered
Tenkile	*Dendrolagus scottae*	Critically Endangered
Seri's Tree Kangaroo	*Dendrolagus stellarum*	Vulnerable

Common Name	Scientific Name	Status
Vogelkop Tree Kangaroo	*Dendrolagus ursinus*	Vulnerable
Black Dorcopsis	*Dorcopsis atrata*	Critically Endangered
Grey Dorcopsis	*Dorcopsis luctuosa*	Vulnerable
Small Dorcopsis	*Dorcopsulus vanheurni*	Near Threatened
Brown's Pademelon	*Thylogale browni*	Vulnerable
Dusky Pademelon	*Thylogale brunii*	Vulnerable
Calaby's Pademelon	*Thylogale calabyi*	Endangered
Mountain Pademelon	*Thylogale lanatus*	Endangered

*The taxonomy of *Dendrolagus dorianus* is currently under investigation and several of the typically recognised subspecies may represent distinct species.

Source: International Union for the Conservation of Nature (IUCN).
For details see: http://www.iucnredlist.org

But if predation by introduced species is the primary factor, what other factors can be associated with the decline and extinction of different macropod species? As we saw in Chapter 8, huge numbers of macropods have been killed since European settlement as result of either bounties or harvesting programmes, however given that most of the species being hunted are (or were, until foxes arrived) abundant, this is not the primary reason for the decline of threatened species. Habitat loss through land clearing may not be a primary cause of the historical decline and extinction of Australian macropods, but it is definitely a contributory factor as it reduced populations of many species of smaller macropods and left those smaller populations less able to withstand attack from the introduced predators.[2]

Concern over the decline in macropod species is not new—as early as 1889 there were suggestions that 'the kangaroo' was threatened with extinction.[3] It was even suggested that unless preventative measures were taken 'the kangaroo' would become a curiosity as a result of the high prices being paid for their skins in the United States. Similar concerns were again raised in 1923 by Herbert Longman, the Director of the Queensland Museum, who suggested that they 'are doomed in all areas of fairly close settlement'.[4] Mr Longman noted that there was no protection for the kangaroos or wallabies in Queensland and that between 300,000 and 400,000 pelts were traded annually through the Brisbane market. Charles Hoy, a collector for the United States National Museum of Natural History, recounts a meeting with a kangaroo hunter who 'had over two thousand kangaroo skins piled on his wagon, the result of a three-months' shooting trip'. During his travels through north-eastern New South Wales in 1919, Hoy noted that the Eastern Grey Kangaroo was 'getting rather scarce' and that other medium-sized wallabies such as the Swamp Wallaby and the Red-necked Wallaby were 'also very scarce'.[5]

As the primary cause of the decline in macropod populations has been identified as predation by introduced foxes and cats, what conservation strategies are being undertaken to halt this decline? One approach is to reintroduce threatened species of macropods into either part of their former distribution or on islands where predators do not occur. Jeff Short reviewed 25 reintroductions of macropods and revealed, not surprisingly, that reintroductions are considerably more successful in areas without exotic predators. Predator control is the key to a successful reintroduction but, as was seen in the Tanami Desert (see page 237), is often difficult to achieve on the ground. Short and his colleagues pointed out that one of the reasons that many reintroductions fail is that the work required to control or exterminate an area's exotic predators is often underestimated.[6] For example, reintroductions of the

Quokka, Tammar Wallaby, Parma Wallaby (at two locations), Banded Hare-wallaby and Brush-tailed Rock-wallaby all failed as a direct result of predation by foxes, cats and dogs, although competition with feral herbivores and disease were also cited as possible causes. Introductions and relocations often fail because they almost never consist of enough individuals and across a great enough area to allow true populations to become established, which is why they are often doomed to fail unless a huge investment is made in predator control.

Of course, as we discussed in Chapter 9, introductions can be successful. The Banded Hare-wallaby has been successfully introduced to Dirk Hartog Island; the Brush-tailed Bettong to several islands off South Australia; and the Bridled Nailtail Wallaby to Idalia National Park west of Longreach and Avocet Nature Refuge west of Rockhampton, both in central Queensland. In Western Australia, the Brush-tailed Bettong has been introduced successfully into Yendicup Block, Perup.[7]

POISON PEAS: DEADLY PROTECTORS OF AUSTRALIAN WILDLIFE

Like the dingo, introduced predators such as foxes are considered as pests by agriculturalists, so they have been hunted and poisoned for decades. In recent years, the most common poison used for controlling exotic predators is sodium monofluroacetate, known colloquially as '1080'. This compound is derived from a toxin found in over 40 species of native shrubs from the genera *Gastrolobium* and *Oxylobium* (known, collectively, as 'poison pea') that occur naturally in south-western Australia.[8] 1080 kills by causing failure of the central nervous system, heart and lungs.[9] As with all ingested poisons, factors such as body mass and the amount of bait eaten can affect an animal's sensitivity to 1080, but there are some general trends that can be exploited by Australian wildlife managers. The key to 1080's success lies in the fact that Australian herbivores have co-evolved with the poison peas, and thus have a high level of genetic tolerance to these plants.[10] Even marsupial carnivores have some level of resistance because they feed on insects that in turn feed on poison pea.[11] This means that to be poisoned, marsupials in general, and especially in those regions where the poison pea occurs, have to ingest far greater quantities of 1080 than introduced mammals.

Introduced eutherian predators such as cats, foxes and dogs are particularly sensitive to 1080. The LD_{50} (that is, the amount of poison required to kill 50 per cent of a sample) for eutherian carnivores is only 0.1 to 0.4 milligrams per kilogram of body weight.[12] For native carnivores such as the Spotted-tailed Quoll the LD_{50} is 1.85 milligrams per kilogram of body weight, and for the smaller carnivorous dunnarts and antechinus the LD_{50} can be as high as 5.2 milligrams per kilogram of body weight.[13] The sensitivity of foxes and cats to 1080 means that the poison baiting of habitats in which endangered species of macropods and other Australian mammals coexist with these introduced predators has considerably reduced fox and cat populations. It has been particularly successful in Western Australia, where widespread baiting of foxes has led to the recovery of several endangered marsupial species, including several macropods— however, cats remain a problem as their numbers typically increase where the foxes are removed.[14]

The Western Australian baiting programme 'Western Shield' is the largest and most successful wildlife conservation programme ever undertaken in Australia. Western Shield is managed by the Western Australian Department of Conservation and Environment and was launched in 1996, with an aim of reducing predation pressure to a level that ensures the continued persistence of native fauna and particularly those within the critical weight range of 35 to 5500 grams.[15] The figures involved are staggering—780,000 dried baits are deployed annually across some 3.4 million hectares from Karratha to Esperance, a straight-line distance of more than 1,500 kilometres. To cover the territory planes drop baits for eight months of the year, and fly more than 50,000 kilometres annually—more than a round-the-world trip.[16] The project was initially overwhelmingly successful: the conservation status of the Tammar Wallaby, the Brush-tailed Bettong and the Southern Brown Bandicoot were downgraded due to the success of baiting programs, and many native animals were re-established in their former habitats.[17] Sadly, though, this programme is now going backwards for the Brush-tailed Bettong, which has declined by 80 per cent since 2001, with the largest and most important populations declining by more than 93 per cent over a two to five year period, with no signs of subsequent recovery. These declines appear to be driven by mesopredator release, which is discussed in Chapter 10, so the foxes (where dingoes have been removed) or cats (where dingoes and foxes have been removed) have been allowed to thrive as a result of decreased competition from larger predators that have been removed by baiting.[18]

Where the reduction of predators through baiting has proved inadequate, the Western Shield programme has opted for complete exclusion, as in the case of 'Project Eden', located within Francois Peron National Park. The park lies within the 1050-square kilometre Peron Peninsula that juts out into the World Heritage-listed Shark Bay. The landward end of the peninsula has a 2-metre high electric fence that extends for more than 3 kilometres across the entire peninsula, effectively sealing it off from the rest of the mainland.[19] When the project was launched in December 1994, its courageous objectives included controlling or eradicating introduced fauna and reconstructing the peninsula's native fauna.[20] Project Eden's early phases involved extensive trapping and baiting inside the fence that all but eliminated introduced foxes. A subsequent trial release of Banded Hare-wallabies within Peron Peninsula National Park in 2001 failed because of excessive cat predation.[21] Although cat numbers have been reduced to about half their carrying capacity, this still seems too high to allow the reintroductions of small macropods to be successful. The project is continuing to undertake research on new ways to control cats—so the work being done at Project Eden might one day benefit other reintroduction and conservation programmes across Australia. Project Eden is also committed to increasing their stock of endangered species for eventual release, and to this end 'threatened' macropods such as the Banded Hare-wallaby and Rufous Hare-wallaby are the subjects of successful captive breeding programmes.

Can the Use of 1080 be Justified?

Despite its effectiveness, the use of 1080 has come under significant criticism in recent years due to the animal welfare aspects of its effects. In carnivores, for example, it appears to lead to mental disorientation and convulsions before the animal loses consciousness. A National Review of the use of 1080 conducted by the Australian Pesticides and Veterinary

Medicines Authority (APVMA) received correspondence from individuals and agencies suggesting there are considerable animal welfare issues based upon the perceived pain and distress experienced by the poisoned animal.[22] Perceptions are one thing, but how real are such concerns? There are conflicting arguments in the literature as to whether 1080 poisoning causes severe pain, and the topic is a contentious one. Humans that present to hospital with 1080 poisoning cite pain as one of their symptoms, however, others argue that the symptoms displayed by dogs are not consistent with a canine response to pain.[23] In a recent review, the APVMA stated 'the issue of humaneness is contentious, as illustrated by accusations of bias from groups opposed to and supportive of the use of 1080, and is unlikely to be resolved through scientific investigation alone'.[24] In the future, 1080 baits might contain analgesics or sedatives to minimise pain and distress, but trials of these compounds are in the early stages. It must also be recognised that without a suitable replacement, 1080 simply must be used to conserve Australian fauna that is being threatened by introduced predators such as cats and foxes. An independent review of the Western Shield programme stated emphatically that 'the 1080 toxin plays a fundamental role in the conservation of the biodiversity and natural heritage of WA ... it would be prudent, if not essential for Australian nature conservation, to retain the wise use of 1080 in Australia'.[25]

Another concern about 1080 is the possibility of accidental poisoning of non-target animals. 1080's potential impact on mainland populations of the Spotted-tailed Quoll is causing considerable concern to conservationists. One study, which assessed whether or not the baits would be dug up by captive animals, suggested that quolls might be at risk from canid control.[26] More recent field studies however that used mortality-sensitive radio collars, which give a different signal when the animal stops moving after a specific period of time, concluded that quolls were not affected by ground baiting programmes for fox control as they did not ingest the baits, and that restrictions that have been imposed to protect the Spotted-tailed Quoll during fox baiting are unnecessary.[27] A related study that assessed the impact of aerial baiting also found that only one quoll died as a result of 1080 poisoning.[28] Similarly, a study by Sally Fenner, an honours student at the University of New England, suggested that smaller mammals such as native rats and antechinus rarely consume meat baits, and that at the current baiting intensity the impact of the programme was likely to be negligible on small mammal populations.[29]

THE IMPORTANCE OF ISLANDS

The islands off Australia's coast have been critical in the conservation of different species of macropods as they generally do not have introduced predators. Three of the best macropod conservation islands are Bernier, Dorre and Dirk Hartog Islands off the coast of Western Australia, all of which have become refuges for macropod species that are now either extinct or in danger of extinction on the Australian mainland. The Banded Hare-wallaby, Rufous Hare-wallaby and Burrowing Bettong are all found on these islands in strong numbers, whereas their mainland counterparts have suffered tremendously from introduced predators.

Tasmania is an island refuge for many endangered mammals, including the Tasmanian Bettong and Tasmanian Pademelon, that no longer occur on mainland Australia. However, the deliberate introduction of foxes to Tasmania in the late 1990s has led to fears for these and other Tasmanian species. Tasmania is now embarking on perhaps the most ambitious island conservation project of all time—the complete eradication of foxes from its 62,000 square kilometres. If eradication is not achieved, mainland Australia's experience shows that the island's fauna will be heavily impacted, and many iconic species of Tasmanian mammals will go to extinction.[30]

CAUGHT IN THE HEADLIGHTS

As anyone who has driven any distance on Australian roads can tell you, collisions with macropods are not uncommon. Although the exact numbers are not known, many thousands are killed annually. Graeme Coulson from the University of Melbourne has been studying the incidence of road-kills in kangaroos and wallabies for a number of years. He has found that in most cases the more common species (for example, Eastern Grey Kangaroos, Red-necked Wallabies and Swamp Wallabies) make up the majority of road-kills, so a high number of fatalities can usually (but not always) be taken as an indication of an overall healthy population size.[31] Coulson's work has also brought to light several interesting trends. For example, drought influences mortality rates, with Eastern Grey Kangaroo and Swamp Wallaby road-kills being higher during a severe drought than during pre- or post-drought conditions. Coulson also showed that over a nine-year period the seasonal frequency of kangaroo road-kills was inversely related to the rainfall of the previous season. Furthermore, up to 90 per cent of road-kills of Western Grey Kangaroos,

Eastern Grey Kangaroos, Red-necked Wallabies, Tasmanian Pademelons and Swamp Wallabies were males, which suggests that male kangaroos are more wide-ranging—or perhaps more focused on finding a female in oestrus than looking out for traffic!

Another study in arid regions of western New South Wales also found that environmental conditions played a key role in determining the patterns and frequencies of kangaroo–vehicle collisions.[32] It appears that in these regions more Euros and Red Kangaroos were killed than Eastern Grey Kangaroos and Western Grey Kangaroos during drought, but not directly after the drought. This appears to be due to the fact that even during drought, the Euro and Red Kangaroo are specialist feeders on the grasses and forbs that often grow along the roadsides, whereas the grey kangaroos are more generalist and can feed over a wider variety of habitats.

In an effort to reduce the impact of macropods on cars, and the significant damage this can cause, various deterrents have been developed. One is an ultrasonic whistle which is affixed to the front of vehicles and is supposed to emit sounds that deter macropods from entering on to the road. There are two main types of ultrasonic whistles, those that produce an electronic noise and those that use an air-driven whistle. The various studies that have been conducted to date, however, show results that are at best equivocal.[33] One particular study of electronic ultrasonic whistles was very blunt when it suggested that the device was not, in fact, ultrasonic, that is, it did not produce sound detectable at a distance of 400 metres, that it did not alter the behaviour of Eastern Grey Kangaroos or Red Kangaroos and that it made no difference in the number of kangaroos hit.[34] A Tasmanian study also tested an ultrasonic whistle and suggested that it should not be considered a genuine road-kill reduction method.[35] Nevertheless, many motorists swear by these devices as deterrents, and vehicles fitted with 'kangaroo whistles' are relatively common in Australia's rural areas.

An alternative to instruments fixed to individual vehicles is the use of roadside reflectors. One design consists of two aluminium mirrors housed in a plastic casing, positioned at a 60° angle to one another, and covered with red prism plates. These reflectors are installed on posts up to 20 metres apart with the aim of reflecting the light from approaching headlights by 90° into the surrounding bushland. This creates an 'optical fence' that deters animals from approaching the roadway until the vehicle has passed. North American and Australian studies have reported mixed success.[36] Few of the macropod studies conducted to date, however, have set up adequate baseline studies to determine what light wavelength is visible to the macropods being studied; what changes in behaviour occur in the presence of reflectors; whether macropods become habituated to reflectors; and what the optimal height of reflectors and different patterns of installation should be.[37] One macropod species prone to collisions with motor vehicles which does seem to respond well to these reflectors is the Proserpine Rock-wallaby, an endangered species that occurs in the Proserpine and Airlie Beach area of north-east Queensland. The Whitsunday Shire Council and the Queensland Department of Transport installed 'optical warning' detectors which had an immediate and dramatic reduction in the road-related mortality rate, prompting further research into their possibilities.[38]

GLOBAL WARMING

So what does the future hold for the different macropod species in relation to global warming? Though the overall impacts are unknown, one study by Dr Euan Ritchie and his colleagues showed that temperature increases will impact on at least some macropods. Their studies predict that the distributions of Antilopine Wallaroo, Red Kangaroo, Common Wallaroo and Eastern Grey Kangaroo in northern Australia will contract as a result of climate change. Their models suggest that fire regimes, water availability, geology, soil type and climate all have large-scale effects on these species, while habitat structure and interspecific species abundance were important at smaller scales. As a result they suggest that the climate changes predicted for Australia could seriously affect the abundance of macropods in tropical Australia. For example, an increase in temperature of 2°C would result in these species decreasing their ranges in northern Australia by an average of 48 per cent, with the Antilopine Wallaroo distribution being reduced by as much as 89 per cent. An increase in temperature of 6°C would result in all four species being reduced in range by an average of 96 per cent, with the Antilopine Wallaroo likely to become extinct under such a scenario.[39]

THREATS TO NEW GUINEAN MACROPODS

The threats to New Guinean macropods relate mainly to over-hunting.[40] People have hunted macropods in New Guinea for thousands of years and, during that time, practices have evolved that serve to conserve wildlife—seasonal hunting, for example, or special protection for particular species or areas.[41] For example, sacred wallabies in the Marshall Lagoon area of Central Province are traditionally never hunted, and when captured in nets by hunters, are decorated 'with flowers and all the good things they could find in the bush' before being released. By treating the animal kindly, the hunters believe they will receive good luck.[42] Certain Moni people in the highlands of west New Guinea believe that the tree kangaroo known as Dingiso is sacred, and that to kill and eat it threatens not just the transgressor, but their entire lineage.[43] Such beliefs not only protect animals from excessive hunting, but also preserve special areas for their conservation. In recent decades, however, an increase in human population coupled with a move away from traditional beliefs and practices, means that much of New Guinea's wildlife is now threatened with overhunting. Changes in hunting practices also place new pressures on wildlife. For example, the widespread use of dogs as hunting companions in the upland meadows of New Guinea has probably contributed to the modern decline of Calaby's Pademelon and other small wallabies previously found in many subalpine regions.[44]

Programmes aimed at reversing the decline of New Guinea's macropods are probably best achieved at the grass-roots level, where campaigns can address directly the needs and concerns of the people that rely on the proceeds of the hunt for their protein. An excellent example of this can be found in the work of the Tenkile Conservation Alliance (TCA). The Tenkile (or Scott's Tree Kangaroo) is endemic to the Torricelli Mountains in Sandaun Province. Since World War II, the region's human population in the area has trebled, and much of the population has turned away from traditional beliefs that placed hunting restrictions on the Tenkile. To make matters even worse, the modern hunting weapon of choice is now the gun, instead of the traditional bow and arrow. These factors had combined to bring the Tenkile to the brink of extinction when it was first brought to scientific attention by Dr Tim Flannery in 1989 as a newly discovered species of tree kangaroo. The TCA's approach includes an education campaign about the importance of maintaining local biodiversity and Tenkile's particular plight in local schools and villages, alongside a rabbit and chicken captive breeding programme that addresses the local inhabitants' protein needs. The programme is proving successful—up to 20 villages are now breeding TCA-supplied chickens and rabbits, and many villages having agreed to a hunting moratorium on local tree kangaroos.[45]

CONCLUSION

As we have explored various aspects of 'the kangaroo' through this book, we have revealed the amazing diversity of this group of animals, which ranges from tiny forest dwellers that scurry around the rainforest floor to large majestic animals that live in mobs in the open plains of central Australia, ever wary of an approaching predator, and the even bigger kangaroos that once roamed the Pleistocene landscape. The success of the macropods has been their remarkable adaptation to Australian's varied landscapes and its changing and unpredictable climate. The extraordinary complex reproduction that allows kangaroos to breed continuously when times are good and switch off when times are bad, their fascinating behaviours, their varied diets, and their unique trademark hopping locomotion all serve to illustrate that kangaroos are remarkable Australian mammals. We hope that one of the enduring thoughts after reading this book is that kangaroos are, quite simply, amazing. It is no wonder then that kangaroos fascinated people from the moment they encountered them, and that a worldwide interest in kangaroos—by scientists and the public alike—has not dwindled with time.

The consumption of kangaroo meat can provide significant benefits not only for the individuals who eat it, because the meat is so lean, but also for the Australian environment if a proportion of domestic livestock were replaced by kangaroos. Even greater environmental benefits may be on the horizon should scientists be successful in replacing the gut flora of sheep and cattle with low-methane-producing equivalents from kangaroos. Indigenous Australians have eaten kangaroo for millennia, and their religious stories and artworks are a testament to the esteem to which they hold the animal. However, for non-indigenous Australians, it is important to point out that the modern-day interest in the eating of kangaroo is not actually new—it is a return to our roots in a sense, because seafarers, explorers and the first European settlers relied on kangaroo for their survival. Perhaps it is time to embrace the kangaroos once again as a key to our sustainable future.

While some species of kangaroo have done well since the arrival of Europeans 200 years ago and increased dramatically in number, many others have fared very badly—with a handful having faded forever to extinction and a number of others being threatened with such. This contradiction in abundance has led to dramatically different management techniques required— one to increase the number of certain species of kangaroos by controlling introduced cats and foxes, and the other to decrease the number of certain kangaroos by culling and harvesting them. Of these, the culling and harvesting has been the most controversial, sparking widespread debate and protest over the welfare of the animals and suggestions that these abundant animals are under threat.

Professor Tim Flannery best described the success of kangaroos when he said 'They are, in short, Australia's most successful evolutionary product'.[46] The challenge now is to ensure the continued evolution for these remarkable mammals with which we are still fortunate to share the planet.

APPENDIX 1

MACROPOD SPECIES WITH THEIR DISTRIBUTION AND CONSERVATION STATUS

Conservation status for each species is according to the IUCN's (International Union for the Conservation of Nature) Red List of Threatened Species. Species names, common names and distributions based on Flannery (1995a, 1995b), Van Dyck and Strahan (2008), Burbidge *et al* (2008) and IUCN (2010). Taxonomy follows Groves (2005).

Appendix 1

Common Name	Scientific Name	Distribution	Status
Superfamily Macropodoidea			
Family Hypsiprymnodontidae			
Musky Rat-kangaroo	*Hypsiprymnodon moschatus*	Australia	Least Concern
Family Potoroidae			
Rufous Bettong	*Aepyprymnus rufescens*	Australia	Least Concern
Tasmanian Bettong	*Bettongia gaimardi*	Australia	Near Threatened
Burrowing Bettong	*Bettongia lesueur*	Australia	Near Threatened
Woylie	*Bettongia penicillata*	Australia	Critically Endangered
Nullarbor Dwarf Bettong	*Bettongia pusilla*	Australia	Extinct
Northern Bettong	*Bettongia tropica*	Australia	Endangered
Desert Rat-kangaroo	*Caloprymnus campestris*	Australia	Extinct
Gilbert's Potoroo	*Potorous gilberti*	Australia	Critically Endangered
Long-footed Potoroo	*Potorous longipes*	Australia	Endangered
Broad-faced Potoroo	*Potorous platyops*	Australia	Extinct
Long-nosed Potoroo	*Potorous tridactylus*	Australia	Least Concern
Family Macropodidae			
Subfamily Macropodinae			
Bennett's Tree Kangaroo	*Dendrolagus bennettianus*	Australia	Near Threatened
Doria's Tree Kangaroo	*Dendrolagus dorianus**	New Guinea	Vulnerable
Goodfellow's Tree Kangaroo	*Dendrolagus goodfellowi*	New Guinea	Endangered
Grizzled Tree Kangaroo	*Dendrolagus inustus*	New Guinea	Vulnerable
Lumholtz's Tree Kangaroo	*Dendrolagus lumholtzi*	Australia	Least Concern

Common Name	Scientific Name	Distribution	Status
Huon Tree Kangaroo	*Dendrolagus matschiei*	New Guinea	Endangered
Golden-mantled Tree Kangaroo	*Dendrolagus pulcherrimus*	New Guinea	Critically Endangered
Tenkile	*Dendrolagus scottae*	New Guinea	Critically Endangered
Lowland's Tree Kangaroo	*Dendrolagus spadix*	New Guinea	Least Concern
Seri's Tree Kangaroo	*Dendrolagus stellarum*	New Guinea	Vulnerable
Vogelkop Tree Kangaroo	*Dendrolagus ursinus*	New Guinea	Vulnerable
Dingiso	*Dendrolagus mbaiso*	New Guinea	Critically Endangered
Black Dorcopsis	*Dorcopsis atrata*	New Guinea	Critically Endangered
White-striped Dorcopsis	*Dorcopsis hageni*	New Guinea	Least Concern
Grey Dorcopsis	*Dorcopsis luctuosa*	New Guinea	Vulnerable
Brown Dorcopsis	*Dorcopsis muelleri*	New Guinea	Least Concern
Macleay's Dorcopsis	*Dorcopsulus macleayi*	New Guinea	Least Concern
Small Dorcopsis	*Dorcopsulus vanheurni*	New Guinea	Near Threatened
Central Hare-wallaby	*Lagorchestes asomatus*	Australia	Extinct
Spectacled Hare-wallaby	*Lagorchestes conspicillatus*	Australia + NG	Least Concern
Rufous Hare-wallaby	*Lagorchestes hirsutus*	Australia	Vulnerable
Eastern Hare-wallaby	*Lagorchestes leporides*	Australia	Extinct
Agile Wallaby	*Macropus agilis*	Australia + NG	Least Concern
Antilopine Wallaroo	*Macropus antilopinus*	Australia	Least Concern

Appendix 1

Common Name	Scientific Name	Distribution	Status
Black Wallaroo	*Macropus bernardus*	Australia	Near Threatened
Black-striped Wallaby	*Macropus dorsalis*	Australia	Least Concern
Tammar Wallaby	*Macropus eugenii*	Australia	Least Concern
Western Grey Kangaroo	*Macropus fuliginosus*	Australia	Least Concern
Eastern Grey Kangaroo	*Macropus giganteus*	Australia	Least Concern
Toolache Wallaby	*Macropus greyi*	Australia	Extinct
Western Brush-wallaby	*Macropus irma*	Australia	Least Concern
Parma Wallaby	*Macropus parma*	Australia	Near Threatened
Whiptail Wallaby	*Macropus parryi*	Australia	Least Concern
Common Wallaroo & Euro	*Macropus robustus*	Australia	Least Concern
Red-necked Wallaby	*Macropus rufogriseus*	Australia	Least Concern
Red Kangaroo	*Macropus rufus*	Australia	Least Concern
Bridled Nailtail Wallaby	*Onychogalea fraenata*	Australia	Endangered
Crescent Nailtail Wallaby	*Onychogalea lunata*	Australia	Extinct
Northern Nailtail Wallaby	*Onychogalea unguifera*	Australia	Least Concern
Allied Rock-wallaby	*Petrogale assimilis*	Australia	Least Concern
Short-eared Rock-wallaby	*Petrogale brachyotis*	Australia	Least Concern
Monjon	*Petrogale burbidgei*	Australia	Near Threatened
Cape York Rock-wallaby	*Petrogale coenensis*	Australia	Near Threatened
Narbalek	*Petrogale concinna*	Australia	Data Deficient
Godman's Rock-wallaby	*Petrogale godmani*	Australia	Least Concern
Herbert's Rock-wallaby	*Petrogale herberti*	Australia	Least Concern
Unadorned Rock-wallaby	*Petrogale inornata*	Australia	Least Concern
Black-footed Rock-wallaby	*Petrogale lateralis*	Australia	Near Threatened

Common Name	Scientific Name	Distribution	Status
Mareeba Rock-wallaby	*Petrogale mareeba*	Australia	Least Concern
Brush-tailed Rock-wallaby	*Petrogale penicillata*	Australia	Near Threatened
Proserpine Rock-wallaby	*Petrogale Persephone*	Australia	Endangered
Purple-necked Rock-wallaby	*Petrogale purpureicollis*	Australia	Least Concern
Rothchild's Rock-wallaby	*Petrogale rothschildi*	Australia	Least Concern
Sharman's Rock-wallaby	*Petrogale sharmani*	Australia	Near Threatened
Yellow-footed Rock-wallaby	*Petrogale xanthopus*	Australia	Near Threatened
Quokka	*Setonix brachyurus*	Australia	Vulnerable
Tasmanian Pademelon	*Thylogale billardierii*	Australia	Least Concern
Brown's Pademelon	*Thylogale browni*	New Guinea	Vulnerable
Dusky Pademelon	*Thylogale brunii*	New Guinea	Vulnerable
Calaby's Pademelon	*Thylogale calabyi*	New Guinea	Endangered
Mountain Pademelon	*Thylogale lanatus*	New Guinea	Endangered
Red-legged Pademelon	*Thylogale stigmatica*	Australia + NG	Least Concern
Red-necked Pademelon	*Thylogale thetis*	Australia	Least Concern
Swamp Wallaby	*Wallabia bicolor*	Australia	Least Concern

Subfamily Sthenurinae

Banded Hare-wallaby	*Lagostrophus fasciatus*	Australia	Endangered

* The taxonomy of *Dendrolagus dorianus* is currently under investigation and several of the typically recognised subspecies may represent distinct species.

Appendix 1

Sources

A.A. Burbidge, N.L. McKenzie, K.E.C. Brennan, J.C.Z. Woinarski, C.R. Dickman, A. Baynes, G. Gordon, P.W. Menkhorst and A.C. Robinson (2008), 'Conservation status and biogeography of Australia's terrestrial mammals', *Australian Journal of Zoology*, 56: 411–22.

T. Flannery (1995a), *Mammals of New Guinea*, 2nd edition, Sydney: Australian Museum/Reed Books.

T. Flannery (1995b), *Mammals of the South-West Pacific & Moluccan Islands*, Sydney: Reed Books.

C. Groves (1993), 'Order Diprotodontia', in D.E. Wilson & D.A. Reeder (eds.) *Mammal Species of the World: A Taxonomic and Geographic Reference*. Baltimore: Johns Hopkins University Press, pp 45–62.

International Union for the Conservation of Nature (IUCN) (2010) *Red List*. Internet address www.iucnredlist.org (accessed 25 May 2010).

S.M. Van Dyck and R. Strahan (eds) (2008), *The Mammals of Australia*, Sydney: Reed New Holland.

APPENDIX 2

MACROPODS INTRODUCED TO AREAS OUTSIDE THEIR KNOWN RANGE FOR REASONS OTHER THAN MODERN CONSERVATION EFFORTS

Species	Source	Destination	Success
Tasmanian Bettong	Tasmania	Maria Island, Tasmania	123 were introduced successfully in 1971.
Long-nosed Potoroo	SE Australia	Maria Island, Tasmania	136 introduced in 1971.
Long-nosed Potoroo	SE Australia	New Zealand	Introduced in 1867 by the Auckland Acclimatisation Society without success.
Huon Tree Kangaroo	New Guinea	Umboi Island	Carried in Holocene, for pets, food and trade.

Species	Source	Destination	Success
Brown Dorcopsis	New Guinea, Misool Island	Halmahera & Gebe Islands. Now extinct on both islands	Probably carried in prehistoric times, for food or trade.
Agile Wallaby	New Guinea	Goodenough, Fergusson, Normanby, Kiriwina Islands	Probably carried in prehistoric times, for food or trade.
Agile Wallaby	Northern Australia	Introduced to Long Island, Queensland	Failed to establish.
Black-Striped Wallaby	Eastern Australia	Kawau Island, New Zealand	Liberated by Sir George Grey in 1870 and became established.
Tammar Wallaby	Southern Australia	Kawau Island and Rotorua area, New Zealand	Liberated by Sir George Grey in 1870 and became established. Also liberated in Rotorua in about 1912.
Western Grey Kangaroo	Southern Australia	Woody Island in Recherche Archipelago before 1948. Single animal to Boullanger Island. Heirisson Island near Perth. Granite Island, South Australia	Appeared to have established, except on Boullanger Island and were removed from Granite Island.
Eastern Grey Kangaroo	Eastern Australia	Heron, Brampton, Long, Middle Percy and South Molle Islands—Queensland. Maria Island, Tasmania	No longer on Long or South Molle Island. Those introduced onto Middle Percy Island may not have been this species.

KANGAROO

Species	Source	Destination	Success
Northern Nailtail Wallaby	Northern Australia	Pulbah Island in Lake Macquarie, New South Wales	Reported to be 're-introduced' in the 1930s but failed to establish.
Parma Wallaby	Eastern Australia	Kawau Island, New Zealand	Introduced in 1870 and established.
Whiptail Wallaby	Northern Australia	Heron Island, North Queensland	Failed to establish.
Common Wallaroo	Eastern and Western Australia	Kangaroo Island, South Australia; Hook Island, Queensland. Carrang Station, Useless Loop, Western Australia. Kawau Island, New Zealand	Only the Useless Loop animals appear to have been successful in Australia. Kawau Island animals introduced between 1860 and 1870 by Sir George Grey but failed to establish.
Red-necked Wallaby	Eastern Australia	Maria Island, Tasmania. South Island, New Zealand. Czechoslovakia, Germany, Hungary, France and United Kingdom	Maria Island and New Zealand Introductions were successful. In Europe only a few small United Kingdom and French introductions successful despite numerous attempts.
Brush-tailed Rock-wallaby	Eastern Australia	Kawau, Rangitoto and Motutapu Islands—New Zealand. Kalihi on Oahu—Hawaiian Islands	Introduced to New Zealand in 1870 and 1873. Introduced to Hawaii in 1916. Became established in both locations.
Brown's Pademelon	New Guinea	Bagabag, Umboi, New Britain, New Ireland, and New Hanover islands	Probably carried in prehistoric times, for pets, food, trade.

Appendix 2

Species	Source	Destination	Success
Dusky Pademelon	New Guinea, Aru	Kai Islands	Probably carried in prehistoric times, for food or trade.
Swamp Wallaby	Eastern Australia	Kawau Island, New Zealand	Introduced by Sir George Grey in 1870.

Sources

T.F. Flannery and J.P. White (1991), 'Animal Translocation: Zoogeography of New Ireland Mammals', *National Geographic Research and Exploration* 7: 96–113.

T.E. Heinsohn (2001), 'Human influences on vertebrate zoogeography: Animal translocation and biological invasions across and to the east of Wallace's Line', in I. Metcalfe, J.M.B. Smith, M. Morwood and I. Davidson (eds), *Faunal and Floral Migrations and Evolution in SE Asia-Australasia*, Lisse: Balkema, pp. 153–70.

T.E. Heinsohn (2003), 'Animal translocation: long-term influences on the vertebrate zoogeogaphy of Australasia (natural dispersal versus ethnophoresy)', *Australian Zoologist* 32: 351–76.

J.L. Long (2003), *Introduced Mammals of the World*, Melbourne: CSIRO Publishing.

ENDNOTES

CHAPTER 1 FANGAROO TO KANGAROO

1 J.C. Beaglehole (1962), *The* Endeavour *Journal of Joseph Banks 1768–1771*, volume 2, Sydney: The Public Library of New South Wales in Association with Angus & Robertson, pp. 116–17.

2 A.J. Dennis and P.M. Johnson (2008), 'Musky Rat-kangaroo *Hypsiprymnodon moschatus*', in S. Van Dyck and R. Strahan (eds), *The Mammals of Australia*, Reed Books, Sydney, pp. 281–3.

3 A. Burk and M.S. Springer (2000), 'Intergeneric relationships among Macropodoidea (Metathera: Diprotodontia) and the chronicle of kangaroo evolution', *Journal of Mammalian Evolution* 7: 213–37.

4 T.F. Flannery, Boeadi and A.L. Szalay (1995), 'A new tree-kangaroo (*Dendrolagus*: Marsupialia) from Irian Jaya, Indonesia, with notes on ethnography and the evolution of tree-kangaroos', *Mammalia* 59: 65–84.

5 J. Hawkesworth (1773), *An account of the voyages undertaken by the order of His Majesty for making discoveries in the Southern Hemisphere,*

and successively performed by Commander Byron, Captain Wallis, Captain Carteret, and Captain Cook, in the Dolphin, *the* Swallow *and the* Endeavour, volume 3, London: W. Strahan & T. Cadell, pp. 173–4.

6   J.B. Haviland (1974), 'A last look at (Cook's) Guugu Yimidhirr wordlist', *Oceania* 44: 216–323.

7   P.P. King (1825), 'Narrative of a survey of the intertropical and western coasts of Australia. Performed between the years 1818 and 1822', London: John Murray (online version http://freeread.com. au/ebooks/e00027.html). Accessed 19 April 2010.

8   J. Troy (1994), *The Sydney Language*, Canberra: Panther Publishing and Printing.

9   P. Van Oosterzee (1997), *Where Worlds Collide: The Wallace Line*, Kew, Victoria: Reed Books; R. Hall (1998), 'The plate tectonics of Cenozoic SE Asia and the distribution of land and sea', in R. Hall and D. Holloway (eds) *Biogeography and Geological Evolution of SE Asia*, Leiden, Netherlands: Backhuys Publishers, pp. 99–131.

10 M.E. White (1994), *After the Greening: The Browning of Australia*, Sydney: Kangaroo Press; H.A. Martin (1994), 'Australian Tertiary phytogeography: Evidence from palynology', in R.S. Hill (ed), *History of the Australian Vegetation: Cretaceous to Recent*, Melbourne: Cambridge University Press, pp. 104–42; and M.O. Woodburne and J.A. Case (1996), 'Dispersal, vicariance, and the Late Cretaceous to Early Tertiary land mammal biogeography from South America to Australia', *Journal of Mammalian Evolution* 3: 121–61.

11 A.P. Kershaw, H.A. Martin and J.R.C. McEwen Mason (1994), 'The Neogene: a period of transition', in R.S. Hill (ed), *History of the Australian Vegetation: Cretaceous to Recent*, Cambridge: Cambridge University Press, pp. 299–327.

12 Martin (1994); M.K MacPhail, N.F. Alley, E.M. Truswell and I.R.K. Sluiter (1994), 'Early Tertiary vegetation: evidence from spores and pollen', in R.S. Hill (ed), *History of the Australian Vegetation: Cretaceous to Recent*. Cambridge University Press, Melbourne, pp. 189–261.

13 G. Singh, A.P. Kershaw and R. Clark (1981), 'Quaternary vegetation and fire history', in I.R. Noble, A.M. Gill and R.H. Groves

(eds), *Fire and the Australian Biota*, Canberra: Australian Academy of Sciences, pp. 23–54; G. Singh and E.A. Geissler (1985), 'Late Cainozoic history of vegetation, fire, lake levels and climate at Lake George, New South Wales, Australia', *Philosophical Transactions of the Royal Society of London* 311: 379–447; A.P. Kershaw, S.C. Bretherton and S. van der Kaars (2007), 'A complete pollen record of the last 230 ka from Lynch's Crater, northeastern Australia', *Palaeogeography, Palaeoclimatology, Palaeoecology* 151: 23–45.

14 J.A. Case (1989), 'Antarctica: The effect of high latitude heterochroneity on the origin of the Australian marsupials', *Geological Society of London Special Publications* 47: 217–26; Burk and Springer (2000).

15 D.J. Tongway and J.A. Ludwig (2002), 'Australian semi-arid lands and savannas', in M.R. Perrow and A.J. Davy (eds), *Handbook of Ecological Restoration*, volume 2, *Restoration in Practice*, Cambridge: Cambridge University Press, pp. 486–502.

16 D.O. Freudenberger, I.R.Wallis and I.D. Hume (1989), 'Digestive adaptations of kangaroos, wallabies and rat-kangaroos', in G. Grigg, P. Jarman and I. Hume (eds), *Kangaroos, Wallabies and Rat-kangaroos*, Sydney: Surrey Beatty & Sons, pp. 179–87.

17 T.J. Dawson (1989), 'Diets of macropodoid marsupials: General patterns and environmental influences', in G. Grigg, P. Jarman and I. Hume (eds), *Kangaroos, Wallabies and Rat-kangaroos*, Surrey Beatty & Sons, Sydney, pp. 129–42.

18 See, for example, B.J. MacFadden (1992), *Fossil Horses: Systematics, Paleobiology, and Evolution of the Family Equidae*, New York: Cambridge University Press.

19 T.F. Flannery (1987), 'The relationships of the macropodoids (Marsupialia) and the polarity of some morphological features within the Phalangeriformes', in M. Archer (ed), *Possums and Opossums: Studies in Evolution*, Sydney: Surrey Beatty & Sons, pp. 741–7; and T.F. Flannery (1989), 'Phylogeny of the Macropodoidea: A study on convergence', in G. Grigg, P. Jarman and I. Hume (eds), *Kangaroos, Wallabies and Rat-Kangaroos*, Sydney: Surrey Beatty & Sons, pp. 1–46.

20 M.S. Springer and J.A.W. Kirsch (1991), 'DNA hybridisation, the compression effect and the radiation of diprotodontian marsu-

pials', *Systematic Zoology* 40: 131–51; M.O. Woodburne, B.J. McFadden, J.A. Case, M.S. Springer, N.S. Pledge, J.D. Power, J.M. Woodburne and K.B. Springer (1993), 'Land mammal biostratigraphy and magnetostratigraphy of the Etadunna Formation (late Oligocene) of South Australia', *Journal of Vertebrate Paleontology* 13: 483–515; J.A.W. Kirsch, F.J. Lapointe and M.S. Springer (1997), 'DNA-hybridisation studies of marsupials and their implications for metatherian classification', *Australian Journal of Zoology* 45: 211–80; A. Burk, M. Westerman and M.S. Springer (1998), 'The phylogenetic position of the musky-rat kangaroo and the evolution of bipedal hopping in kangaroos (Macropodidae: Diprotodontia)', *Systematic Biology* 47: 457–74; and A. Burk and M.S. Springer (2000).

21 W.D.L. Ride (1993), '*Jackmahoneya* gen. nov. and the genesis of the macropodiform molar', *Memoirs of the Association of Australasian Palaeontology* 15: 441–59; and Kirsch *et al.* (1997).

22 Springer and Kirsch (1991); Kirsch *et al.* (1997); Burk *et al.* (1998); R.W. Meredith, M. Westerman and M.S. Springer (2008), 'A phylogeny and timescale for the living genera of kangaroos and kin (Macropodiformes: Marsupialia) based on nuclear DNA sequences', *Australian Journal of Zoology* 56: 395–410.

23 Burk and Springer (2000).

24 M.O. Woodburne, B.J. McFadden, J.A. Case, M.S. Springer, N.S., Pledge, J.D. Power, J.M. Woodburne and K.B. Springer (1993), 'Land mammal biostratigraphy and magnetostratigraphy of the Etadunna Formation (late Oligocene) of South Australia', *Journal of Vertebrate Paleontology* 13: 483–515; G.J. Prideaux (1999), 'Systematics and evolution of the extinct kangaroo subfamily Sthenurinae', Unpublished PhD Dissertation. Flinders University of South Australia; Burk and Springer (2000).

25 Ibid.

26 Burk *et al.* (1998); and Meredith *et al.* (2008).

27 Burk and Springer (2000).

28 Flannery (1989); and J. Long, M. Archer, T.F. Flannery and S. Hand (2002), *Prehistoric Mammals of Australia and New Guinea: One Hundred Million Years of Evolution*, Sydney: University of New South Wales Press.

29 Burk and Springer (2000).

30 Flannery (1989).

31 C. Johnson (2006), *Australia's Mammal Extinctions: A 50,000 Year History*, Cambridge: Cambridge University Press.

32 N. Bishop (1997), 'Functional anatomy of the macropodid pes', *Proceedings of the Linnean Society of New South Wales* 117: 17–50; and Long *et al.* (2002).

33 B.N. Cooke (2000), 'Cranial remains of a new species of balbarine kangaroo (Marsupialia: Macropodoidea) from the Oligo-Miocene freshwater limestone deposits of Riversleigh World Heritage Area, northern Australia', *Journal of Paleontology* 74: 317–26; and Long *et al.* (2002).

34 Long *et al.* (2002); and H. Tyndale-Biscoe (2005), *Life of Marsupials*, Melbourne: CSIRO Publishing.

35 B.P. Kear, B.N. Cooke, M. Archer and T.F. Flannery (2007), 'Implications of a new species of Oligo-Miocene kangaroo (Marsupialia: Macropodoidea) *Nambaroo*, from the Riversleigh World Heritage Area, Queensland, Australia', *Journal of Paleontology* 81: 1147–67; La Trobe University (2008), 'Skippy's ancestor a galloping kangaroo?', at www.latrobe.edu.au/bulletin/2008/0208/research2.html (date accessed 6 December 2009).

36 S. Wroe, J. Brammall and B.N. Cooke (1998), 'The skull of *Ekaltadeta ima* (Marsupialia, Hypsiprymnodontidae?): An analysis of some marsupial cranial features and a re-investigation of propleopine phylogeny, with notes on the inference of carnivory in mammals', *Journal of Paleontology* 72: 738–51; S. Wroe (2001), 'The killer rat-kangaroo's tooth', *Nature Australia* 27(1): 28–31; and Long *et al.* (2002).

37 B.N. Cooke and B. Kear (1999), 'Evolution and diversity of kangaroos (Macropodoidea, Marsupialia)', *Australian Mammalogy* 21: 27–9.

38 Gröcke, D.R. (1997), 'Distribution of C3 and C4 plants in the Late Pleistocene of South Australia recorded by isotope biogeochemistry of collagen in megafauna', *Australian Journal of Botany* 45: 607–617 ; and Long *et al.* (2002).

39 T.F. Flannery and M. Archer (1985), '*Palorchestes* Owen, 1874. Large and small palorchestes', in P.V. Rich and G.F. van Tets (eds),

Kadimakara: Extinct Vertebrates of Australia, Melbourne: Pioneer Design Studio, pp. 234–9.

40 Long *et al.* (2002); and Johnson (2006).

41 Flannery and Archer (1985).

42 Long *et al.* (2002).

43 R.T. Wells, D.R. Horton and P. Rogers (1982), '*Thylacoleo carnifex* Owen (Thylacoleonidae): marsupial carnivore?', in M. Archer and G. Clayton (eds), *Carnivorous Marsupials*, Sydney: Royal Zoological Society of New South Wales, pp. 573–86; S. Wroe, T.J. Myers, R.T. Wells and A. Gillespie (1999), 'Estimating the weight of the Pleistocene marsupial lion, *Thylacoleo carnifex* (Thylacoleonidae: Marsupialia): implications for the ecomorphology of a marsupial super-predator and hypotheses of impoverishment of Australian marsupial carnivore faunas', *Australian Journal of Zoology* 47: 489–98.

44 Proponents of the climate change argument include A.R. Main (1978), 'Ecophysiology: Towards an understanding of late Pleistocene marsupial extinction', in D. Walker and J.C. Guppy (eds), *Biology and Quaternary Environments*, Canberra: Australian Academy of Science, pp. 169–84; M. Archer (1984), 'Effects of humans on the Australian vertebrate fauna', in M. Archer and G. Clayton (eds), *Vertebrate Zoogeography and Evolution in Australia*, Perth: Hesperian Press, pp. 151–61; D. Horton (1984), 'Red kangaroos: last of the Australia megafauna', in P.S. Martin and R.G. Klein (eds), *Quaternary Extinctions: A Prehistoric Revolution*, Tucson, Arizona: University of Arizona Press, pp. 639–80; J.L. Kohen (1995), *Aboriginal Environmental Impacts*, Sydney: University of New South Wales Press; J. Field and J. Dodson (1999), 'Late Pleistocene megafauna and archaeology from Cuddie Springs, southern-eastern Australia', *Proceedings of the Prehistoric Society* 65: 275–301; and Prideaux (1999). For landscape burning see D. Merrilees (1968), 'Man the destroyer; late Quaternary changes in the Australian marsupial fauna', *Journal of the Royal Society of Western Australia* 51: 1–24; R. Jones (1968), 'The geographical background to the arrival of man in Australia and Tasmania', *Archaeology and Physical Anthropology in Oceania* 3: 186–215; and G.H. Miller, M.L. Fogel,

J.W. Magee, M.K. Gagan, S.J. Clarke and B.J. Johnson (2005), 'Ecosystem collapse in Pleistocene Australia and a human role in megafauna extinction', *Science* 309: 287–90. For overhunting, see T. Flannery (1994) *The Future Eaters*, Sydney: Reed New Holland; and Johnson (2006).
45 Johnson (2006).

CHAPTER 2 DREAMTIME

1   R.B. Smyth (1878), *The Aborigines of Victoria: With notes relating to the habits of the natives of other parts of Australia and Tasmania. Compiled from various sources for the Government of Victoria*, Melbourne: John Curry O'Neil, pp. 186–7.
2   Aboriginal Art and Culture Centre, Alice Springs (2009), 'The Dreamtime', at http://aboriginalart.com.au (date accessed 22 October 2009).
3   C. Dean. (1996), *The Australian Aboriginal Dreamtime: An Account of its History, Cosmogenesis, Cosmology and Ontology*, Geelong, Victoria: Gamahucher Press, pp. 3, 6.
4   D. Yerbury (2003), 'A journey from Dreamtime to machine time: Australian history through the eyes of Australian indigenous artists', *Museologia* 3: 139–48.
5   Dean (1996), pp. 3, 6.
6   C.W. Peck (1925), *Australian Legends: Tales Handed Down from the Remotest Times by the Autocthonous Inhabitants of Our Land*, Sydney: C.W. Peck. Available at www.holyebooks.org/australia/australian_legends/ peck13.html (accessed 25 April 2010).
7   A. Massola (1968), *Bunjil's Cave: Myths, Legends and Superstitions of the Aborigines of South-east Australia*, Melbourne: Landsdowne Press, p. 17.
8   K.L. Parker (1953), *Australian Legendary Tales*, collected by K. Langloh Parker, selected and edited by H. Drake-Brockman. Sydney: Angus & Robertson, pp. 93–5.
9   Ibid.
10 Anon. (1975), *Djugurba: Tales from the Spirit Time*, Canberra: Australian National University Press, pp. 62–4.
11 Massola (1968), p. 47.

12 Anon. (1975), pp. 12–14.

13 U. Beier and G. Beier (1972), *When the Moon was Big, and Other Legends from New Guinea*, Sydney: William Collins Ltd, p. 40.

14 T.F. Flannery, R. Martin and A. Szalay (1996), *Tree Kangaroos: A Curious Natural History*, Sydney: Reed Books, pp. 34–5.

15 Massola (1968).

16 Yerbury (2003).

17 A.P. Elkin (1954), *Legends and Dreaming: Legends of the Dream-Time of the Australian Aborigines as Related to Roland Robinson by Men of the Djauan, Rimberunga, Mungarai-Ngalarkan and Yungmun Tribes of Arnhem; Illustrated from Paintings of the Legendary Figures Made by the Narrators in Earth Colours and Charcoal*, Sydney: Edwards and Shaw, pp. 35–6; see also K.W. Porter (1956), 'Review: Myths of the Australian Dreamtime', *The Journal of American Folklore* 69 (272): 194–9.

18 J.G. Steele (1983), *Aboriginal Pathways in Southeast Queensland and the Richmond River*, St Lucia: University of Queensland Press, pp. 35–7.

19 Ibid.

20 D.B. Croft (1991), 'The relationship between people and animals: an Australian perspective', in D.B. Croft (ed), *Australian People and Animals in Today's Dreamtime: The Role of Comparative Psychology in the Management of Natural Resources,* New York: International Society for Comparative Psychology, Praeger Publishing, p. 7.

21 A.E. Newsome (1980), 'The eco-mythology of the red kangaroo in central Australia', *Mankind* 12: 327–33.

22 L. Taylor (1989), 'Seeing the 'inside': Kunwinjku paintings and the symbol of the divided body', in H. Morphy (ed), *Animals into Art*, London: Unwin Hyman, pp. 371–389; Yerbury (2003).

23 J.M. Thomson, J.L. Long and D.R. Horton (1987), 'Human exploitation of and introductions to the Australian flora', in G.R. Dyne and D.W. Walton (eds), *Fauna of Australia. Vol. 1A: General Articles*, Canberra: Australian Government Publishing Service. pp. 227–249; T.J. Dawson (1995), *Kangaroos: Biology of the Largest Marsupials*, Sydney: University of New South Wales Press.

24 J.C. Altman (1984), 'The dietary utilisation of flora and fauna by contemporary hunter-gatherers at Momega Outstation, north-central Arnhem Land', *Australian Aboriginal Studies* 2(1): 35–46.

25 Thomson *et al.* (1987).

26 P.P. King (1825), *Narrative of a survey of the intertropical and western coasts of Australia. Performed between the years 1818 and 1822*, London: John Murray, p. 355.

27 D. Tunbridge (1991), *The Story of the Flinders Ranges Mammals*, Sydney: Kangaroo Press.

28 Ibid.

29 E.J. Eyre (1845), *Journals of expeditions Of discovery into Central Australia and overland from Adelaide To King George's Sound in the years 1840–1: Sent by the colonists of South Australia, with the sanction and support of the government: including an account of the manners and customs of the aborigines and the state of their relations with Europeans*, volume 2, London: T & W Boone, pp. 276–7.

30 G. Grey (2006), *Journals of two expeditions of discovery in north-west and Western Australia*, Volumes 1 and 2, Middlesex: The Echo Library, pp. 397–8.

31 P. Clarke. (2003), *Where the Ancestors Walked: Australia as an Aboriginal Landscape*, Sydney: Allen & Unwin, pp. 78–85.

32 For the different uses of kangaroo 'byproducts', see J.F. O'Connell (1980), 'Notes on the manufacture and use of a kangaroo skin waterbag', *Australian Institute of Aboriginal Studies N. S.* 13: 26–9; Tunbridge (1991); S.J. Meagher and W.D.L. Ride (1979), 'Use of natural resources by the Aborigines of south-western Australia', in R.M. Berndt and C.H. Berndt (eds), *Aborigines in the West: Their Past and Their Present*, Perth: UWA Press, pp. 66–80; and R.B. Smyth (1878), *The Aborigines of Victoria: With notes relating to the habits of the natives of other parts of Australia and Tasmania. Compiled from various sources for the Government of Victoria*, Melbourne: John Curry O'Neil, pp. 186–7; M.J. Morwood, and D.R. Hobbs (2002), *Visions from the Past: the Archaeology of Australian Aboriginal Art*, Sydney: Allen and Unwin, pp. 13–14; R.A. Gould (1980), *Living Archaeology*, Cambridge: Cambridge University Press, pp. 247–8; and A. Garton and K. Williamson (2005), *Science*

for Life, Volume 8, South Yarra: MacMillan Education Australia, p. 165.

33 T.F. Flannery, R. Martin and A. Szalay (1996), *Tree Kangaroos: A Curious Natural History*, Sydney: Reed Books, pp. 34–5.

34 Morwood and Hobbs (2002).

35 H. Morphy (1991), *Ancestral Connections*, Chicago: University of Chicago Press; W. Caruna (1993), *Aboriginal Art*, London: Thames and Hudson.

CHAPTER 3 CIVET CATS, GIANT RATS AND JUMPING RACCOONS

1 J. Banks (1896). *Journal of the Right. Hon. Sir Joseph Banks During Captain Cook's First Voyage in H.M.S. Endeavour in 1768–71 to Terra Del Fuego, Otahite, New Zealand, Australia, The Dutch East Indies, Etc.* London: Macmillan and Co. Ltd, p. 301.

2 C. de Jode (1593), *Speculum Orbis Terrae*, Antwerp.

3 D. Clode (2006), *Continent of Curiosities: A Journey Through Australian Natural History*, Cambridge: Cambridge University Press.

4 D. Clode (2006).

5 H.N. Stevens (1930), *New Light on the Discovery of Australia as revealed by the Journal of Captain Don Diego de Prado y Tovar*, London: Henry, Stevens, Son and Stiles, p. 139; see also J.H. Calaby (1965), 'Early European description of an Australian mammal', *Nature* 205: 516–17.

6 M. Dash (2002), *Batavia's Graveyard*, London: Weidenfeld & Nicholson.

7 H. Drake-Brockman and E.D. Drok (1963), *Voyage to Disaster: The Life of Francisco Pelsaert: Covering his Indian Report to the Dutch East India Company, and the Wreck of the Ship Batavia in 1629 off the coast of Western Australia, together with the full text of his Journals concerning the rescue voyages*, Sydney: Angus & Robertson, pp. 235–6.

8 J.E. Heeres (1899), *The Part Borne by the Dutch in the Discovery of Australia 1616–1765*, Leiden: Brill, p. 168.

9 G. Schilder (1985), *Voyage to the Great South Land Willem de Vlamingh 1696–1697*, The Hague, Netherlands: Martinus Nijhoff, p. 123.

10 P. Playford (1998), *Voyage of Discovery to Terra Australis by William De Vlamingh*, Perth: Western Australian Museum, p. 18.

11 Schilder (1985), p. 217.

12 M. Lister (1698), 'Part of a letter from Mister Witsen, Burger Master of Amsterdam, and F.R.S., to Dr Martin Lister, fellow of the College of Physicians, and R.S., Concerning some later observations in Nova Hollandia', *Philosophical Transactions of the Royal Society of London* 20: 361–3, p. 362.

13 W. Dampier (1703), *A Voyage to New Holland, &c. In the Year, 1699*, volume III, London: Knapton, p. 123.

14 D. de Bruin (1714), *Reizen over Moskovie door Persie en Indie*, Amsterdam: R. & G. Wetstein, J. Oestwewwyk & H. van de Gaete; J. Lendering, 'Cornelis de Bruijn'. Livius: Articles on Ancient History at http://www.livius.org/bn-bz/bruijn/cornelis_de_bruijn. html (date accessed 22 February 2010).

15 J.C. Beaglehole (1962), *The* Endeavour *Journal of Joseph Banks 1768– 1771*, Volume 2, Sydney: The Public Library of New South Wales in Association with Angus & Robertson, pp. 84, 85, 89, 93–94, 100, 116–117; J. Hawkesworth (1773), *An account of the voyages undertaken by the order of His Majesty for making discoveries in the Southern Hemisphere, and successively performed by Commander Byron, Captain Wallis, Captain Carteret, and Captain Cook, in the* Dolphin, *the* Swallow *and the* Endeavour, volume 3, London: W. Strahan & T. Cadell, pp. 157, 173–4. The quotes from pp. 55–6 are from these sources.

16 P.L.S. Müller (1776), *Des Ritters Carl von Linné*: vollständiges Natursystem nach der zwölften lateinischen Ausgabe und nach Anleitung des Holländischen Houttuynischen Werks. Bey Gabriel Nicolaus Raspe, Nürnberg: Supplements und Register-Band, p. 62; E.A.W. Zimmerman (1777), *Specimen zoologiae geographicaem quadrupedum domicilia et migrations sistens. Dedit, tabulamque muni zoographicam adjunxit*, Lugduni Batavorum: *Theodorum Haak et socios*, p. 526.

17 For a review see T. Iredale and E. Troughton (1962), 'The actual identity of Captain Cook's kangaroo', *Proceedings of the Linnean Society of New South Wales* 87: 177–84; see also T.C.S. Morrison-Scott and F.C. Sawyer (1950), 'The identity of Captain Cook's

kangaroo', *Bulletin of the British Museum (Natural History), Zoology* 1(3): 45–50.

18 J.C. Beaglehole (1967), *The Journals of Captain James Cook on His Voyages of Discovery. The Voyage of the* Resolution *and* Discovery *1776–1780*, Cambridge: Hakluyt Society and Cambridge University Press, pp. 792–3.

19 State Library of New South Wales (2008), 'David Blackburn (1753–1795), Letter to Richard Knight dated12 July 1788', at www.sl.nsw.gov.au/discover_collections/history_nation/terra_australis/letters/Blackburn/index.html (date accessed 18 September 2008).

20 W. Tench (1996), 'A Narrative of the Expedition to Botany Bay', in T.F. Flannery (ed), *1788 Comprising a Narrative of the Expedition to Botany Bay and A Complete Account of the Settlement at Port Jackson*, Melbourne: The Text Publishing Company; and I. Merle (2009), 'Watkin Tench's fieldwork: The journal of an "ethnographer" in Port Jackson, 1788–1791', in M. Jolly, S. Tcherkézoff and Darrell Tryon (eds), *Oceanic Encounters: Exchange, Desire, Violence*, Canberra: ANU E Press, pp. 199–19.

21 W. Tench (1996), 'A Narrative of the Expedition to Botany Bay', in T.F. Flannery (ed), *1788 Comprising a Narrative of the Expedition to Botany Bay and A Complete Account of the Settlement at Port Jackson*, Melbourne: The Text Publishing Company, pp. 13–84, quoted material from pp. 74–5.

22 W. Tench (1996), 'A Complete Account of the Settlement at Port Jackson', in T.F. Flannery (ed), *1788 Comprising a Narrative of the Expedition to Botany Bay and A Complete Account of the Settlement at Port Jackson*, Melbourne: The Text Publishing Company, pp. 85–274, quoted material from p. 237.

23 Ibid., pp. 237–8. Both quotes on p. 61 are from these pages.

24 A. Phillip (1789), *The Voyage of Governor Phillip to Botany Bay, With an Account of the Establishment of the Colonies of Port Jackson & Norfolk Island Compiled from Authentic Papers…To which are added the Journals of Lieuts. Shortland, Watts, Ball & Capt. Marshall, With an Account of their Discoveries*, London: John Stockdale, p. 277.

25 G. Perry (1810–11), *Arcana, or, The Museum of Natural History, Containing the most Recent Discovered Objects. Embellished with Coloured*

Plates and Corresponding Descriptions, with Extracts Relating to Animals and Remarks of Celebrated Travellers, Combining a General Survey of Nature, London: James Stafford, two unnumbered pages next to Plate 27.

26 Ibid.

28 T.F. Flannery, R. Martin and A.L. Szalay (1996), *Tree Kangaroos: A Curious Natural History*, Sydney: Reed Books, p. 3.

30 S. Müller and J. Yeats (1858), 'Contributions to the knowledge of New Guinea', *Journal of the Royal Geographical Society of London* 28: 264–72.

31 J. MacGillivray (1852), *Narrative Of The Voyage Of H.M.S.* Rattlesnake, *Commanded By The Late Captain Owen Stanley, R.N., F.R.S. Etc. During The Years 1846–1850. Including Discoveries And Surveys In New Guinea, The Louisiade Archipelago, Etc. To Which Is Added The Account Of Mr. E.B. Kennedy's Expedition For The Exploration Of The Cape York Peninsula*. Project Gutenberg e-book: http://www.gutenberg.org/files/12433/12433-h/12433-h.htm (date accessed 22 February 2010).

32 J. Seebeck and P.G. Johnson (1980), '*Potorous longipes* (Marsupialia: Macropodidae); a new species from eastern Victoria', *Australian Journal of Zoology* 28: 119–134; and G.M. Maynes (1982), 'A new species of rock-wallaby, *Petrogale persephone* (Marsupialia, Macropodidae), from Proserpine, central Queensland', *Australian Mammalogy* 5: 47–58.

33 T.F. Flannery and L. Seri (1990), '*Dendrolagus scottae* n. sp. (Marsupialia: Macropodidae) a new tree-kangaroo from Papua New Guinea', *Records of the Australian Museum* 42: 237–45; T.F. Flannery, Boeadi and A.L. Szalay (1995), 'A new tree-kangaroo (*Dendrolagus*: Marsupialia) from Irian Jaya, Indonesia, with notes on ethnography and the evolution of tree-kangaroos', *Mammalia* 59: 65–84.

34 R. Rienits and T. Rienits (1963), *Early Artists of Australia*, Sydney: Angus & Robertson, p. 10.

35 A. Graves (1907), *The Society of Artists of Great Britain 1760–1791 and The Free Society of Artists 1761–1791. A Complete Dictionary of Contributors and their Work from the Foundation of the Societies to 1791*, London: George Bell and Sons, p. 250; W. Blunt (1976), *The Ark*

in the Park: The Zoo in the Nineteenth Century, London: Hamish Hamilton and The Tryon Gallery and Parham House and Garden (2006), at www.parhaminsussex.co.uk/?contentId=2 (date accessed 28 November 2008).

36 S. Parkinson (1773), *A Journal Of A Voyage To The South Seas, In His Majesty's Ship, The* Endeavour. *Faithfully Transcribed From The Papers Of The Late Sydney Parkinson, Draughtsman To Joseph Banks, Esq. On His Late Expedition. With Dr. Solander, Round The World. Embellished With Views And Designs, Delineated By The Author, And Engraved By Capital Artists*, London, Stanfield Parkinson, p. 188.

37 J. White (1790), *Journal of a Voyage to New South Wales; with Sixty-five Plates of Non descript Animals, Birds, Lizards, Serpents, Curious Cones of Trees and Other Natural Productions*, London: J. Debrett.

38. A.H. Chisholm (1962), 'Editor's introduction', in J. White (1962), *Journal of a Voyage to New South Wales; with Sixty-five Plates of Non descript Animals, Birds, Lizards, Serpents, Curious Cones of Trees and Other Natural Productions*, Sydney: Angus & Robertson, pp. 9–16, quoted material p. 11.

39 J. Hunter (1793), *An Historical Journal of the Transactions at Port Jackson and Norfolk Island*, London: John Stockdale; D. Collins (1798), *An Account Of The English Colony In New South Wales: With Remarks On The Dispositions, Customs, Manners, etc. of The Native Inhabitants of That Country*, London: T. Cadwell (Jnr) & W. Davies.

40 Rienits and Rienits (1963), pp. 17, 20.

41 Phillip (1789); Rienits and Rienits (1963), p. 46.

42 Rienits and Rienits (1963), p. 27.

43 R. Rienits (1962), 'Biographical introduction', in J. White (1962), *Journal of a Voyage to New South Wales; with Sixty-five Plates of Non descript Animals, Birds, Lizards, Serpents, Curious Cones of Trees and Other Natural Productions*, Sydney: Angus & Robertson, pp. 17–34, quoted material p. 26.

44 R. Rienits (1962), p. 26.

45 Natural History Museum (2007), 'The Watling Collection', at www.nhm.ac.uk/jdsml/nature-online/first-fleet/collections.dsml?coll=watling (date accessed 20 January 2010).

46 T. Skottowe (1821), *The Skottowe Manuscript, Volume 1 – Thomas Skottowe's Select Specimens from Nature of the birds, animals, &c of New South Wales 1813*, Sydney: David Ell Press, Hordern House, pp. 33–4; T. Bonyhady and J.C. Calaby (1988), *The Skottowe Manuscript, Volume 2, Commentary*, Sydney: David Ell Press, p. 28.

47 Bonyhady and Calaby (1988), p. 59.

48 Bonyhady and Calaby (1988), p.34.

49 Skottowe (1821), pp. 33–4.

50 P. Watts, J.A. Pomfrett and D. Mabberley (1997), *An Exquisite Eye: The Australian Flora and Fauna Drawings 1801–1820 of Ferdinand Bauer*, Sydney: Historic Houses Trust of New South Wales, pp. 50–3.

51 Ibid., p. 9.

52 Perry (1810–1811), two unnumbered pages next to Plate 73.

53 G. Krefft (1871), *Mammals of Australia*, Sydney: Thomas Richards. Text associated with the first Great Kangaroo (*Macropus major*) Plate.

CHAPTER 4 SUSPENDED ANIMATION

1 W. Tench (1996), 'A Complete Account of the Settlement at Port Jackson', in T.F. Flannery (ed), *1788 Comprising a Narrative of the Expedition to Botany Bay and A Complete Account of the Settlement at Port Jackson*, Melbourne: The Text Publishing Company. pp. 85–274, quoted material from p. 236.

2 H. Tyndale-Biscoe (2005), *Life of Marsupials*, Melbourne: CSIRO Publishing.

3 See, for example, S.M. Jackson (2003), *Australian Mammals: Biology and Captive Management*, Melbourne: CSIRO Publishing, pp. 140, 285.

4 H. Tyndale-Biscoe and M. Renfree (1987), *Reproductive Physiology of Marsupials*, Cambridge: Cambridge University Press.

5 G.B. Sharman (1954), 'Reproduction in marsupials', *Nature* 173302–3; M.J. Smith (1981), 'Morphological observations on the diapausing blastocyst of some macropodid marsupials', *Journal of Reproduction and Fertility* 61: 483–886.

6　See Sharman (1954); G.B. Sharman (1955a), 'Studies on marsu-
　　pial reproduction. III. Normal and delayed pregnancy in *Setonix
　　brachyurus*', *Australian Journal of Zoology* 3: 56–70; and G.B.
　　Sharman (1955b), 'Studies on marsupial reproduction. IV. Delayed
　　birth in *Protemnodon eugenii* Desmarest', *Australian Journal of Zoology*
　　3: 156–61.

7　See Jackson (2003), p. 287.

8　B.J. Berger (1966), 'Eleven-month 'embryonic diapause' in a
　　marsupial', *Nature* 211: 435–6; M.B. Renfree and C.H. Tyndale-
　　Biscoe (1973), 'Intra-uterine development after diapause in the
　　marsupial *Macropus eugenii*', *Development Biology* 32: 28–40; and
　　D.C. Catt (1977), 'The breeding biology of Bennett's wallaby
　　(*Macropus rufogriseus fruticus*) in south Canterbury, New Zealand',
　　New Zealand Journal of Zoology 4: 401–11.

9　W.E. Poole and P.C. Catling (1974), 'Reproduction in the two
　　species of grey kangaroo, *Macropus giganteus* Shaw and *M. fuligino-
　　sus* (Desmarest). I. Sexual maturity and oestrus', *Australian Journal
　　of Zoology* 22: 277–302.

10　A.E. Newsome (1964a), 'Anoestrus in the red kangaroo *Megaleia
　　rufa* (Desmarest)', *Australian Journal of Zoology* 12: 9–17; H.J. Frith
　　and G.B. Sharman (1964), 'Breeding in wild populations of the
　　red kangaroo, *Megaleia rufa*', *CSIRO Wildlife Research* 9: 86–114.

11　See Tyndale-Biscoe and Renfree (1987).

12　E.L. Troughton (1947), 'Kangaroo twins—and triplets', *Austra-
　　lian Museum Magazine* November 9: 160–4.

13　S. Van Dyck and R. Strahan (2008), *The Mammals of Australia*,
　　Sydney: Reed Books.

14　For discussions of the birth process in macropods, see G.B.
　　Sharman and J.H. Calaby (1964), 'Reproductive behaviour in
　　the red kangaroo, *Megaleia rufa*, in captivity', *CSIRO Wildlife
　　Research* 9: 58–85; G.B. Sharman, J.H. Calaby and W.E. Poole
　　(1966), 'Patterns of reproduction in female diprotodont marsu-
　　pials', *Symposia of the Zoological Society of London* 15: 205–32;
　　W.E. Poole and P.E. Pilton (1964), 'Reproduction in the grey
　　kangaroo *Macropus canguru*, in captivity', *CSIRO Wildlife Research*
　　9: 218–34; and D.M. Beeck (1955), 'Observations on the birth of

the grey kangaroo (*Macropus ocydromus*)', *Western Australian Naturalist* 5: 9.

15 See Sharman and Calaby (1964).

16 See Tyndale-Biscoe (2005).

17 J.E. Heeres (1899), *The Part Borne by the Dutch in the Discovery of Australia 1616–1765*, Leiden: Brill, p. 61.

18 H. Drake-Brockman and E.D. Drok (1963), *Voyage to Disaster: The Life of Francisco Pelsaert : Covering his Indian Report to the Dutch East India Company, and the Wreck of the Ship* Batavia *in 1629 off the coast of Western Australia, together with the full text of his Journals concerning the rescue voyages*, Sydney: Angus & Robertson, p. 236.

19 See Drake-Brockman and Drok (1963).

20 E. Tyson (1698), 'Carigueya, seu Marsupiale Americanum, or the anatomy of an opossum, dissected at Gresham College', *Philosophical Transactions of the Royal Society* 20: 105–64.

21 F. Valentyn (1726), *Oud en nieuw Oost-Indien*, Dooordrecht: J. Van Braam & G.O. den Linden; see Tyndale-Biscoe and Renfree (1987).

22 Tyndale-Biscoe (2005).

23 E. Home (1795), 'Some observations on the mode of generation of the kangaroo: a particular description of the organs themselves', *Philosophical Transactions of the Royal Society* 85: 221–30; Tyndale-Biscoe and Renfree (1987).

24 J. Morgan (1833a), 'A description of the mammary organs of the kangaroo', *Transactions of the Linnean Society of London* 16: 61–84, p. 61.

25 J. Morgan (1833b), 'A further description of the anatomy of the mammary organs of the kangaroo', *Transactions of the Linnean Society of London* 16: 455–63, pp. 456–7.

26 Ibid., pp. 457–8.

27 A. Collie (1830), 'Letter dated 26 January 1830. Birth of a kangaroo', *Zoological Journal* 5: 238–241, p. 240.

28 R. Owen (1834), 'On the generation of the marsupial animals, with a description of the impregnated uterus of the kangaroo', *Philosophical Transactions of the Royal Society* 1834: 333–64, p. 334.

29 Ibid., p. 340.

30 Ibid., p. 345.

31 J.L. Stokes (1846), *Discoveries in Australia, with an account of the coasts and rivers explored and surveyed during the voyage of H.H.S.* Beagle *in the years 1837, 38, 39, 40, 41, 42, 43*. Volume II. London: T. & W. Boone, pp. 156–61.

32 J.J. Fletcher (1881), 'On the existence after parturition of a direct communication between the median vaginal cul-de-sac so called, and the urogenital canal, in certain species of kangaroo', *Proceedings of the Linnean Society of New South Wales* 6: 796–811; and J.J. Lister and J.J. Fletcher (1881), 'On the condition of the median portion of the vaginal apparatus in the Macropodidae', *Proceedings of the Zoological Society of London* 1881: 976–96.

33 J. Bancroft (1882), 'On the mode of birth of the kangaroo, communicated by the Hon. L. Hope, with remarks on the echidna and platypus', *Proceedings of the Philosophical Society of Queensland* 3: 1–4, p. 1.

34 D. Le Souef (1900), 'Mode in which the newborn kangaroo is transferred to the maternal pouch and affixed to the nipple', *Nature* 61: 423. March 1.

35 A.S. Le Souef and H. Burrell (1926), *The Wild Animals of Australasia*, London: Harrap, pp. 169–70.

36 See Tyndale-Biscoe and Renfree (1987); Tyndale-Biscoe (2005).

37 See Owen (1834), p. 348.

38 See Tyndale-Biscoe (2005).

39 Ibid.

40 P.B. Frappell and P.M. MacFarlane (2006), 'Development of the respiratory system in marsupials', *Respiratory Physiology & Neurobiology* 154: 252–67.

41 P.M. MacFarlane and P.B. Frappell (2001), 'Convection requirement is established by total metabolic rate in the newborn tammar wallaby', *Respiratory Physiology* 126: 221–31; P.M. MacFarlane, P.B. Frappell and J.P. Mortola (2002), 'Mechanics of the respiratory system in the newborn tammar wallaby', *Journal of Experimental Biology* 205: 533–8; and Frappell and MacFarlane (2006).

42. J.P. Mortola, P.B. Frappell and P.A. Woolley (1999), 'Breathing through the skin in a newborn mammal', *Nature* 397: 660.

43 See Van Dyck and Strahan (2008).

44 See Tyndale-Biscoe and Renfree (1987).

45 See Tyndale-Biscoe (2005).

46 A.E. Newsome (1966), 'The influence of food on breeding in the red kangaroo in central Australia', *CSIRO Wildlife Research* 11: 187–96; A.E. Newsome (1975), 'An ecological comparison of the two arid-zone kangaroos of Australia, and their anomalous prosperity since the introduction of ruminant stock to their environment', *The Quarterly Review of Biology* 50: 389–424; and Tyndale-Biscoe and Renfree (1987).

47 Sharman and Calaby (1964); G.B. Sharman and P.E. Pilton (1964), 'The life history and reproduction of the red kangaroo (*Megaleia rufa*)', *Proceedings of the Zoological Society of London* 142: 29–48.

48 See Frith and Sharman (1964); Newsome (1964a); and A.E. Newsome (1965), 'Reproduction in natural populations of the red kangaroo, *Megaleia rufa* (Desmarest), in central Australia', *Australian Journal of Zoology* 13: 735–759.

49 A.E. Newsome (1964b), 'Oestrus in the lactating red kangaroo *Megaleia rufa* (Desmarest)', *Australian Journal of Zoology* 12: 315–21; G.B. Sharman and M.J. Clark (1967), 'Inhibition of ovulation by the corpus luteum in the red kangaroo, *Megaleia rufa*', *Journal of Reproduction and Fertility* 14: 129–37.

50 H.G. Andrewartha and S. Barker (1969), 'Introduction to a study of the ecology of the Kangaroo Island Wallaby, *Protemnodon eugenii* (Demarest), within Flinders chase, Kangaroo Island South Australia', *Transactions of the Royal Society of South Australia* 93: 127–32; see also Tyndale-Biscoe and Renfree (1987).

51 Berger (1966); M.B. Renfree and C.H. Tyndale-Biscoe (1973), 'Intra-uterine development after diapause in the marsupial *Macropus eugenii*', *Development Biology* 32: 28–40.

52 See Andrewartha and Barker (1969); G.B. Sharman and P.J. Berger (1969), 'Embryonic diapause in marsupials', *Advances in Reproductive Physiology* 4: 211–40; C.H. Tyndale-Biscoe. and J. Hawkins (1977), 'The corpora lutea of marsupials, aspects of function and control', in J.H. Calaby and C.H. Tyndale-Biscoe (eds), *Reproduction and Evolution*, Canberra: Australian Academy of Science,

pp. 245–52; and J.C. Merchant and J.H. Calaby (1981), 'Reproductive biology of the red-necked wallaby (*Macropus rufogriseus banksianus*) and Bennett's wallaby (*M. r. rufogriseus*) in captivity', *Journal of Zoology* (London) 194: 203–17.

53 See Jackson (2003), p. 285.

54 Ibid, p. 249.

55 Ibid, p. 250.

56 D.A. Taggart, D. Schultz and P. Temple-Smith (1997), 'Development and application of assisted reproductive technologies in marsupials: their value for the conservation of rock-wallabies', *Australian Mammalogy* 19: 183–90.

57 Jackson (2003), p. 294.

58 D.A. Taggart, G.A. Shimmin, G. Underwood and K. Phillips (2002), 'Survival of very small macropod pouch young following short-term isolation from the pouch at various environmental temperatures', *Animal Conservation* 5: 275–82.

CHAPTER 5 BOXING KANGAROO

1 A.S. Le Souef and H. Burrell (1926), *The Wild Animals of Australasia*, London: Harrap, pp. 168–9.

2 D.B. Croft (1989), 'Social organisation of the Macropodoidea', in G. Grigg, P. Jarman and I. Hume (eds), *Kangaroos, Wallabies and Rat-Kangaroos*, Sydney: Surrey Beatty & Sons, pp. 505–25.

3 J. H. Kaufmann (1974), 'The ecology and evolution of social organisation in the kangaroo family (Macropodidae)', *American Zoologist* 14: 51–62; and G.E. Heinsohn (1968), 'Habitat requirements and reproductive potential of the macropod marsupial *Potorous tridactylus* in Tasmania', *Mammalia* 32: 30–43.

4 Kaufmann (1974).

5 P.J. Jarman (1987), 'Group size and activity in eastern grey kangaroos', *Animal Behaviour* 35: 1044–50; and D.T. Blumstein, J.C. Daniel and C.S. Evans (2001), 'Yellow-footed rock-wallaby group size effects reflect a trade-off', *Ethology* 107: 655–64.

6 P.J. Jarman and S.M. Wright (1993), 'Macropod studies at Wallaby Creek. IX. Exposure and responses of eastern grey kangaroos to dingoes', *Wildlife Research* 20: 833–43.

7   A.M.L. Colagross and A. Cockburn (1993), 'Vigilance and grouping in the Eastern Grey Kangaroo, *Macropus giganteus*', *Australian Journal of Zoology* 41: 325–34.

8   P. Banks (2001), 'Predation-sensitive grouping and habitat use by eastern grey kangaroos: a field experiment', *Animal Behaviour* 61:1013–21.

9   D.O. Fisher and I.P.F. Owens (2000), 'Female home range size and the evolution of social organization in macropod marsupials', *Journal of Animal Ecology* 69: 1083–98.

10 See Croft (1989).

11 P.J. Jarman (1991), 'Social behaviour and organisation in the Macropodoidea', *Advances in the Study of Behaviour* 20: 1–50.

12 C.N. Johnson (1989), 'Dispersal and philopatry in the macropodoids', in G. Grigg, P. Jarman and I. Hume (eds), *Kangaroos, Wallabies and Rat-Kangaroos*, Sydney: Surrey Beatty & Sons, pp. 593–601.

13 See Jarman (1991); and Fisher and Owens (2000).

14 Fisher and Owens (2000).

15 For the tree kangaroos, see R. Martin (2005), *Tree-Kangaroos of Australia and New Guinea*, Melbourne: CSIRO Publishing; for the potoroos, see D.J. Scotts and J.H. Seebeck (1989), 'Studies of *Potorous longipes* (Marsupialia: Potoroidae): with preliminary recommendations for its conservation in Victoria', *Technical Report Series No. 62*, Heidelberg, Victoria: Arthur Rylah Institute for Environmental Research; J.H. Seebeck and R.W. Rose (1989), 'Potoroidae' in D.W. Walton and B.J. Richardson (eds), *Fauna of Australia Volume 1B: Mammalia*, Canberra: Australian Government Publishing Service, pp. 716–39; and K. Green, A.T. Mitchell and P. Tennant (1998), 'Home range and microhabitat use by the long-footed potoroo, *Potorous longipes*', *Wildlife Research* 25: 357–72.

16 G.R. Newell (1999), 'Responses of Lumholtz's tree-kangaroo (*Dendrolagus lumholtzi*) to loss of habitat within a tropical rainforest fragment', *Biological Conservation* 91: 181–9.

17 See Jarman (1991).

18 L. Pope (2000), Population structure of the Northern Bettong, unpublished PhD thesis, Brisbane: University of Queensland.

19 A.B. Horsup (1994), 'Home range of the allied rock-wallaby, *Petrogale assimilis*', *Wildlife Research* 21: 65–84; and A.B. Horsup (1996), The behavioural ecology of the allied rock-wallaby, *Petrogale assimilis*, unpublished PhD thesis, James Cook University, Townsville.

20 P.B.S. Spencer, A.B. Horsup and H.D. Marsh (1998), 'Enhancement of reproductive success through mate choice in a social rock-wallaby, *Petrogale assimilis* (Macropodidae) as revealed by microsatellite markers', *Behavioural Ecology and Sociobiology* 43: 1–9.

21 Ibid.

22 G. Coulson (1989), 'Repertoires of social behaviour in the Macropodoidea', in G. Grigg, P. Jarman and I. Hume (eds), *Kangaroos, Wallabies and Rat-Kangaroos*, Sydney: Surrey Beatty & Sons, pp. 457–73.

23 G.M.Coulson and D.B. Croft (1981), 'Flehmen in kangaroos', *Australian Mammalogy* 4: 139–40.

24 See Coulson (1989).

25 D.B. Croft (1981), 'Behaviour of red kangaroos, *Macropus rufus*, (Desmarest, 1822) in northwestern New South Wales', *Australian Mammalogy* 4:5–58.

26 Ibid.

27 T. Dawson (1995), *Kangaroos: Biology of the Largest Marsupials*, Sydney: University of New South Wales Press.

28 Ibid.

29 Ibid.

30 Ibid.

31 See Jarman (1991).

32 Jarman (1991).

33 See Jarman (1991).

34 See Coulson and Croft (1981); and Coulson (1989).

35 S.W. Wright (1993), 'Observations of the behaviour of male eastern grey kangaroos when attacked by dingoes', *Wildlife Research* 20: 845–9.

36 P.C. Thompson (1992), 'The behavioural ecology of dingoes in north-western Australia. III. Hunting and feeding behaviour, and diet', *Wildlife Research* 19: 531–41.

37 See Wright (1993).

38 T.A. Rose, A.J. Munn, D. Ramp and P.B. Banks (2006), 'Foot-thumping as an alarm signal in macropodoid marsupials: prevalence and hypotheses of function', *Mammal Review* 36: 281–98.

39 H. Bender (2006), 'Structure and function of the eastern grey kangaroo (*Macropus giganteus*) foot thump', *Journal of Zoology* 268: 415–22.

CHAPTER 6 TRUFFLES, FRUIT, LEAVES AND GRASS

1 J. White (1790), *Journal of a Voyage to New South Wales*, London: J. Debrett, p. 193.

2 G.D. Sanson (1989), 'Morphological adaptations of teeth to diets and feeding in the Macropodoidea', in G. Grigg, P. Jarman and I. Hume (eds), *Kangaroos, Wallabies and Rat-kangaroos*, Sydney: Surrey Beatty & Sons, pp. 151–68.

3 A.J. Dennis (2002), 'The diet of the Musky Rat-kangaroo, *Hypsiprymnodon moschatus*, a rainforest specialist', *Wildlife Research* 29: 209–19.

4 P.M. Johnson and R. Strahan (1982), 'A further description of the Musky-Rat Kangaroo, *Hypsiprymnodon moschatus* Ramsay, 1876 (Marsupialia, Potoroidae), with notes on its biology', *Australian Zoologist* 21: 27–46.

5 A.J. Dennis (1997), Musky Rat-kangaroos, *Hypsiprymnodon moschatus*: Cursorial Frugivores in Australia's Wet-Tropical Rain Forests, unpublished PhD Thesis, James Cook University, Townsville.

6 M. Murphy (2010), The relationship between *Bettongia penicillata ogilbyi* (the woylie) and *Santalum spicatum* (sandalwood): Implications for functional processes in Dryandra, a semi-arid woodland in Western Australia, unpublished PhD Thesis, Perth: Murdoch University.

7 A.W. Claridge, J. Seebeck and R. Rose (2007), *Bettongs, Potoroos and the Musky Rat-kangaroo*, Melbourne: CSIRO Publishing.

8 Jim Trappe, Oregon State University, Corvallis, Oregon, personal

communication to Karl Vernes dated 2 May 2003 and unpublished data.

9   A.W. Claridge and T.W. May (1994), 'Mycophagy among Australian mammals', *Australian Journal of Ecology* 19: 251–75; K. Vernes, (2007), 'Are diverse mammal communities important for maintaining plant-fungal associations and ecosystem health?', *Australasian Plant Conservation* 15:16–18.

10 J.M. Trappe and C. Maser (1977), 'Ectomycorrhizal fungi: Interactions of mushrooms and truffles with beasts and man', in T. Walters (ed), *Mushrooms and Man, an Interdisciplinary Approach to Mycology*, Albany, Oregon: Linn-Benton Community College, pp. 165–79; I.R. Caldwell, K. Vernes and F. Bärlocher (2005), 'The northern flying squirrel as a vector for inoculation of red spruce (*Picea rubens*) seedlings with ectomycorrhizal fungi', *Sydowia* 57: 166–78.

11 Claridge and May (1994); K. Vernes, S. Blois, and F. Bärlocher (2004), 'Seasonal consumption of hypogeous fungi by northern flying squirrels (*Glaucomys sabrinus*) and red squirrels (*Tamiasciurus hudsonicus*) in old-growth forest, New Brunswick', *Canadian Journal of Zoology* 82: 110–17.

12 A.W. Claridge and S.J. Cork (1994), 'Nutritional value of hypogeal fungal sporocarps for the long-nosed potoroo (*Potorous tridactylus*), a forest-dwelling mycophagous marsupial', *Australian Journal of Zoology* 42: 701–10.

13 R. Donaldson and M. Stoddart (1994), 'Detection of hypogeous fungi by the Tasmanian bettong (*Bettongia gaimardi*: Marsupialia; Macropodoidea)', *Journal of Chemical Ecology* 20: 1201–7.

14 K. Vernes, M. Castellano and C.N. Johnson (2001), 'Effects of season and fire on the diversity of hypogeous fungi consumed by a tropical mycophagous marsupial', *Journal of Animal Ecology* 70: 945–54.

15 C.N. Johnson (1994), 'Fruiting of hypogeous fungi in a dry sclerophyll forest in Tasmania, Australia: seasonal variation and annual production', *Mycological Research* 98: 1173–82; V.P. Nguyen, A.D. Needham and J.S. Friend (2005), 'A quantitative dietary study of the critically endangered Gilbert's potoroo, *Potorous gilbertii*', *Australian Mammalogy* 27: 1–6; and A.W. Claridge, M.T. Tanton and R.B. Cunningham (1993), 'Hypogeal fungi in the diet of

the long-nosed potoroo (*Potoroos tridactylus*) in mixed-species and regrowth eucalypt forest stands in south-eastern Australia', *Wildlife Research* 20: 321–38.

16 Claridge and May (1994).

17 K. Vernes (2009), 'Mycophagy in a community of macropodoid species', in: G.M. Coulson and M.D.B. Eldridge (eds), *Macropods: The Biology of Kangaroos, Wallabies and Rat-kangaroos*, Melbourne: CSIRO Publishing, pp. 155–70.

18 B.B. Lamont, C.S. Ralph and P.E.S. Christiensen (1985), 'Mycophagous marsupials as dispersal agents for ectomycorrhizal fungi on *Eucalyptus calophylla* and *Gastrolobium bilobum*', *New Phytologist* 101: 651–6; N. Malajckuk, J.M. Trappe and R. Molina (1987), 'Interrelationships among some ectomycorrhizal trees, hypogeous fungi and small mammals: Western Australian and northwestern America parallels', *Australian Journal of Ecology* 12: 53–5.

19 I.D. Hume (1982), *Digestive Physiology of Marsupials*, Cambridge: Cambridge University Press.

20 D.O. Freudenberger, I.R. Wallis and I.D. Hume (1989), 'Digestive adaptations of kangaroos, wallabies and rat-kangaroos', in G. Grigg, P. Jarman and I. Hume (eds), *Kangaroos, Wallabies and Rat-kangaroos*, Sydney: Surrey Beatty & Sons, pp. 179–87.

21 Hume (1982); J. Seebeck, A.F. Bennett and D.J. Scott (1989), 'Ecology of the Potoroidae: A review', in G. Grigg, P. Jarman and I. Hume (eds), *Kangaroos, Wallabies and Rat-kangaroos*, Sydney: Surrey Beatty & Sons, pp. 67–88.

22 See Sanson (1989).

23 See Freudenberger *et al.* (1989).

24 See Sanson (1989).

25 See Hume (1982).

26 See Sanson (1989).

27 See Freudenberger *et al.* (1989).

28 See Sanson (1989).

29 T.J. Dawson (1989), 'Diets of macropodoid marsupials: General patterns and environmental influences', in G. Grigg, P. Jarman and I. Hume (eds), *Kangaroos, Wallabies and Rat-kangaroos*, Sydney: Surrey Beatty & Sons, pp. 129–42.

30 S. Barker, G.D. Brown and J.H. Calaby (1963), 'Food regurgitation in the Macropodidae', *Australian Journal of Science* 25: 4302.

31 See Hume (1982).

32 M.L. Dudzinski, W.A. Lowe, W.J. Miller and B.S. Low (1982), 'Joint use of habitat by red kangaroos and shorthorn cattle in central Australia', *Australian Journal of Ecology* 7: 69–74.

33 See Dawson (1989).

34 R.D. Barker (1987), 'The diet of herbivores in the sheep rangelands', in G. Caughley, N. Shepherd and J. Short (eds), *Kangaroos: Their Ecology and Management in the Sheep Rangelands of Australia*, Cambridge: Cambridge University Press, pp. 69–83.

35 T.J. Kempton, R.M. Murray and R.A. Length (1976), 'Methane production and digestibility measurements in the grey kangaroos and sheep', *Australian Journal of Biological Sciences* 29: 209–14.

36 W.H. Beijer (1952), 'Methane fermentation in the rumen of cattle', *Nature* 170: 576–7; K.A. Johnson and D.E. Johnson (1995), 'Methane emissions from cattle', *Journal of Animal Science* 73: 2483–92.

37 D. Ouwerkerk, A.V. Klieve, R.J Forster, J.M. Templeton and A.J Maguire (2005), 'Characterisation of culturable anaerobic bacteria from the forestomach of an eastern grey kangaroo, *Macropus giganteus*', *Letters in Applied Microbiology* 41: 327–33.

38 L. Milich (1999), 'The role of methane in global warming: where might mitigation strategies be focused?', *Global Environmental Change* 9: 179–201.

39 R.T. Watson, M.C. Zinyowera and R.H. Moss (eds) (1996), 'Technical summary: impacts, adaptations, and mitigation options', in *Climate Change 1995—Impacts, Adaptations and Mitigation of Climate Change: Scientific-Technical Analyses. Contribution of Working Group II to the Second Assessment Report of Intergovernmental Panel on Climate Change*, Cambridge: Cambridge University Press, pp. 20–53.

40 Milich (1999); National Greenhouse Gas Inventory (2005), *The Australian Government Submission to the UN Framework Convention on Climate Change*, Canberra: Australian Greenhouse Office; and G.R. Wilson and M.J. Edwards (2008), 'Native wildlife on rangelands to minimize methane and produce lower-emission meat: kangaroo versus livestock', *Conservation Letters* 1(3): 119–28.

41 M.R. Manning, G.I. Pearman, D.M. Etheridge, P.J. Fraser, D.C. Lowe and L.P. Steele (1996), 'The changing composition of the atmosphere', in W.J. Bouma, G.I. Pearman and M.J. Manning (eds), *Greenhouse: Coping with Climate Change*, Melbourne: CSIRO Publishing, pp. 3–26; Food and Agriculture Organization of the United States (2006), 'Livestock's Long Shadow. United Nations, Rome', at www.fao.org/docrep/010/a0701e/a0701e00.HTM (date accessed 14 February 2010).

42 A. Moss (1992), 'Methane from ruminants in relation to global warming', *Chemistry and Industry* 9: 334–6; Milich (1999).

43 R. Hegarty (2001), *Greenhouse Gas Emissions from the Australian Livestock Sector*, Canberra: Australian Greenhouse Office.

44 Wilson and Edwards (2008).

45 M. Diesendorf (2007), *Paths to a Low Carbon Future: Reducing Australia's Greenhouse Gas Emissions by 30 Per Cent by 2020*, Sydney: Sustainability Centre.

46 Ibid.

47 S.M. Howden and P.J. Reyenga (1999), 'Methane emissions from Australian livestock: implications of the Kyoto Protocol', *Australian Journal of Agricultural Research* 50: 1285–91.

48 Howden and Reyenga (1999).

49 D. Ouwererk, A.J. Maguire, L. McMillen and A.V. Klieve (2007), 'Why kangaroos do not produce methane', *Recent Advances in Animal Nutrition in Australia* 16: 101–4.

50 D. Ouwerkerk, A.J. Maguire, L. McMillen and A.V. Klieve (2009), 'Hydrogen utilising bacteria from the forestomach of eastern grey (*Macropus giganteus*) and red (*Macropus rufus*) kangaroos', *Animal Production Science* 49: 1043–51.

51 M. Willacy (2007), 'Scientists aiming to cut livestock emissions,' LandLine, dated 15 April 2007, at www.abc.net.au/landline/content/2006/s1897018.htm (date accessed 22 April 2007).

52 Willacy (2007).

CHAPTER 7 HIGH JUMPERS

1 T. Bewick (1790), *A General History of Quadrupeds*, London: Windward, republished 1980, pp. 439–40.

2   J.L. Patton (2005), 'Family Heteromyidae', in D.E. Wilson and
    D.M. Reeder (eds), *Mammal Species of the World: A Taxonomic
    and Geographic Reference*, Baltimore: Johns Hopkins Univer-
    sity Press, pp. 844–58; M. Silva and J.A. Downing (1995),
    CRC Handbook of Mammalian Body Masses, Boca Raton:
    CRC Press.

3   M.E. Holden and G.G. Musser (2005), 'Family Dipodidae', in
    D.E. Wilson and D.M. Reeder (eds), *Mammal Species of the World:
    A Taxonomic and Geographic Reference*. Baltimore: Johns Hopkins
    University Press, pp. 871–93; Silva and Downing (1995); and
    R.M. Nowak (1991), *Walker's Mammals of the World*, 5th edition,
    Baltimore: Johns Hopkins University Press.

4   S. Van Dyck and R. Strahan (2008), *The Mammals of Australia*,
    3rd edition, Sydney: Reed/New Holland.

5   Silva and Downing (1995); F. Dieterlen (2005), 'Family Pedeti-
    dae', in D.E. Wilson and D.M. Reeder (eds), *Mammal Species of
    the World: A Taxonomic and Geographic Reference*, Baltimore: Johns
    Hopkins University Press, p. 1535.

6   E.A.W. Zimmerman (1777), *Specimen zoologiae geographicaem
    quadrupedum domicilia et migrations sistens. Dedit, tabulamque muni
    zoographicam adjunxit*, Lugduni Batavorum: *Theodorum Haak, et
    socios*.

7   R. McN. Alexander and A. Vernon (1975), 'The mechanics of
    hopping by kangaroos (Macropodidae)', *Journal of Zoology* (London)
    177: 265–303.

8   Alexander and Vernon (1975); R.V. Baudinette (1994), 'Loco-
    motion in macropodoid marsupials: gaits, energetics and heat
    balance', *Australian Journal of Zoology* 42: 103–23.

9   Alexander and Vernon (1975); W.G. Cuming, R. McN. Alexan-
    der and A.S. Hayes (1978), 'Rebound resilience of tendons in the
    feet of sheep (*Ovis aries*)', *Journal of Experimental Biology* 74: 75–81;
    Baudinette (1994).

10 G.A. Cavagna, N.N. Heglund and C.R. Taylor (1977), 'Mechani-
    cal work in terrestrial locomotion: two basic mechanisms for
    minimising energy expenditure', *American Journal of Physiology*
    233: R243-R261.

11 A.A. Biewener, R.McN. Alexander and N.C. Heglund (1981), 'Elastic energy storage in the hopping of kangaroo rats (*Dipodmys spectabilis*)', *Journal of Zoology* (London) 195: 369–83.

12 S. Dennington and J. Baldwin (1988), 'Biochemical correlates of energy metabolism used to power hopping by kangaroos', *Australian Journal of Zoology* 36: 229–40.

13 H. Tyndale-Biscoe (2005), *Life of Marsupials*, Melbourne: CSIRO Publishing, p. 310.

14 Alexander and Vernon (1975); D.L. Morgan, U. Proske and D. Warren (1978), 'Measurements of muscle stiffness and the mechanism of elastic storage of energy in hopping kangaroos', *Journal of Physiology* 282: 253–61; and Tyndale-Biscoe (2005), p. 310.

15 G.J. Kenagy (1973), 'Daily and seasonal patterns of activity and energetics in a heteromyid rodent community', *Ecology* 54: 1201–19; Biewener *et al.* (1981); A.A. Biewener and R. Blickhan (1988), 'Kangaroo rat locomotion: design for elastic energy storage or acceleration', *Journal of Experimental Biology* 140: 243–55.

16 A.A. Biewener and J.E.A. Bertram (1991), 'Efficiency and optimisation in the design of skeletal support systems', in R.W. Blake (ed), *Efficiency and Economy in Animal Physiology*, Cambridge: Cambridge University Press, pp. 65–82.

17 T.J. Dawson and C.R. Taylor (1973), 'Energetic cost of locomotion in kangaroos', *Nature* 246: 313–14; R.V. Baudinette, B.J. Gannon, W.B. Runcieman and S. Wells (1987), 'Do cardiorespiratory frequencies show entrainment with hopping in the tammar wallaby?', *Journal of Experimental Biology* 129: 251–63; and R.V. Baudinette, G.K. Snyder and P.B. Frappell (1992), 'Energetic cost of locomotion in the tammar wallaby', *American Journal of Physiology* 262: R771–R778.

18 Cavagna *et al.* (1977); Alexander and Vernon (1975); and R.F. Ker, N.J. Dimery and R.McN. Alexander (1986), 'The role of tendon elasticity in hopping in a wallaby (*Macropus rufogriseus*)', *Journal of Zoology* (London) 208: 417–428.

19 M.B. Bennett and G.C. Taylor (1995), 'Scaling of elastic strain energy in kangaroos and the benefits of being big', *Nature* 378: 56–59.

20 C.R. Taylor, K. Schmidt-Nielsen and J.L. Raab (1970), 'Scaling of energetic cost of running to body size in mammals', *American Journal of Physiology* 219: 1104–7; R.V. Baudinette, K. Nagle and R.A.D. Scott (1976), 'Locomotory energetics in dasyurid marsupials', *Journal of Comparative Physiology* 109: 159–68; M.A. Fedak and H.J. Seeherman (1979), 'Reappraisal of energetics of locomotion shows identical cost in bipeds and quadrupeds including ostrich and horse', *Nature* 282: 713–16; and C.R. Taylor, N.C. Heglund and G.M.O. Maloiy (1982), 'Energetics and mechanics of terrestrial locomotion. I. Metabolic energy consumption as function of speed and size in birds and mammals', *Journal of Experimental Biology* 97: 1–21.

21 Dawson and Taylor (1973); T.J. Dawson (1977), 'Kangaroos', *Scientific American* 237(2): 78–89.

22 T.J. Dawson (1983), *Monotremes and Marsupials: The Other Mammals*, London: Edward Arnold; T.J. Dawson, E. Finch, L. Freedman, I.D. Hume, M.B. Renfree and P.D. Temple-Smith (1989), 'Morphology and physiology of the metatherian', in D.W. Walton and B.J. Richards (eds), *Fauna of Australia. Volume 1B. Mammalia*, Canberra: Australian Government Publishing Service, pp. 451–504.

23 Dawson (1983); D.E. Windsor and A.I. Dagg (1971), 'The gaits of the Macropodinae (Marsupialia)', *Journal of Zoology* (London) 163: 165–75; and M.B. Bennett (1987), 'Fast locomotion of some kangaroos', *Journal of Zoology* (London) 212: 457–64.

24 K.N. Webster and T.J. Dawson (2003), 'Locomotion energetics and gait characteristics of a rat-kangaroo, *Bettongia penicillata*, have some kangaroo-like features', *Journal of Comparative Physiology B* 173: 549–57; Dawson and Taylor (1973); R.V. Baudinette, B.J. Gannon and W.B. Wells (1987), 'Do cardiorespiratory frequencies show entrainment with hopping in the tammar wallaby?', *Journal of Experimental Biology* 129: 251–63; H. Tyndale-Biscoe (2005), *Life of Marsupials*, Melbourne: CSIRO Publishing.

25 Dawson (1983); Windsor and Dagg (1971); and Bennett (1987).

26 R.V. Baudinette (1989), 'The biomechanics and energetics of locomotion in Macropodidae', in G. Grigg, P. Jarman and I. Hume

(eds), *Kangaroos, Wallabies and Rat-Kangaroos*, Sydney: Surrey Beatty & Sons, pp. 245–53.

27 R.V. Baudinette, E.A. Halpern and D.S. Hinds (1993), 'Energetic cost of locomotion as a function of ambient temperature and during the growth in the marsupial *Potorous tridactylus*', *Journal of Experimental Biology* 174: 81–95; Webster and Dawson (2003); S.D. Thompson, R.E. MacMillen, E.M. Burke and C.R. Taylor (1980), 'The energetic cost of bipedal hopping in small mammals', *Nature* 287: 223–4. The species mentioned are Spring Hares (*Pedetes capensis*, Rodentia, Petetidae), Brush-tailed Rat-kangaroos (Marsupialia, Potoroidae) and Desert Rat-kangaroos (*Dipodomys deserti* Rodentia, Heteromyidae) and Merriam's Kangaroo Rat (*Dipodomys merriami*); Baudinette *et al.* (1993); and Thompson *et al.* (1980).

28 Webster and Dawson (2003).

29 Dawson and Taylor (1973); Baudinette *et al.* (1987); and Webster and Dawson (2003).

30 N.C. Heglund, N.C. and C.R. Taylor (1988), 'Speed, stride frequency and energy cost per stride: how do they change with body size and gait?', *Journal of Experimental Biology* 138: 301–18.

31 A. Burk, M. Westerman and M.S. Springer (1998), 'The phylogenetic position of the musky-rat kangaroo and the evolution of bipedal hopping in kangaroos (Macropodidae: Diprotodontia)', *Systematic Biology* 47: 457–74.

32 R.McN. Alexander (1987), 'Wallabies vibrate to breath', *Nature* 328: 477; R.McN. Alexander (1989), 'On the synchronisation of breathing with running in wallabies (*Macropus* spp.) and horses (*Equus caballus*)', *Journal of Zoology* (London) 218: 69–85; and Baudinette (1989).

33 Alexander (1987); Alexander (1989); and Baudinette *et al.* (1987).

34 T.J. Dawson, D. Robertshaw and C.R. Taylor (1974), 'Sweating in the kangaroo: a cooling mechanism during exercise, but not in heat', *American Journal of Physiology* 227: 494–8.

35 R. Martin (2005), *Tree-Kangaroos of Australia and New Guinea*, Melbourne: CSIRO Publishing.

36 S. Vogel (2003), *Comparative Biomechanics: Life's Physical World*, Princeton, NJ: Princeton University Press, p. 497.

37 C.P. McGowan, J. Skinner and A.A. Biewener (2008), 'Hind limb scaling of kangaroos and wallabies (Superfamily Macropodoidea): implications for hopping performance, safety factor and elastic savings', *Journal of Anatomy* 212: 153–63.

38 Bennett and Taylor (1995); M.B. Bennett (2000), 'Unifying principles in terrestrial locomotion: do hopping Australian marsupials fit in?', *Physiological and Biochemical Zoology* 73: 726–35.

39 Bennett and Taylor (1995); Bennett (2000).

40 C.N. Johnson and G.J. Prideaux (2004), 'Extinctions of herbivorous mammals in the late Pleistocene of Australia in relation to their feeding ecology; No evidence for environmental change as cause of extinction', *Austral Ecology* 29: 553–7; P. Murray (1991), 'The Pleistocene megafauna of Australia', in P. Vickers-Rich, J.M. Monaghan, R.F. Baird and T.H. Rich (eds), *Vertebrate Palaeontology of Australia*, Melbourne: Pioneer Design Studios and Monash University, pp. 1071–1164; and K.M. Helgen, R.T. Well, B.P. Kear, W.R. Gerdtz and T.F. Flannery (2006), 'Ecological and evolutionary significance of sizes of giant extinct kangaroos', *Australian Journal of Zoology* 54: 293–303.

41 F.S. Szalay (1994), *The Evolutionary History of Marsupials and an Analysis of Osteological Characters*, Cambridge: Cambridge University Press.

42 Helgen *et al.* (2006).

43 McGowan *et al.* (2008).

44 C. Johnson (2006), *Australia's Mammal Extinctions: A 50,000-year History*, Cambridge: Cambridge University Press; McGowan *et al.* (2008).

45 McGowan *et al.* (2008).

46 C.P. McGowan, R.V. Baudinette and A.A. Biewener (2006), 'Differential design for hopping in two species of wallabies', *Comparative Biochemical Physiology* A 150: 151–8.

47 McGowan *et al.* (2008).

48 Bennett (2000).

49 Burk *et al.* (1998).

50 R.V. Baudinette (1991), 'The energetics and cardiorespiratory correlates of mammalian terrestrial locomotion', *Journal of Experimental Biology* 160: 209–31; Tyndale-Biscoe (2005), p. 311.

51 Dawson (1977).

52 T.J. Dawson and. K.N. Webster (2010) 'Energetic characteristic of macropod locomotion', in G. Coulson and M. Eldridge (eds), *Macropods: The Biology of Kangaroos, Wallabies and Rat-Kangaroos*, Melbourne: CSIRO Publishing, pp. 99–108.

53 K.N. Webster and T.J. Dawson (2004), 'Is the energetics of mammalian hopping locomotion advantageous in arid environments?', *Australian Mammalogy* 26: 153–60.

CHAPTER 8 KANGAROO COMMODITY

1 G. Bennett (1834), *Wanderings in New South Wales; Batavia, Pedir Coast, Singapore, and China: Being the Journals of a Naturalist in those Countries during 1832, 1833, and 1834*, volume 1, London, Richard Bentley, pp. 285, 289.

2 H.N. Stevens (1930), *New Light on the Discovery of Australia as revealed by the Journal of Captain Don Diego de Prado y Tovar*, London: Henry, Stevens, Son and Stiles, p. 139; J.H. Calaby (1965), 'Early European description of an Australian mammal', *Nature* 205: 516–17.

3 H. Drake-Brockman and E.D. Drok (1963), *Voyage to Disaster: The Life of Francisco Pelsaert: Covering his Indian Report to the Dutch East India Company, and the Wreck of the Ship* Batavia *in 1629 off the coast of Western Australia, together with the full text of his Journals concerning the rescue voyages*, Sydney: Angus & Robertson, p. 214.

4 W. Dampier (1729), *A voyage to New Holland Etc. in the Year 1699*, A Project Gutenberg of Australia eBook: http://freeread.com.au/ebooks/e00046.html (date accessed 7 March 2010).

5 J. Banks (1962), *The* Endeavour *Journal of Sir Joseph Banks 1768–1771*. Sydney: State Library of New South Wales A Project Gutenberg of Australia eBook: http://gutenberg.net.au/ebooks05/0501141h.html (date accessed 7 March 2010).

6 W. Tench (1996), 'A Narrative of the Expedition to Botany Bay', in T.F. Flannery (ed), *1788 Comprising a Narrative of the Expedition*

to Botany Bay and A Complete Account of the Settlement at Port Jackson, Melbourne: The Text Publishing Company, pp. 13–85, quoted material p. 75.

7   G. Worgan (1978), *Journal of a First Fleet Surgeon (1788)*, Sydney: Library Council of New South Wales, p. 34.

8   J. White (1790), *Journal of a Voyage to New South Wales*, London: J. Debrett, pp. 183–4.

9   Anon (1789), *Whitehall Evening Post* (London, England), Thursday, 28 May 1789; Issue 6558. 17th–18th Century Burney collection newspapers, British Library.

10 W. Tench (1996), 'A Narrative of the Expedition to Botany Bay', in T.F. Flannery (ed), *1788 Comprising a Narrative of the Expedition to Botany Bay and A Complete Account of the Settlement at Port Jackson*, Melbourne: The Text Publishing Company, pp. 87–274, quoted material pp. 122–3.

11 D. Collins (1804), *General and garrison orders, 1803–1808*, entry for 10 September 1804, p. 103.

12 D. Collins (1804), *General and garrison orders, 1803–1808*, entry for 14 September 1805, p. 174

13 J. Boyce (2009), *Van Diemen's Land*, Melbourne: Black Inc., p. 44.

14 J. West (1852), *The History of Tasmania, Volume 1*, Launceston: Henry Dowling, p. 41.

15 Boyce (2009), p. 53.

16 Ibid., p. 63.

17 Ibid., p. 68.

18 M. Flinders (1814), *A Voyage to Terra Australis: undertaken for the purposes of completing the discovery of that vast country, and prosecuted in the years 1801, 1802 and 1803, in His Majesty's Ship the* Investigator, *and subsequently in the armed vessel* Porpoise *and* Cumberland *schooner*, London: G. & W. Nicol, Volume 1. Available at: http://ia331334.us. archive.org/2/items/avoyagetoterraau12929gut/12929-h/12929-h. htm (date accessed 25 April 2010).

19 M.F. Peron (1809), *Voyage of Discovery to the Southern Hemisphere, Performed by order of the Emperor Napoleon During the Years 1801, 1802, 1803, and 1804*, translated from the French, Phillips, London. Reproduced Melbourne 1975, pp. 93–4.

20 N. Baudin (1800–1803), *The Journal of Post Captain Nicolas Baudin, Commander-in-Chief of the corvettes* Le Geographe *and* Le Naturaliste, *assigned by order of the government to a voyage of discovery*, translated from the French by Christine Cornell (1974), Adelaide: Libraries Board of South Australia.

21 E. Giles (1880), *Australia Twice Traversed: The Romance Of Exploration, Being A Narrative Compiled From The Journals Of Five Exploring Expeditions Into And Through Central South Australia, And Western Australia, From 1872 To 1876.* A Project Gutenberg of Australia eBook: http://freeread.com.au/ebooks/e00052.html (date accessed 7 March 2010).

22 L. Leichhardt (1847), *Journal Of An Overland Expedition In Australia: From Moreton Bay To Port Essington, A Distance Of Upwards Of 3000 Miles, During The Years 1844–1845*, London: T & W Boone. A Project Gutenberg of Australia eBook: http://freeread.com.au/ebooks/e00030.html (date accessed 7 March 2010).

23 E.J. Eyre (1845), *Journals of Expeditions of Discovery into Central Australia and Overland from Adelaide to King George's Sound*, London: T. and W. Boone. A Project Gutenberg of Australia eBook: http://freeread.com.au/ebooks/e00048.html (date accessed 7 March 2010).

24 J. Forrest (1875), *Explorations in Australia*, London: Gilbert and Rivington. A Project Gutenberg of Australia eBook: http://freeread.com.au/ebooks/e00051.html (date accessed 7 March 2010).

25 J. Oxley (1823), *Journals Of Two Expeditions Into The Interior Of New South Wales, By Order Of The British Government In The Years 1817–18.* A Project Gutenberg of Australia eBook: http://freeread.com.au/ebooks/e00037.txt (date accessed 7 March 2010).

26 G. Grey (2006), *Journals of Two Expeditions of Discovery in North-West and Western Australia, Volumes 1 & 2*, Middlesex: The Echo Library, p. 389

27 Ibid., p. 398.

28 Bennett (1834), p. 289.

29 I.D. Hume, P.J. Jarman, M.B. Renfree and P.D. Temple-Smith (1989), 'Macropodidae', in D.W. Walton (ed), *Fauna of Australia. Volume 1B. Mammalia*, Canberra: Australian Government Publishing Service, pp. 679–715.

30 T.H. Kirkpatrick and P.J. Amos (1985), 'The kangaroo industry', in H.J. Lavery (ed), *The Kangaroo Keepers*, Brisbane: University of Queensland Press, pp. 75–102.

31 C. Lumholtz (1889), *Among Cannibals: Account of Four Years Travels in Australia and of Camp Life with the Aborigines of Queensland*, London: John Murray. p. 29, 33–34.

32 E. Rolls (1969), *They All Ran Wild*, Sydney: Angus & Robertson; R.B. Smyth (1878), *The Aborigines of Victoria: With notes relating to the habits of the natives of other parts of Australia and Tasmania. Compiled from various sources for the Government of Victoria*, Melbourne: John Curry O'Neil.

33 J.D. Robertshaw and R.H. Harden (1989), 'Predation on Macropodoidea: A Review', in G. Grigg, P. Jarman and I. Hume (eds), *Kangaroos, Wallabies and Rat-kangaroos*, Sydney: Surrey Beatty & Sons, pp. 735–53.

34 P.J. Jarman and K.A. Johnson (1977), 'Exotic mammals, indigenous mammals and land-use', *Proceedings of the Ecological Society of Australia* 10: 146–66.

35 T.H. Kirkpatrick and P.J. Amos (1985), 'The kangaroo industry', in H.J. Lavery (ed), *The Kangaroo Keepers*, Brisbane: University of Queensland Press, pp. 75–102.

36 J. Gould (1863), *The Mammals of Australia*, 3 volumes, London: The Author; F.W. Jones (1924), *The Mammals of South Australia. Part II. The Bandicoots and Herbivorous Marsupials*, Adelaide: Government Printer.

37 A.W. Cameron (1975), 'Changes in the wild life community of the Waterloo Valley Between 1866 and 1975', in Agriculture, Forestry & Wildlife: Conflict or Coexistence, Armidale: University of New England, pp. 19–25.

38 Jarman and Johnson (1977).

39 Robertshaw and Harden (1989).

40 J. Short (1998), 'The extinction of rat-kangaroos (Marsupialia: Potoroidae) in New South Wales, Australia', *Biological Conservation* 86: 365–77; J. Short and G. Milkovits (1990), 'Distribution and status of the brush-tailed rock-wallaby in south-eastern Australia', *Australian Wildlife Research* 17: 169–79.

41 T. Livanes (1971), 'Kangaroos as a resource', *Australian Zoologist* 16: 68–72; G. Grigg (1987), 'Kangaroos—a better economic base for our marginal grazing lands?', *Australian Zoologist* 24: 72–80; and G. Grigg (1988), 'Kangaroo harvesting and the conservation of the sheep rangelands', *Australian Zoologist* 24: 124–8.

42 Kirkpatrick and Amos (1985).

43 Rolls (1969); I.D. Hume, P.J. Jarman, M.B. Renfree and P.D. Temple-Smith (1989), 'Macropodidae', in D.W. Walton (ed), *Fauna of Australia. Volume 1B. Mammalia*, Canberra: Australian Government Publishing Service, pp. 679–715.

44 J.D. Macfarlane (1971), 'Exports of kangaroo meat', *Australian Zoologist* 16: 62–4; P. Corrigan (1988), 'Export of kangaroo meat', *Australian Zoologist* 24: 179–80; N. Shepherd and G. Caughley (1987), 'Options for management of kangaroos', in G. Caughley, N. Shepherd and J. Short (eds), *Kangaroos: Their Ecology and Management in the Sheep Rangelands of Australia*, Sydney: Cambridge University Press, pp. 188–219; *The Age* (1973), 'Government Bans export of all kangaroo product', 12 January, p. 2, at http://news.google.com/n ewspapers?id=C5IQAAAAIBAJ&sjid=2ZADAAAAIBAJ&pg=7 186,1796345&dq=government+bans+export+of+all+kangaroo+ product&hl=en (date accessed 25 April 2010); M. Grattan (1975), 'Kangaroo export ban to be eased', *The Age,* 21 February 1975, p. 3, at http://news.google.com/newspapers?id=bHsQAAAAIBAJ &sjid=NJIDAAAAIBAJ&pg=1660,4353208&dq=kangaroo+b an+imposed+1975&hl=en (date accessed 25 April 2010); Anon (1981), 'Kangaroo hide ban is lifted', *St. Petersburg Times*, 29 April, at http://news.google.com/newspapers?id=X_oNAAAAIBAJ&sji d=CnsDAAAAIBAJ&pg=6742,4577921&dq=kangaroo+ban+lif ted+us+1981&hl=en (date accessed 25 April 2010).

45 A.R. Pople and G.C. Grigg (1999), 'Commercial harvesting of kangaroos in Australia. Environment Australia, Canberra, at www. ea.gov.au/biodiversity/trade-use/wild-harvest/kangaroo/harvest-ing/index.html (date accessed 22 October 2008); G. Wilson personal communication to S. Jackson 23 April 2010.

46 B.J. Ramsay (1994), *Commercial Use of Wild Animals in Australia*, Canberra: Australian Government Publishing Service; Pople and Grigg (1999).

47 G.R. Wilson and M.J. Edwards (2008), 'Native wildlife on range-lands to minimize methane and produce lower-emission meat: kangaroos versus livestock', *Conservation Letters* 1: 119–28; G.C. Grigg (1989), 'Kangaroo harvesting and the conservation of arid and semi-arid rangelands', *Conservation Biology* 3: 194–7.

48 Grigg (1989).

49 J.C. Newman and R.W. Condon (1969), 'Land use and present condition', in R.O. Slatyer and R.A. Perry (eds), *Arid Lands of Australia*, Canberra: Australian National University Press, pp. 105–32; L.E. Woods (1984), *Land Degradation in Australia*, Canberra: Australian Government Publishing Service.

50 Grigg (1987); Grigg (1989); and Grigg (1988).

51 Pople and Grigg (1999).

52 Grigg (1989); G. Grigg (2002), 'Conservation benefit from harvesting kangaroos: status report at the start of a new millen-nium—a paper to stimulate discussion and research' in D. Lunney and Chris Dickman (eds), *A Zoological Revolution: Using Native Fauna to Assist in its Own Survival*, Sydney: Royal Zoological Society of New South Wales and Australian Museum; D. Lunney (2010), 'A history of the debate (1948–2009) on the commercial harvesting of kangaroos, with particular reference to New South Wales and the role of Gordon Grigg', *Australian Zoologist* 35: (in press); Gordon Grigg, personal communication to K. Vernes 1 May 2010.

53 Pople and Grigg (1999); Parliment of Australia—Senate (2003), Commercial use of Australian Wildlife. Chapter 9. Macropod, at www.aph.gov.au/senate/committee/rrat_ctte/completed_inqui-ries/1996–99/wild/report/contents.htm (date accessed 23 April 2010).

54 J.H. Gilroy (2004), 'New South Wales Kangaroo Management Program: 2002 and beyond', *Australian Mammalogy* 26: 3–8.

55 Pople and Grigg (1999).

56 G. Caughley and G.C. Grigg (1981), 'Surveys of the distribution and density of kangaroos in the pastoral zone South Australia and their bearing on the feasibility of aerial survey in large remote areas', *Australian Wildlife Research* 8: 1–11.

57 G. Caughley (1987), 'Ecological relationships', in G. Caughley, N. Shepherd and J. Short (eds), *Kangaroos: Their Ecology and Management in the Sheep Rangelands of Australia*, Sydney: Cambridge University Press, pp. 159–87.

58 Department of Environment, Water and Heritage (2000), 'Commercial kangaroo harvest quotas—National quotas', at www.environment.gov.au/biodiversity/trade-use/wild-harvest/kangaroo/national.html (date accessed 23 October 2008).

59 Caughley (1987); G.C. Grigg (1997), 'A crossroads in kangaroo politics', *Australian Biologist* 10: 12–22; and Pople and Grigg (1999).

60 Pople and Grigg (1999).

61 George Wilson personal communication to S. Jackson 23 April 2010; Department of Environment, Water and Heritage (2007), 'Wildlife trade and conservation—kangaroos', at www.environment.gov.au/biodiversity/trade-use/wild-harvest/kangaroo/index.html (date accessed 17 February 2009).

62 Pople and Grigg (1999); and Wilson and Edwards (2008).

63 G. Coulson, P. Alviano, D. Ramp and S. Way (1999), 'The kangaroos of Yan Yean: History of a problem population', *Proceedings of the Royal Society of Victoria* 111: 121–30.

64 C.A. Herbert (2004), 'Long-acting contraceptives: A new tool to manage overabundant kangaroo populations in nature reserves and urban areas', *Australia Mammalogy* 26: 67–74.

65 A.C. Dufty, J.H. Seebeck, J. McKay and A.J. Watson (1995), 'Reintroduction of Eastern Barred Bandicoots at Gellibrand Hill Park, Victoria', in M. Serena (ed), *Reintroduction Biology of Australian and New Zealand Fauna*, Sydney: Surrey Beatty and Sons, pp. 219–25. S. Jackson pers. obs.; A.L. Winnard and G. Coulson (2008). 'Sixteen years of Eastern Barred Bandicoot *Perameles gunnii* reintroductions in Victoria: a review', *Pacific Conservation Biology* 14: 34–53.

66 ABC Online (2008), 'Kangaroo cull mooted for Canberra', 13 May 2008, at www.abc.net.au/news/newsitems/200705/s1921538.htm (date accessed 15 May 2008).

67 Adelaide Now (2008), 'Roo cull "threatens whale ban"', 15 March 2008 at www.news.com.au/adelaidenow/story/0,22606, 23382079–

910,00.html (date accessed 15 March 2008); George Wilson personal communication to S. Jackson 23 April 2010.

68 D.W. Cooper and C.A. Herbert (2001), 'Genetics, biotechnology and population management of overabundant mammalian wildlife in Australasia', *Reproduction Fertility and Development* 13: 451–8; and George Wilson personal communication to S. Jackson 23 April 2010.

69 C.D. Nave, G. Shaw, R.V. Short and M.B. Renfree (2000), 'Contraceptive effects of levonorgestrel implants in a marsupial', *Reproduction, Fertility and Development* 12: 81–6; Cooper and Herbert (2001); and Herbert (2004).

70 Jones (1924).

71 G.C. Grigg (1984), 'Roo Harvesting: Are kangaroos really under threat?', *Australian Natural History* 21(4): 123–9; Rawlingson (1988); S. Arnold (1988), 'The morality of harvesting kangaroos', *Australian Zoologist* 24: 143–6; P. Preuss and J. Rogers (1995), 'Consumptive use of wildlife: Conservation or exploitation?', in G.C. Grigg, P.T. Hale and D. Lunney (eds), *Conservation Through Sustainable Use of Wildlife*, Brisbane: University of Queensland, pp. 69–72; M. Wilson (ed) (1999), *The Kangaroo Betrayed: World's Largest Wildlife Slaughter*, Melbourne: Hill of Content; M. Wilson and D.B. Croft (eds) (2005), *Kangaroos: Myths and Realities*, Melbourne: Australian Wildlife Protection Council.

72 Pople and Grigg (1999).

73 Grigg (1984); Grigg (1989); Croft (2000); Arnold (1988); and R. Linden (2005), 'Kangaroo killing', in M. Wilson and D.B. Croft (eds), *Kangaroos: Myths and Realities*, Melbourne: The Australian Wildlife Protection Council Inc, pp. 85–90.

74 N. Clayton, J.C. Wombey, I.J. Mason, R.T. Chesser and A. Wells (2006), *CSIRO List of Australian Vertebrates: A Reference with Conservation Status*, Melbourne: CSIRO Publishing.

75 Pople and Grigg (1999); D.B. Croft (2000), 'Sustainable use of wildlife in western New South Wales: Possibilities and problems', *Rangelands Journal* 22: 88–104.

76 P.T. Hale (2004), 'Genetic effects of kangaroo harvesting', *Australian Mammalogy* 26: 75–86.

77 Arnold (1988).

78 P.A. Rawlinson, P.A. (1988), 'Kangaroo conservation and kangaroo harvesting: intrinsic value versus instrumental value of wildlife', *Australian Zoologist* 24: 129–37.

79 L. Stacker (1988), 'The case against free range kangaroo harvesting', *Australian Zoologist* 24: 153–8.

80 Linden (2005).

81 A.E. Andrew (1988), 'Kangaroo meat—Public health aspects', *Australian Zoologist* 24: 138–40; and D. Obendorf (2008), 'Diseases in kangaroo meat' at www.awpc.org.au/kangaroos/book_files/diseases.htm (date accessed 24 October 2008); P. O'Brien (2005), 'And we call ourselves civilised?', in M. Wilson and D.B. Croft (eds), *Kangaroos: Myths and Realities*, Melbourne: The Australian Wildlife Protection Council Inc, pp. 68–76.

82 Pople and Grigg (1999).

83 D.R. Butcher (1988), 'Animal welfare aspects of kangaroo management', *Australian Zoologist* 24: 164–5.

84 Department of Environment and Heritage (2008), 'National Code of Practice for the Humane Shooting of Kangaroos and Wallabies for Commercial Purposes. Environment Australia, Canberra', at www.environment.gov.au/biodiversity/trade-use/wild-harvest/kangaroo/pubs/practice.pdf (date accessed 14 February 2010).

85 RSPCA (2002), 'Kangaroo Shooting Code of Compliance: A survey of the extent of compliance with the requirements of the Code of Practice for the Humane Shooting of Kangaroos', at www.environment.gov.au/biodiversity/trade-use/publications/kangaroo-report/index.html (date accessed 24 October 2008).

86 R. Garnaut (2008), *The Garnaut Climate Change Review*, Cambridge: Cambridge University Press.

87 A. Klieve and D. Ouwekerk (2007), 'Comparative greenhouse gas emissions from herbivores', in Q.X. Meng, L.P. Ren and Z.J. Cao (eds), *Proceedings of the VIII International Symposium on the Nutrition of Herbivores*, Beijing: China Agriculture University Press, pp. 487–500.

88 Garnaut (2008).

89 Wilson and Edwards (2008); Gordon Grigg, personal communication to K. Vernes 1 May 2010.

90 R. Boswell (2008), 'Media Release. Kangaroo Farms—A Eureka Moment from Garnaut', at http://ronboswell.com/?p=697 (accessed 20 October 2008); and ABC News (2008), 'Roo industry backs climate change report', at www.abc.net.au/news/stories/2008/10/02/2379803.htm (date accessed 10 October 2008).

91 ABC News (2008).

92 R. Cooney, A. Baumber, P. Ampt and G. Wilson (2009), 'Sharing skippy: how can landholders be involved in kangaroo production in Australia?', *The Rangeland Journal* 31; 283–92.

93 W. Tench (1961), *Sydney's First Four Years*, Sydney: Angus & Robertson, p. 268

94 P.M. Cunningham (1827), *Two Years in New South Wales: A series of letters, comprising sketches of the actual state of society in that colony; of its peculiar advantages to emigrants; of its topography, natural history etc*, London: Henry Colburn, p. 309.

95 Worgan (1978), p. 13.

96 K. O'Dea (1988), 'Kangaroo meat—polyunsaturated and low in fat: ideal for cholesterol-lowering diets', *Australian Zoologist* 24: 140–3; A.J. Sinclair (1988), 'Nutritional properties of kangaroo meat', *Australian Zoologist* 24: 146–8.

97 O'Dea (1988).

98 Andrew (1988).

99 Pople and Grigg (1999).

100 P. Ampt and K. Owen (2008), *Consumer Attitudes to Kangaroo Meat Products*, Canberra: Rural Industries Research and Development Corporation. Available at: https://rirdc.infoservices.com.au/downloads/08–026.pdf (date accessed 21 April 2010).

101 G.B. Sharman (1971), 'Management of kangaroos', *Australian Zoologist* 16: 73–9; N.C. Shepherd (1983), 'The feasibility of farming kangaroos', *Australian Rangelands Journal* 5: 35–44; and Rawlinson (1988).

102 Rawlinson (1988).

CHAPTER 9 FLYING KANGAROOS

1 An early handbill that captures the amazement of Europeans when they first saw the kangaroo. Quote taken from P. Stanbury and G. Phipps (1980), *Australia's Animals Discovered*, Sydney: Pergamon Press, p. 32. Also available at the National Library of Australia: www.nla.gov.au/pub/nlanews/2004/may04/article2.html (date accessed 23 December 2008).

2 Department of Foreign Affairs and Trade (2006) *Australia's Coat of Arms*: www.dfat.gov.au/fcats/coat_of_arms.html (date accessed 22 February 2006).

3 Postage stamps and postal history of Australia, at http://en.wikipedia.org/wiki/Postage_stamps_and_postal_history_of_Australia (date accessed 10 September 2009).

4 Wikipedia (2010), Coins of Australia, at http://en.wikipedia.org/wiki/Coins_of_Australia (accessed 26 April 2010); QANTAS (2010), The kangaroo symbol, at www.qantas.com.au/travel/airlines/history-kangaroo-symbol/global/en (date accessed 26 April 2010).

5 H. Golder and D. Kirkby (2003), 'Mrs. Mayne and Her Boxing Kangaroo: A Married Woman Tests Her Property Rights in Colonial New South Wales', *Law and History Review* 21: 585–605.

6 Boxing kangaroo, at http://en.wikipedia.org/wiki/ Boxing Kangaroo (date accessed 16 November 2008).

7 D. Inwood (2010), 'IOC will allow Australians' boxing kangaroo flag to stay', *The Vancouver Sun*, 7 February 2010 (Online Edition). http://www.vancouversun.com (date accessed 3 March 2010).

8 Dot and the Kangaroo, at http://en.wikipedia.org/wiki/ Dot_and_the_Kangaroo (date accessed 16 November 2008).

9 The Encyclopedia of Disney Animated Shorts (2008), at www.disneyshorts.org/ years/1935/mickeyskangaroo.html (date accessed 16 November 2008).

10 Classic Cartoons (2005), Introducing...Kiko the Kangaroo!, at http://classiccartoons.blogspot.com/2005/12/introducingkiko-kangaroo.html (date accessed 16 November 2008).

11 Bigpond News (2010), Boxing kangaroo act cancelled, at http://bigpondnews.com/ articles/TopStories/2010/03/06/Outcry_over_boxing_kangaroo_436752.html (date accessed 6 March 2010).

12 TvParty (2008), The Good Captain, at www.tvparty.com/lostter-rytoons.html (date accessed 16 November 2008).

13 Captain Kangaroo, at http://en.wikipedia.org/wiki/ Captain_Kangaroo (date accessed 16 November 2008).

14 Skippy the Bush kangaroo, at http://en.wikipedia.org/wiki/ Skippy_the_Bush_Kangaroo (date accessed 16 November 2008).

15 IMBD (2008), Kangaroo Jack at www.imdb.com/title/tt0257568 (accessed 16 November 2008).

16 University of Missouri, Kansas City (2010), UMKC History, at www.umkc.edu/history (date accessed 29 January 2010).

17 T.E. Heinsohn (1998), 'Captive ecology', *Nature Australia* 26 (2): 36–43.

18 T.E. Heinsohn (2001), 'Human influences on vertebrate zoogeography: Animal translocation and biological invasions across and to the east of Wallace's Line', in I. Metcalfe, J.M.B. Smith, M. Morwood and I. Davidson (eds), *Faunal and Floral Migrations and Evolution in SE Asia-Australasia*, Lisse: Balkema, pp. 153–70; and T.E. Heinsohn (2003), 'Animal translocation: long-term influences on the vertebrate zoogeography of Australasia (natural dispersal versus ethnophoresy)', *Australian Zoologist* 32: 351–376. Also see Appendix 2.

19 T.E. Heinsohn (2005), 'Wallaby extinctions at the macropodid frontier: Changing status of the northern pademelon *Thylogale browni* in New Ireland Province, Papua New Guinea', *Australian Mammalogy* 27(2): 175–83.

20 Heinsohn (1998).

21 Stanbury and Phipps (1980), p. 32.

22 *Morning Post and Daily Advertiser* (London, England), Friday, December 9, 1791; Issue 5812. 17–18th Century Burney Collection Newspapers at the British Library. Electronic Access at National Library of Australia (date accessed 23 April 2010).

23 W. Blunt (1976), *The Ark in the Park: The Zoo in the Nineteenth Century*, London: Hamish Hamilton and The Tryon Gallery.

24 *The Morning Chronicle* (London, England), Saturday, August 7, 1802; Issue 10364. 19th Century British Library Newspapers. Electronic Access at National Library of Australia.

25 W. Bingley (1804), *Animal Biography; or Authentic Anecdotes of the Lives, Manners, and Economy, of the Animal Creation, Arranged According to the System of Linnaeus*, Richard Phillips, London, p. 391.

26 T.F. Flannery (2004), *Country: A Continent, a Scientist and a Kangaroo*, Melbourne: The Text Publishing Company, Melbourne, p. 24.

27 C.H. Keeling (2001), 'The Zoological Gardens of Great Britain', in C.H. Kisling (ed), *Zoo and Aquarium History: Ancient Animal Collections to Zoological Gardens*, Boca Raton: CRC Press, pp. 49–74, p. 58.

28 J. Gould (1845–1863), *The Mammals of Australia*, London: the Author. Three volumes republished in one with modern notes by J.M. Dixon (1983), Melbourne: Macmillan, p. 147.

29 S. Stewart (2009), 'Scotland's only wallabies face extermination', *Scottish Daily Record* (Online Edition), 4 June 2009 at http://www.dailyrecord.co.uk/news/scottish-news/2009/06/04/ (date accessed 3 March 2010).

30 M. McLean (2009), 'Campaign to save Loch Lomond's wallabies gains pace', *Lennox Herald* (Online Edition), 6 June 2009 at http://www.lennoxherald.co.uk/dunbartonshire-news/dunbartonshire-news/loch-lomondside-news/2009/06/26/ (date accessed 3 March 2010); The Scottish Parliament (2009), *Business Bulletin No. 115/2009, Section E: Written Questions lodged from 20 to 24 July 2009*. Question No. S3W–25978 athttp://www.scottish.parliament.uk/business/businessBulletin/ (date accessed 3 March 2010).

31 S. Stewart (2009), 'Wallabies bid to escape Loch Lomond island cull by swimming ashore', *Scottish Daily Record* (Online Edition), 11 June 2009, at http://www.dailyrecord.co.uk/news/scottish-news/2009/06/11/ (date accessed 3 March 2010)

32 D. Fleming, R.N. Cinderey and J.P. Hearn (1983), 'The reproductive biology of Bennett's wallaby (*Macropus rufogriseus rufogriseus*) ranging free at Whipsnade Park', *Journal of Zoology* (London) 201: 283–91.

33 C. Lever (1977), *The Naturalised Animals of the British Isles*, London, Hutchinson; R.S.R. Fitter (1959), *The Ark in our Midst*, London: Collins; D.W. Yalden and G.R. Hosey (1971), 'Feral wallabies in the Peak District', *Journal of Zoology* (London)

165: 513–20; D.W. Yalden (1988), 'Feral wallabies in the Peak District, 1971–1985', *Journal of Zoology* (London) 215: 369–74;

34 D.W. Yalden, personal communication K. Vernes received 10 September 2009; and S.J. Baker (1990), 'Escaped exotic animals in Britain', *Mammal Review* 20: 75–90.

35 The Roaches (2010), 'Welcome the Roaches Website', at www. roaches.org.uk (date accessed 29 January 2010).

36 J.L. Long (2003), *Introduced Mammals of the World: Their History, Distribution and Influence*, Melbourne: CSIRO Publishing.

37 V. Elliott (2009), 'Home-grown wallabies hop in to help gardeners keep their lawns trim', *Times* on Line at www.timesonline.co.uk/tol/ news/environment/article6261351.ece (date accessed 15 May 2009)

38 Long (2003).

39 Ibid.

40 CERF (2007), Centre d'Etudes de et de sa Forêt: Enquête sur le Wallaby de Bennett en la Forêt d'Yvelines at http://www.cerf78.fr (date accessed 9 September 2009).

41 A. Crabb (2006), 'Roos are driving French hopping mad', *Sydney Morning Herald* at www.smh.com.au/news/world/roos-are-driving-french-hopping-mad/2006/02/11/1139542445052.html (date accessed 7 April 2009).

42 Long (2003).

43 J.D. Lazell (1987), 'Evolution of the hop', *BBC Wildlife* 6: 666–8; J.D. Lazell, T.W. Sutterfield and W.D. Giezentanner (1984), 'The population of rock-wallabies (genus *Petrogale*) on Oahu, Hawaii', *Biological Conservation* 30: 99–108.

44 M.D.B. Eldridge and T.L. Browning (2002), 'Molecular genetic analysis of the naturalized Hawaiian population of the brush-tailed rock-wallaby, *Petrogale penicillata* (Marsupialia: Macropodidae)', *Journal of Mammalogy* 83(2):437–44.

45 *The Ottawa Citizen*, 14 November, 2008. 'Wendell the Wallaby died close to home' at http://www.canada.com/ottawacitizen/news/ city/story.html?id=4db0348e-c8ab–43aa-afca–4f98e7edcbf2 (date accessed 10 September 2009).

46 'Phantom Kangaroos' at http://en.wikipedia.org/wiki/Phantom_ kangaroo (date accessed 5 March 2010; 'Hunters Kill Big Lynx, Tennessee's Kangaroo', *New York Times*, 30 January 1934.

47 K. Wodzicki and J.E.C. Flux (1967), 'Guide to introduced walla-
    bies in New Zealand', *Tuatara* 15(2): 48–58.
48 George Grey at http://en.wikipedia.org/wiki/George_Grey (date
    accessed 3 March 2010).
49 E. Wilson (1935), 'Kawau—Island of Dreams: Memories of Sir
    George Grey', *The New Zealand Railways Magazine* 10, (9): 33–38;
    Wodzicki and Flux (1967).
50 Department for Environment and Heritage (2006), *Re-introduction
    of Mainland SA Tammar Wallaby to Innes National Park Progress Report*,
    Department for Environment and Heritage: Adelaide, South Australia.

CHAPTER 10 EXTINCT?

1   T.F. Flannery (1990), *Australia's Vanishing Mammals: Endangered
    and Extinct Native Species*, Sydney: RD Press, p. 11.
2   T. Flannery and P. Schouten (2001), *A Gap in Nature: Discovering
    the World's Extinct Animals*, Melbourne: Text Publishing.
3   Flannery and Schouten (2001); S. Van Dyck and R. Strahan (2008),
    The Mammals of Australia, Sydney: Reed Books.
4   Van Dyck and Strahan (2008); C. Johnson (2006), *Australia's
    Mammal Extinctions: A 50,000 year history*, Cambridge: Cambridge
    University Press; and C. Dickman (2007), *A Fragile Balance: The
    Extraordinary Story of Australian Marsupials*, Fishermans Bend,
    Victoria: Craftsman House.
5   A.A. Burbidge and N.L. McKenzie (1989), 'Patterns in the modern
    decline of Western Australia's vertebrate fauna: Causes and conser-
    vation implications', *Biological Conservation* 50: 143–98.
6   C. Johnson and J.L. Isaac (2009), 'Body mass and extinction risk
    in Australian marsupials: The "Critical Weight Range" revisited',
    Austral Ecology 34: 35–40; Johnson (2006).
7   Johnson (2006).
8   D.J. Kitchener and J.A. Friend (2008), 'Broad-faced Potoroo
    Potorous platyops', in S. Van Dyck and R. Strahan (eds), *The Mammals
    of Australia*, 3rd edition, Sydney: Reed New Holland, pp. 301–2.
9   J.A. McNamara (1997), 'Some smaller macropod fossils of South
    Australia', *Proceedings of the Linnean Society of New South Wales* 117:
    97–105; A.A. Burbidge, N.L. McKenzie, K.E.C. Brennan, J.C.Z.

Woinarski, C.R. Dickman, A. Baynes, G. Gordon, P.W. Menkhorst and A.C. Robinson (2008), 'Conservaion status and biogeography of Australia's terrestrial mammals', *Australian Journal of Zoology* 56: 411–422.

10 J. Gould (1845–63), *The Mammals of Australia*, London: The Author. The three volumes are combined as one with modern notes by J. Dixon (1983), Melbourne: Macmillan, pp. 260, 258.

11 Flannery and Schouten (2001).

12 A.A. Burbidge, K.A. Johnson, P.J. Fuller and P.F. Aitken (2008), 'Central hare-wallaby', in S. Van Dyck and R. Strahan (eds), *The Mammals of Australia*, 3rd edition, Sydney: Reed New Holland, pp. 312–13; A.A. Burbidge, K.A. Johnson, P.J. Fuller and R.I. Southgate (1988), 'Aboriginal knowledge of mammals of the central deserts of Australia', *Australian Wildlife Research* 15: 9–39.

13 R. Tate (1878), 'The natural history of the country around the head of the Great Australian bight', *Transactions of the Philosophical Society of South Australia* 8: 94–28, see p. 124.

14 H.H. Finlayson (1931), 'Notes on some south and central Australian mammals. Part 2', *Transactions of the Royal Society of South Australia* 55: 161–2.

15 H.H. Finlayson (1943), *The Red Centre*, Sydney: Angus & Robertson, pp. 101–3.

16 S.G. Carr and A.C. Robinson (1997). 'The present status and distribution of the Desert Rat-kangaroo *Caloprymnus campestris* (Marsupialia: Potoroidae)', *The South Australian Naturalist* 72: 4–27.

17 Finlayson (1943), pp. 101–2.

18 Finlayson (1943), pp. 103–4.

19 G.C. Shortridge (1909), 'An account of the geographical distribution of macropods of south-west Australia, having special reference to the specimens collected during the Balston Expedition of 1904–1907', *Proceedings of the Zoological Society of London* 1909: 803–48.

20 Gould (1845–63), p. 258.

21 IUCN (2009), 'IUCN Red List of Threatened Species', at www.iucnredlist.org (date accessed 22 January 2010).

22 B.J. Marlow (1958), 'A survey of the marsupials of New South Wales', *CSIRO Wildlife Research* 3: 71–114.

23 G.M. Maynes (1977), 'Distribution and aspects of the biology of the parma wallaby, *Macropus parma*, in New South Wales', *Australian Journal of Wildlife Research* 4: 109–25.

24 K.A. Wodzicki and J.E.C. Flux (1967), 'Re-discovery of the white-throated wallaby, Macropus parma Waterhouse 1846, on Kawau Island, New Zealand', *Australian Journal of Science* 29: 429–30.

25 Maynes (1977).

26 Gould (1845–63), p. 255.

27 G. Krefft (1866), 'On the vertebrated animals of the lower Murray and Darling, their habits, economy and geographical distribution', *Transactions of the Philosophical Society of New South Wales* 1862–1865: 1–33.

28 A.S. Le Souef (1923), 'The Australian native animals, how they stand today and the cause of scarcity of certain species', *Australian Zoologist* 3: 108–11.

29 H.H. Finlayson (1931), 'On mammals from the Dawson Valley, Queensland. Part 1', *Transactions of the Royal Society of South Australia* 55: 67–89.

30 Gould (1845–63), p. 288.

31 E.A. Sinclair, A. Danks and A.F. Wayne (1996), 'Rediscovery of Gilbert's potoroo, *Potorous tridactylus*, in Western Australia', *Australian Mammalogy* 19: 69–72.

32 R. Broom (1896), 'On a small fossil marsupial with large grooved premolars', *Proceedings of the Linnean Society of New South Wales* (2)10: 563–7.

33 W.D.L. Ride (1964), 'A review of Australian fossil marsupials', *Journal and Proceedings of the Royal Society of Western Australia* 47: 97–131.

34 Anon. (1966), 'A relict marsupial', *Nature* 212: 255; J. Epstein (1981), *The Friends of Burramys*, Melbourne: Oxford University Press.

35 L.S. Broom (2008), 'Mountain Pygmy-possum *Burramys parvus*', in S. Van Dyck and R. Strahan (eds), *The Mammals of Australia*, 3rd edition, Sydney: Reed New Holland, pp. 210–12.

36 Johnson (2006), pp. 197–206; E. Rolls (1969), *They All Ran Wild*, Sydney: Angus & Robertson.

37 G. Saunders, C. Lane, S. Harris and C. Dickman (2006), *Foxes in Tasmania: A Report on the Incursion of an Invasive Species*, Invasive Animals Cooperative Research Centre.

38 C.M. Hoy (1923). 'The present status of the Australian mammal fauna', *Journal of Mammalogy* 4: 164–166; F.W. Jones (1925), *The Mammals of South Australia Part III: The Monodelphia*, Adelaide, Government Printer, p. 358. E.L.G. Troughton (1938), 'Australian mammals: their past and future', *Journal of Mammalogy* 19: 401–11.

39 Johnson (2006), pp. 188–97.

40 J. Short (1998), 'The extinction of rat-kangaroos (Marsupialia; Potoroidae) in New South Wales, Australia', *Biological Conservation* 86: 365–77.

41 J. Short and J.H. Calaby (2001), 'The status of Australian mammals in 1922: Collections and field notes of museum collector Charles Hoy', *Australian Zoologist* 31: 533–62.

42 P. Jarman and K. Vernes (2006), 'Wildlife', in A. Atkinson, A. Piper, J.S. Ryan and I. Davidson (eds), *High Lean Country: Land, People and Memory in New England*, Sydney: Allen and Unwin, pp. 44–56.

43 I. Abbott (2002), 'Origin and spread of the cat, *Felis catus*, on mainland Australia, with a discussion of the magnitude of its early impact on native fauna', *Wildlife Research* 29: 51–74.

44 C.R. Dickman, R.L. Pressey, L. Lim and H.E. Parnaby (1993), 'Mammals of particular concern in the western division of New South Wales', *Biological Conservation* 65: 219–48.

45 A.A. Burbidge and B.J.F. Manly (2002), 'Mammal extinctions on Australian islands: causes and conservation implications', *Journal of Biogeography* 29: 465–73.

46 D.F. Gibson, G. Lundie-Jenkins, D.G. Langford, J.R. Cole, D.E. Clarke and K.A. Johnson (1994), 'Predation by feral cats, *Felis catus*, on the rufous hare wallaby, *Lagorchestes hirsutus*, in the Tanami Desert', *Australian Mammalogy* 17: 103–107.

47 P. Spencer (1994), 'Evidence of predation by a feral cat, *Felis catus* (Carnivora: Felidae) on an isolated rock-wallaby colony in tropical Queensland', *Australian Mammalogy* 14: 143–4.

48 Johnson (2006), pp. 207–10.

49 Rolls (1969).

50 K. Williams, I. Parer, B. Coman, J. Burley and M. Braysher (1995), *Managing Vertebrate Pests: Rabbits*, Canberra: Australian Government Publishing Service; G.C. Caughly (1977), *Analysis of Vertebrate Populations*, London: John Wiley; P. Jarman (1986), 'The brown hare—a herbivorous mammal in a new ecosystem', in R.L. Kitching (ed), *The Ecology of Exotic Animals and Plants*, Brisbane: Wiley, pp. 62–76; and P. Jarman (1986), 'The red fox—an exotic large predator', in R.L. Kitching (ed), *The Ecology of Exotic Animals and Plants*, Brisbane: Wiley, pp. 44–61.

51 Johnson (2006), p. 209.

52 Williams *et al.* (1995).

53 A.P. Smith and D.G. Quin (1996), 'Patterns and causes of extinction and decline in Australian conilurine rodents', *Biological Conservation* 77: 243–67.

54 Johnson (2006), p. 214.

55 R. Breckwoldt (1988), *The Dingo: A Very Elegant Animal*, Sydney: Angus & Robertson. Lovell, J. (2006), *The Great Wall: China Against The World 1000BC–2000AD*, Picador, Sydney.

56 P. Fleming, L. Corbett, R. Harden and P. Thomson (2001), *Managing the Impacts of Dingoes and Other Wild Dogs*, Canberra: Bureau of Rural Sciences.

57 A.S. Glen and C.R. Dickman (2005), 'Complex interactions among mammalian carnivores in Australia, and their implications for wildlife management', *Biological Reviews* 80: 1–15.

CHAPTER 11 KANGAROO CONSERVATION

1 K.A. Johnson (1999), 'Recovery and discovery: Where we have been and where we might go with species recovery?', *Australian Mammalogy* 21: 75–86, see p. 75.

2 K.A. Johnson, A.A. Burbidge and N.L. McKenzie (1989), 'Australian Macropodoidea: Status, causes of decline and future and management', in G. Grigg, P. Jarman and I. Hume (eds), *Kangaroos, Wallabies and Rat-Kangaroos*, Sydney: Surrey Beatty & Sons, pp. 641–57.

3 A.F. Robin (1889), 'Threatened with extinction', *The Zoologist* (3)13: 225–26.

4 H.A. Longman (1923), 'Is the kangaroo doomed?', *Australian Zoologist* 3: 103–7.

5 C.M. Hoy (1923), 'The present status of the Australian mammal fauna', *Journal of Mammalogy* 4: 164–6; J. Short and J.H. Calaby (2001), 'The status of Australian mammals in 1922—collections and field notes of museum collector Charles Hoy', *Australian Zoologist* 31: 533–62.

6 J. Short, S.D. Bradshaw, J. Giles, R.I.T. Prince and G.R. Wilson (1992), 'Reintroduction of macropods (Marsupialia: Macropodoidea) in Australia—a review', *Biological Conservation* 62: 189–204.

7 G. Lundie-Jenkins and J. Lowry (2005), 'Recovery plan for the bridled nailtail wallaby (*Onychogalea fraenata*) 2005–2009', Report to the Department of Environment and Heritage (DEH), Canberra and Environmental Protection Agency/Queensland Parks and Wildlife Service, Brisbane; Short *et al.* (1992).

8 A.J. Oliver, D.R. King and R.J. Mead (1979), 'Fluoroacetate tolerance, a genetic marker is some Australian mammals', *Australian Journal of Zoology* 27: 363–72.

9 Queensland Department of Primary Industries (2008), *Dog Aware Fact, 1080-Sodium Fluoroaceteate,* Brisbane: Queensland Department of Primary Industries.

10 D.R. King, A.J. Oliver and R.J. Mead (1978), 'The adaptations of some Western Australian mammals to food plants containing fluoroacetate', *Australia Journal of Zoology* 26: 699–712; A.J. Oliver, D.R. King and R.J. Mead (1977), 'The evolution of resistance to fluoroacetate intoxication in mammals', *Search* (Syd.) 8: 130–2.

11 R.J. Mead, A.J. Oliver, D.R. King and P.H. Hubach (1985), 'The co-evolutionary role of fluoroacetate in plant-animal interactions in Australia', *Oikos* 44: 55–60.

12 J.C. McIlroy (1981), 'The sensitivity of Australian animals to 1080 poison. II. Marsupial and eutherian carnivores', *Australian Wildlife Research* 8: 385–99; J.C. McIlroy and D.R. King (1990), 'Appropriate amounts of 1080 poison in baits to control foxes,

Vulpes vulpes', *Australian Wildlife Research* 17: 11–13; and J.C. McIlroy (1992), 'The Effect of Australian animals of 1080-poisoning campaigns', *Proceedings of the Fifteenth Vertebrate Pest Conference*, Lincoln, Nebraska: University of Nebraska, pp. 356–9.

13 Australian Pesticides and Veterinary Medicines Authority (2008), *The Reconsideration of Registrations of Products Containing Sodium Fluoroacetate (1080) and the Associated Labels. Preliminary Review and Findings*, Canberra: Australian Pesticides and Veterinary Medicines Authority; McIlroy (1981).

14 H. Possingham, P. Jarman and A. Kearns (2004), 'Independent review of Western Shield. February 2003', *Conservation Science Western Australia* 5(2): 2–18.

15 A.A. Burbidge and N.L. McKenzie (1989), 'Patterns in the modern decline of Western Australia's vertebrate fauna: causes and conservation implications', *Biological Conservation* 50: 143–98; A.A. Burbidge, A.N. Start, K.D. Morris and R. Armstrong (1995), *Western Shield—Bringing back our Wildlife*, Perth: Department of Conservation and Land Management.

16 R. Armstrong (2004), 'Baiting operations: Western Shield review—February 2003', *Conservation Science Western Australia* 5(2): 31–50; Department of Environment and Conservation (2008), 'Western Shield', at www.dec.wa.gov.au/programs/western-shield/index.html (date accessed 20 November 2008).

17 Possingham *et al.* (2004).

18 A. Wayne (2009), *Woylie declines: what are the causes?* Department of Environment and Conservation. Information Sheet 7. Science Division.

19 Department of Environment and Conservation (2008), 'Project Eden', at www.dec.wa.gov.au/programs/project-eden/index.html (date accessed 20 November 2008).

20 K. Morris, C. Sims, K. Himbeck, P. Christensen, N. Sercombe, B. Ward and N. Noakes (2004), 'Project Eden—fauna recovery on Peron peninsula, Shark Bay: Western Shield review—February 2003', *Conservation Science Western Australia* 5(2): 202–34.

21 B. Hardman (2003), 'Response of banded hare-wallabies and mala to reintroduction at Peron Peninsula, Shark Bay', Master of Science

thesis, Edith Cowan University; B. Hardman and D. Moro (2006), 'Importance of diurnal refugia to a hare-wallaby reintroduction in Western Australia', *Wildlife Research* 33: 355–9.

22 Australian Pesticides and Veterinary Medicines Authority (2008).

23 C.H. Chi, K.W. Chen, S.H. Chan, M.U. Wu and J.J. Huang (1996), 'Clinical presentation and prognostic factors in sodium monofluoroacetate intoxication', *Clinical Toxicology* 3: 707–12; G. Gregory (1996), 'Perception of pain associated with 1080 poisoning', in P.M. Fisher and C.A. Marks (eds), Seminar Proceedings (27 March 1996): *Humaneness and Vertebrate Pest Control, Report Series No 2,* Victorian Department of Natural Resources and Environment, pp. 62–4.

24 Australian Pesticides and Veterinary Medicines Authority (2008).

25 Possingham *et al.* (2004).

26 C.A. Belcher (1998), 'Susceptibility of the tiger quoll, *Dasyurus maculatus*, and the eastern quoll, *D. viverrinus*, to 1080-poisoned baits in control programmes for vertebrate pests in eastern Australia', *Wildlife Research* 25: 33–40.

27 G. Körtner, S. Gresser and B. Harden (2003), 'Does fox baiting threaten the spotted-tailed quoll (*Dasyurus maculatus*)?', *Wildlife Research* 30: 111–18.

28 G. Körtner and P. Watson (2005), 'The immediate impact of 1080 aerial baiting to control wild dogs on a spotted-tailed quoll population', *Wildlife Research* 32: 673–80.

29 S. Fenner, G. Körtner and K. Vernes (2009), 'Aerial baiting with 1080 to control wild dogs does not affect the populations of two common small mammal species', *Wildlife Research* 36: 528–32.

30 G. Saunders, C. Lane, S. Harris and C. Dickman (2006), *Foxes in Tasmania: A Report on the Incursion of an Invasive Species.* Invasive Animals Cooperative Research Centre; Parks and Wildlife Service, Tasmania (2008), 'Threatening Processes—Foxes in Tasmania', at www.parks.tas.gov.au/index.aspx?base=3026 (date accessed 20 November 2008).

31 G. Coulson (1989), 'The effect of drought on road mortality of macropods', *Wildlife Research* 16: 79–83; G. Coulson (1997), 'Male bias in road-kills of macropods', *Wildlife Research* 24: 21–5.

32 E. Lee, U. Klöcker, D.B. Croft and D. Ramp (2004), 'Kangaroo-vehicle collisions in Australia's sheep rangelands, during and following drought periods', *Australian Mammalogy* 26: 215–26.

33 S. Muirhead, D. Blache, B. Wykes and R. Bencini (2006), 'Roo-Guard® sound emitters are not effective at deterring tammar wallabies (*Macropus eugenii*) from a source of food', *Wildlife Research* 33: 131–6.

34 H. Bender (2001), 'Deterrence of Kangaroos from Roadways Using Ultrasonic Frequencies—efficiency of the Shu Roo', A report to: NRMA Insurance Limited, Royal Automobile Club of Victoria, Road Traffic Authority of New South Wales, Transport South Australia. Melbourne: University of Melbourne, Department of Zoology.

35 Z. Magnus, L.K. Kriwoken, N.J. Mooney and M.E. Jones (2004), *Reducing the Incidence of Wildlife Roadkill: Improving the Visitor Experience in Tasmania*. Technical Report. Cooperative Research Centre for Sustainable Tourism, Gold Coast.

36 G.H. Waring, J.L. Griffis and M.E. Vaughn (1991), 'White-tailed deer roadside behaviour, wildlife warning reflectors, and highway mortality', *Applied Animal Behaviour Science* 29: 215–23; A.F. Reeve and S.H. Anderson (1993), 'Ineffectiveness of Swareflex reflectors sat reducing deer-vehicle collisions', *Wildlife Society Bulletin* 21: 127–32; and ACT Kangaroo Advisory Committee (1997), *Living with Eastern Grey Kangaroos in the A.C.T.—Public Land*, Third Report to the minister for the Environment, Land and Planning, at www.tams.act.gov.au/__data/assets/pdf_file/ 0010/13051/actkangarooadvisorycommitteereport3pdf.pdf (date accessed 29 November 2008).

37 ACT Kangaroo Advisory Committee (1997).

38 P. Johnson, B. Nolan and B. Moore (1993), *The Use of Wildlife Reflectors as a Means of Reducing Kangaroo Road Deaths—The Proserpine Rock-wallaby Experience*, Internal Report, Brisbane: Queensland Department of Environment and Heritage.

39 E.G. Ritchie and E.E. Bolitho (2008), 'Australia's savanna herbivores: bioclimatic distributions and an assessment of the potential impact of regional climate change' *Physiological and Biochemical Zoology* 81: 880–90; E.G. Ritchie, J.K. Martin,

A.K. Krockenberger, S. Garnett and C.N. Johnson (2008), 'Large-herbivore distribution and abundance: Intra- and interspecific niche variation in the tropics', *Ecological Monographs* 78: 105–22.

40 R. Martin (2005), *Tree-kangaroos of Australia and New Guinea*, Melbourne: CSIRO Publishing, pp. 138–9.

41 N. Kwapena (1984), 'Traditional conservation and utilization of wildlife in Papua New Guinea', *The Environmentalist* 4 (Supplement 7): 22–6.

42 Kwapena (1984).

43 T.F. Flannery, R. Martin. and A. Szalay (1996), *Tree Kangaroos: A Curious Natural History*, Sydney: Reed Books, p. 33.

44 K.M. Helgen (2007), 'The mammal fauna of the Kaijende Highlands, Enga Province, Papua New Guinea', in S.J. Richards (ed), 'A rapid biodiversity assessment of the Kaijende Highlands, Enga Province, Papua New Guinea', *RAP Bulletin of Biological Assessment 45*, Arlington, VA: Conservation International, pp. 52–68.

45 Tenkile Conservation Alliance (2010), 'Tenkile Conservation Alliance', at www.tenkile.com (date accessed 10 February 2010); Martin (2005), p. 142.

46 T.F. Flannery (2004), *Country: A Continent, a Scientist and a Kangaroo*, Melbourne: The Text Publishing Company, Melbourne. p. 3.

CITATIONS FOR
FIGURES AND TABLES

Pages 14–15 – Table

B.P. Kear and B.N. Cooke (2001), 'A review of macropodoid (Marsupialia) systematics with the inclusion of a new family', *Memoirs of the Association of Australasian Palaeontologist* 25: 83–101.

B.P. Kear (2002), 'Phylogenetic implications of macropodid (Marsupialia: Macropodoidea) postcranial remains from Miocene deposits of Riversleigh, northwestern Queensland', *Alcheringa*, 26: 299–318.

J. Long, M. Archer, T. Flannery and S. Hand (2002), *Prehistoric Mammals of Australia and New Guinea: One Hundred Million Years of Evolution*: Sydney: University of NSW Press.

G.J. Prideaux (2004), 'Systematics and evolution of the sthenurine kangaroos', *Geological Sciences – University of California Publications* 146: 1–622.

K.M. Helgen, R.T. Wells, B.P. Kear, W.R. Gerdtz and T.F. Flannery (2006), 'Ecological and evolutionary significance of sizes of giant extinct kangaroos', *Australian Journal of Zoology* 54: 293–303.

C. Johnson (2006), *Australia's Mammal Extinctions: A 50,000 Year History*. Cambridge: Cambridge University Press.

B.P. Kear, B.N. Cooke, M. Archer and T.F. Flannery (2007), 'Implications of a new species of Oligo-Miocene kangaroo, (Marsupialia: Macropodoidea) *Nambaroo*, from the Riversleigh World Heritage Area, Queensland, Australia', *Journal of Paleontology* 81: 1147–67.

B.P. Kear and N.S. Pledge (2007), 'A new fossil kangaroo from the Oligocene-Miocene Etadunna Formation of Ngama Quarry, Lake Palankarinna, South Australia', *Australian Journal of Zoology* 55: 331–9.

Page 33 – Illustration

J.M. Dixon and L. Huxley (1985), *Donald Thompson's Mammals and Fishes of Northern Australia*, Melbourne: Thomas Nelson, p. 90.

Page 37 – Illustration

D. Tunbridge (1991), *The Story of the Flinders Ranges Mammals*, Sydney: Kangaroo Press.

Page 48 – Illustration

C. de Jode (1593), *Speculum Orbis Terrae*, Antwerp.

Page 83 – Illustration

S.M. Jackson (2007), *Koala: Origins of an Icon*. Sydney: Allen & Unwin, p. 3.

Page 98 – Illustration

H. Tyndale-Biscoe and M. Renfree (1987), *Reproductive Physiology of Marsupials*, Cambridge: Cambridge University Press, p. 82.

Page 100 – Illustration

H. Tyndale-Biscoe (2005), *Life of Marsupials*, Melbourne: CSIRO Publishing, p. 323.

Page 113 – Illustration

D.B. Croft (1981), 'Behaviour of Red Kangaroos, *Macropus rufus* (Desmarest, 1822) in northwestern New South Wales', *Australian Mammalogy* 4: 5–58, p. 38.

Page 129 – Illustration

I.D. Hume (1982), *Digestive Physiology of Marsupials*, Cambridge: Cambridge University Press, p. 115.

Page 139 – Illustration

R.V. Baudinette (1994), 'Locomotion in macropodoid marsupials:

gaits, energetics and heat balance', *Australian Journal of Zoology* 42: 103–23, p. 107.

Page 140 – Illustration
S. Dennington and J. Baldwin (1988), 'Biochemical correlates of energy metabolism used to power hopping by kangaroos', *Australian Journal of Zoology* 36: 229–40, p. 231.

Page 142 – Illustration
H. Tyndale-Biscoe (2005), *Life of Marsupials*, Melbourne: CSIRO Publishing, p. 309.

T.J. Dawson and C.R. Taylor (1973), 'Energetic cost of locomotion in kangaroos', *Nature* 246: 313–14, p. 314.

R.V. Baudinette, G.K. Snyder and P.B. Frappell (1992), 'Energetic cost of locomotion in the tammar wallaby', *American Journal of Physiology* 262: R771–R778, p. R775.

K.N. Webster and T.J. Dawson (2003), 'Locomotion energetics and gait characteristics of a rat-kangaroo, *Bettongia penicillata*, have some kangaroo-like features', *Journal of Comparative Physiology* B 173: 549–57, p. 553.

Page 144 – Illustration
T.J. Dawson (1977), 'Kangaroos', *Scientific American* 237(2): 78–89, p. 79.

Page 172 – Illustration
G.R. Wilson and M.J. Edwards (2008), 'Native wildlife on rangelands to minimize methane and produce lower-emission meat: kangaroo versus livestock', *Conservation Letters* 1(3): 119–28, p. 122.

Page 176 – Illustration
A.R. Pople and G.C. Grigg (1999), 'Commercial harvesting of kangaroos in Australia. Environment Australia, Canberra, at www.ea.gov.au/biodiversity/trade-use/wild-harvest/kangaroo/harvesting/index.html (accessed 22 October 2008).

Page 178 – Illustration
G.R. Wilson and M.J. Edwards (2008), 'Native wildlife on rangelands to minimize methane and produce lower-emission meat: kangaroo versus livestock', *Conservation Letters* 1(3): 119–28, p. 122.

Page 219 – Illustration

J. Gould (1863), *The Mammals of Australia*, 3 volumes, London: The Author.

Page 220 – Table

C. Johnson (2006), *Australia's Mammal Extinctions: A 50,000 Year History*. Cambridge: Cambridge University Press.

S. Van Dyck and R. Strahan (2008), *The Mammals of Australia*, Sydney: Reed Books.

Pages 232–3 – Table

P.F. Aitken (1971), 'Rediscovery of the large desert Sminthopsis (*Sminthopsis psammophilus* Spencer) on Eyre Peninsula, South Australia', *Victorian Naturalist* 88: 103–111.

Anon (1966), 'A relict marsupial', *Nature* 212: 255.

G. Armstrong and J. Reid (1992), 'The rediscovery of the Adelaide Pygmy Bluetongue *Tiliqua adelaidensis* (Peters, 1863)', *Herpetofauna* 22 (2): 3–6.

G. Armstrong, J.R.W. Reid and M.N. Hutchinson (1993), Discovery of a population of the rare scincid lizard *Tiliqua adelaidensis* (Peters),' *Records of the South Australian Museum* 36: 153–5.

W. Boles, W. Longmore and M. Thomson (1991), 'The fly-by-night parrot', *Australian Natural History* 23: 689–95.

C.W. Brazener (1962), 'Rediscovery of a rare Australian possum', *Proceedings of the Zoological Society of London* 139: 529–631.

K. Brisbane (1998), 'A rare occasion! The re-discovery of the central rock rat *Zyzomys pedunculatus* in the West MacDonnell National Park', pp. 225–30. In AAZPA/Conference Proceedings. Taronga Zoo. 22–27 March 1998.

A.A. Burbidge and N.L. McKenzie (1976), 'A further record of *Sminthopsis longicaudata* (Marsupialia, Dasyuridae)', *Western Australian Naturalist* 13: 144–5.

J. Covacevich (2008), 'The rediscovery of the Western Taipan', at www.qm.qld.gov.au/features/snakes/taipan/rediscovery.asp (date accessed 2 September 2008).

L. Glauert (1954), 'Herpetological miscellanea, IV. A new swamp tortoise from the Swamp River District', *Western Australian Naturalist* 4: 125–7.

KANGAROO

G. Gordon and B.C. Lawrie (1980), 'The rediscovery of the bridled nail-tailed wallaby, *Onychogalea fraenata* (Gould) (Marsupialia; Macropodidae) in Queensland', *Australian Wildlife Research* 7: 339–45.

K. Keith and J.H. Calaby (1968), 'The New Holland Mouse, *Pseudomys novaehollandiae* (Waterhouse), in the Port Stephens District, New South Wales', *CSIRO Wildlife Research* 13: 45–58.

J.A. Mahoney and B.J. Marlow (1968), 'The rediscovery of the New Holland Mouse', *Australian Journal of Science* 31: 221–3.

I.A. May (1977), 'Recent Re-discovery of the Eyrean Grasswren', *Emu* 77: 230–1.

M.K. Morcombe (1967), 'The rediscovery after 83 years of the dibbler *Antechinus apicalis* (Marsupialia, Dasyuridae)', *Western Australian Naturalist* 10: 103–11.

J. Short and A. Smith (1994), 'Mammal decline and recovery in Australia', *Journal of Mammalogy* 75: 288–97.

E.A. Sinclair, A. Danks and A.F. Wayne (1996), 'Rediscovery of Gilbert's potoroo, *Potorous tridactylus*, in Western Australia', *Australian Mammalogy* 19: 69–72.

T. Start, A. Burbidge, E. Sinclair, and A. Wayne (1995), 'Lost & Found: Gilbert's Potoroo', *Landscope* 10: 29–33.

S. Van Dyck (1993), 'The taxonomy and distribution of *Petaurus gracilis* (Marsupialia: Petauridae), with notes on its ecology and conservation status', *Memoirs of the Queensland Museum* 33: 77–122.

H.O. Webster (1962), 'Rediscovery of the Noisy Scrub-bird *Atrichornis clamosus*', *Western Australian Naturalist* 8: 57–79.

H.E. Wilkinson (1961), 'The rediscovery of Leadbeater's possum, *Gymnobelideus leadbeateri* McCoy', *Victorian Naturalist* 78: 97–102.

E.E. Williams (1958), 'Rediscovery of the Australian chelid genus *Pseudemydura* (Chelidae, Testudines)', *Breviora* 84: 1–8.

H. Wilson (1937), 'Notes on the night parrot, with references to recent occurrences', *Emu* 37: 79–87.

K.A. Wodzicki and J.E.C. Flux (1967), 'Re-discovery of the white-throated wallaby, *Macropus parma* Waterhouse 1846, on Kawau Island, New Zealand', *Australian Journal of Science* 29: 429–30.

Page 234 – Illustration

J. Gould (1863), *The Mammals of Australia*, 3 volumes, London: The Author.

INDEX

Index

Index